WITHDRAWN

)01

24.00

A HISTORY OF BRITISH
TRADE
UNIONISM
c. 1770–1990

Keith Laybourn

Professor in History,
The Polytechnic of Huddersfield

ALAN SUTTON

First published in the United Kingdom in 1992
Alan Sutton Publishing Ltd
Phoenix Mill · Far Thrupp · Stroud · Gloucestershire

First published in the United States of America in 1992
Alan Sutton Publishing Inc · Wolfeboro Falls · NH 03896–0848

British Library Cataloguing in Publication Data

Laybourn, Keith
    A history of British trade unionism c.1770–1990.
    I. Title
    331.880941
    ISBN 0-86299-785-2

Library of Congress Cataloging in Publication Data applied for

Jacket illustrations: (above) demonstrators during the 1889 dock
strike *(courtesy of the Trades Union Congress); (below)* on the picket line
at Selby coalfield in June 1984 during the 1984/5 miners' strike
(courtesy of the Yorkshire Evening Press).

Typeset in 11/12 Garamond.
Typesetting and origination by
Alan Sutton Publishing Limited.
Printed in Great Britain by
The Bath Press, Bath, Avon.

CONTENTS

To Peter Wood and David Wright for their help and
guidance over many years

ACKNOWLEDGEMENTS

There are many individuals to whom I owe thanks for their help in the preparation of this book. The librarians and archivists of West Yorkshire, particularly, have given generously of their time and I would especially like to express my thanks to Dr Alan Betteridge, Dr David James and the library and archive staff in Leeds, Bradford, Huddersfield and Halifax. In addition, I must also thank the staff of the British Library of Economic and Social Science, at the London School of Economics.

Among other friends and colleagues, I wish to acknowledge my debt to the late Jack Reynolds, Professor Chris Wrigley, and to my colleagues at Huddersfield Polytechnic, most particularly Peter Wood and David Wright, to whom this book is dedicated. I must also thank Keith Dockray, with whom I share a room, for his constant ability to raise me out of the slough which afflicts all writers and researchers from time to time.

All photographs have been reproduced courtesy of the Trades Union Congress, London, except where otherwise indicated.

Keith Laybourn

ABBREVIATIONS

AEU	Amalgamated Engineering Union
APEX	Association of Professional, Executive, Clerical and Computer Staff
AUEW	Amalgamated Union of Engineering Workers
ASE	Amalgamated Society of Engineers
ASRS	Amalgamated Society of Railway Servants
CWC	Clyde Workers' Committee
DORA	Defence of the Realm Act
GNCTU	Grand National Consolidated Trade Union
ILP	Independent Labour Party
IPMS	Institution of Professionals, Managers and Scientists
LRC	Labour Representation Committee
LRL	Labour Representation League
NAPL	National Association for the Protection of Labour
NIRC	National Industrial Relations Court
NUM	National Union of Mineworkers
NUPE	National Union of Public Employees
SRB	Special Review Body
SWMF	South Wales Miners' Federation
TASS	Technical, Administrative and Supervisory Section
TGWU	Transport and General Workers' Union
UDM	Union of Democratic Mineworkers
WTUL	Women's Trade Union League

INTRODUCTION

The emergence of the trade union movement has been one of the most significant events in recent British history, not least because for almost three centuries it has been rejected, both formally and informally, by the state and the employers who saw it as a dangerous movement which threatened the free operation of the market and restricted the introduction of much needed technological change. In recent years unions have been considered to be a major reason for the failure of the British economy, 'the British disease'. Only during the two world wars and from 1945 to the mid-1970s has there been any significant honeymoon period between trade unions, employers and government – even though many unions have enjoyed good long-standing relations with their employers through established negotiating arrangements. At the present time, the consensus gone, they are once again seen as being in conflict with the aims of the state – a situation which has led to the imposition of restrictions on their freedom of action and to a substantial decline in membership.

The structure of trade unions has, of course, changed substantially over time. In the eighteenth century trade unions were small, often insecure, societies of skilled or semi-skilled workers. Many quite clearly emerged to deal with a particular dispute and disappeared once the issue was reconciled. By the late nineteenth century unions had widened their base as their legal right to exist became more socially acceptable and their membership broadened out to include many of the unskilled. Local societies of skilled workers came together to form national organizations, both of a federal and centralized nature. The formation of the Trades Union Congress in the 1860s also added impetus to the movement and enabled it to campaign for improvements in trade union rights. Nevertheless, the trade union movement still had many deficiencies. The number of workers organized by unions was only a small proportion of the total workforce and was something of an exclusive body, even though most of them were by no means a skilled aristocracy of labour. There were few female trade unionists and, as in the case of the Victorian and Edwardian clerks, they were often seen as a potential weakness to the trade union movement accepting low wages and having no life-time commitment to their work. Not surprisingly, then, trade unions frequently ran campaigns to get women out of the industry, most obviously in the textile industry where mothers were encouraged to stay at home.

During the twentieth century many of these weaknesses have been reduced. There has been an enormous widening of the trade union base in most industries to a situation where, by the late 1970s, about 57 per cent of the workforce were members of unions – although the proportion had fallen to around 49 per cent by the mid-1980s. The increasing move towards amalgamations has also greatly strengthened the movement to such an extent that while in 1917 266 trade unions represented just over four and a half million workers affiliated to the TUC there were only 83 unions affiliated in 1988, with just over nine million members. The twentieth century has also seen the increased involvement of women in trade unionism, although the union structure is still overwhelmingly dominated by men.

The move from exclusivity to openness has meant that the involvement and place of the individual within unions has changed. Until the mid-nineteenth century the majority of workers in any union would have participated directly in the affairs of the local branch. From the late nineteenth century onwards, however, when mass unionism became more common, the move was, increasingly, to pay professional organizers. This was the major feature adopted by the Gasworkers' and General Labourers' Union and by the other large 'new unions' of the late 1880s and the early 1890s. The problem, of course, is that the officials often lose touch with their members, as was evidenced on Clydeside during the First World War and in the Hull dockers' dispute of 1954. Unofficial strike action by trade unionists is often a reflection of this type of situation.

As the trade union movement has developed, many debates and issues have emerged to fascinate historians and it is the examination of these which forms the basis of this book. On the history of early British trade unionism there has been much discussion about the extent to which trade unions existed prior to the Industrial Revolution. Whereas it is often suggested that trade unionism only emerged in permanent form at the beginning of the Industrial Revolution an increasing amount of evidence now suggests that

INTRODUCTION

Britain was a far more industrialized society in the seventeenth century than is often supposed, or was indicated by Gregory King's survey, and that there were many small industrial disputes by bodies of workmen who, if the brevity of their organization can be ignored, might be regarded as being members of trade unions.[1]

Another debate has focused upon the importance and effectiveness of the Combination Acts of 1799 and 1800 in restricting trade unionism. It has been argued that the acts were a new attempt by the state to oppress the working classes.[2] Yet others have argued that there was nothing new in the legislation and that it was a rather ineffective instrument of oppression. Recent opinion is still divided. John Rule claims that the acts as well as extending old restrictions also introduced new penalties for actions that were purely industrial and which would not have been, by themselves, acted upon by other eighteenth-century legislation directed against combinations; while J. Moher considers the legislation to have been ineffective.[3] There may well have been a class dimension to the acts.[4] Connected with this is a third debate associated with the repeal of the Combination Acts in 1824 and 1825. Why did the repeal take place? Was it simply a product of the lobbying of Francis Place or did other factors come into play?

For the decades of the 1830s and 1840s the most controversial debate concerns the extent to which trade unionism can be seen as part of the wider political Labour movement. In other words, the question is – were trade unions deeply involved in the radical, republican and chartist periods of the 1830s and the 1840s or did they remain aloof from such activities? In the early 1970s Dr John Foster wrote that trade unionism was very closely associated with the political consciousness of the working classes.[5] This view was countered by that of A.E. Musson who denied the connection.[6] However, recent evidence does tend to suggest a connection and involvement of type.[7]

The years of the mid-Victorian prosperity, 1850–75, have drawn historians to speculate upon the degree of accommodation which trade unions came to with capitalism. There is, on the one hand, the image of the fobwatched and top-hatted trade union leaders hobnobbing with the chief industrialists and employers of the day, a situation reflected in the relationship between Alexander Mac-Donald, the miners' leader, and Lord Elcho, who had extensive coal interests. Left-wing writers have particularly pressed this view

3

forward, cultivating the impression of respectability presented by the trade union 'Junta' and the Webbs' interpretation of the events of this period.[8] Yet other historians have questioned the extent to which there could be such an accommodation and suggest that in reality the interests between labour and capital were antagonistic and could not easily be reconciled.

For the late nineteenth century the focus changes once again, in an attempt to measure the political impact of 'new unionism' and the threat of de-skilling. This has led to many questions. Were the Webbs correct in their estimation of 'new unionism'? What was distinctive about the 'new' unions? Was there de-skilling and the development of a homogeneous working class or did differences between the skilled, semi-skilled and unskilled still persist? In general there is less of a debate about 'new unionism' and more consensus that 'new unionism' refers to both the formation of new unions, among the unskilled, semi-skilled and skilled, and the opening up of existing unions to new members. Many of the 'new unionists' were committed to the eight-hour day and state intervention but, it is argued, one should not expect all the new unions to be general in form nor socialist in intent. The fact is that there were marked differences within the working classes due to the uneven pattern of the development of capitalism. The working class may not have been de-skilled and was most certainly not homogeneous.

By the early twentieth century the trade union movement was expanding rapidly in periods of economic prosperity. There was an amalgamation movement, more officials were appointed, and trade unions were becoming associated with the emergent Labour Party, the independent political party of the working class. The features of these trends have been closely scrutinized. Nevertheless, there remains an underlying feeling among some writers that the revival of the pre-First World War trade union movement had a lot to do with the emergence of the industrial syndicalist movement led by Tom Mann.[9] Yet, although Bob Holton may argue that British syndicalism was tremendously important in this period, it is clear that the evidence for this is all rather slim. There appear to have been few syndicalists and their influence upon the pattern of trade unionism appears to have been rather slim.[10] They were not directly associated with many of the major industrial conflicts of this period, the vast majority of strikes had no intention of threatening and overthrowing society, and the views of syndicalists were clearly not widespread.

4

INTRODUCTION

The First World War saw the rapid increase in trade union membership and, despite the contrary impression given by the events on Clydeside, the vast majority of trade unions clearly did well out of the war effort. In the post-war years, however, the movement fell back and the major focus of attention has been placed upon the General Strike. Numerous questions have been asked about the event. What were the causes of the General Strike? Was it the culmination of the rise of industrial militancy since 1910? How effective was it? Did it fail? What were the consequences of the end of the dispute? Bitter debate still divides historians on many of these questions. Nevertheless, the issue which divides most concerns the extent to which the General Strike can be seen as a watershed in Britain's industrial relations. Some Marxist writers certainly see the General Strike as a watershed, as do other writers of a right-wing perspective.[11] These two groups do, however, differ on the meaning of the defeat. On the other hand, a body of opinion, represented by Gordon Phillips, maintains that the General Strike did little to alter the pattern of industrial relations and did not force the TUC to change direction.[12] This view is further reflected in the work of Professor H.A. Clegg who has recently suggested that, in any case, the General Strike should not be seen as a defeat for it checked employers, made them think about industrial action, and actually slowed down the pace of wage reductions.[13]

Since the Second World War trade unions have assumed an increasingly important part of the British economy. Herein lies both their strength and weakness. Because of their heightened importance they have been drawn more closely into decision-making, into the National Economic Development Council and similar bodies. At the same time, their greater importance has made them a target for those who see many of Britain's industrial ills in terms of restrictive attitudes of trade unions. Thus, the 'Thatcherite' attack upon trade unions throughout the 1980s can be seen as an attack upon the restrictive nature of trade unionism. Yet, although there are many issues, there have been few major debates about the history of trade unionism of the last forty-five years – except perhaps the issue of consensus and the extent to which trade unions have contributed to the 'British Disease': Was there a political consensus in the post-war years? and Are trade unions responsible for Britain's industrial decline? The majority of opinion on the first question appears to be that there was a political consensus. On the second question there are still marked differences between Conservative writers, who see trade unions as the great beneficiaries of the welfare state which has imposed an enormous burden upon British industry, and others who are prepared to argue that there is little evidence to suggest that trade unionism has added considerably to Britain's economic decline.[14] There are also many subsidiary questions to these main themes, pertaining to the relationship between the trade union bureaucracy and the rank and file, and to the way in which trade unions are responding to the challenges of the 1980s and 1990s.

Final Note

The history of British trade unionism has been intensely controversial, due largely to the partisan nature of much of what has been written. But the increasing availability of trade union records has opened up the history of British trade unionism to wider scrutiny. During the last twenty years many collections of records have become available, and some, such as the George Howell collection, the TUC Annual Reports and the records of trades councils, have been microfilmed for more general circulation. Government and Cabinet records have also become available up to 1960 and add to the considerable amount of published government material in the form of, for example, annual reports on trade unions and royal commissions. Many libraries and trade union organizations have kept their own records. The National Union of Mineworkers' headquarters at Barnsley contains, for instance, a superb collection of trade union documents, government reports relating to mining and extensive collections of newspaper cuttings. The Calderdale archives at Halifax contain one of the most impressive collections of trade union archives, although it can in no way rival the Webb collection, of trade union rule books, annual reports, pamphlets and other sources which are to be found in the British Library of Political and Economic Science. Also, the *Bulletin of the Society for the Study of Labour History*, now renamed as the *Labour History Review*, has often reproduced primary material on trade unions as well as report-backs on conference dealing with trade union history.

As a result of the increasing availability of primary material, the approach to the study of trade union history has changed greatly since the 1950s. It is now far more common to look at trade unionism from below than it once was, even though there is still a

INTRODUCTION

preponderance of viewing trade unionism from above, through its major unions and the TUC. Indeed, the rank-and-file and shop-floor dimensions have become more evident in recent writings. Furthermore, the dramatic decline in membership which the British trade union movement has faced in the 1980s has certainly revived an interest in the movement, partly in the hope of some that research might provide clues as to the possible reasons for the decline and the suggestions for its future recovery.

The primary aim of this book is to produce a clear pathway through the forest of detailed research which has appeared in recent years in order to enable the general, rather than specialist, reader to appreciate the major debates which have convulsed the study of British trade union history and to reflect upon how the increased availability of new primary sources has affected and altered the state of our knowledge. Although it contains the details of some of my own research, it is, by and large, to others that I owe a debt, for it is into their debates that I enter.

NOTES

This introductory chapter is based upon that written at the beginning of K. Laybourn, *British Trade Unionism c. 1770–1990: A Reader in History* (Alan Sutton, Stroud, 1991).

1. P.H. Lindert, 'English occupations, 1670–1811', *Journal of Economic History*, XL, No. 4 (1980), pp. 685–712.
2. E.P. Thompson, *The Making of the English Working Class* (Penguin, 1968), p. 546; J. Foster, *Class Struggle and the Industrial Revolution: early industrial capitalism in three English towns* (Unwin, 1977), pp. 38, 49–50.
3. J. Rule, *The Labouring Classes in Early Industrial England 1750–1850* (Longman, 1986), p. 274; J. Moher, 'From Suppression to Containment: Roots of Trade Union Law to 1825', *British Trade Unionism 1750–1850* (Longman, 1988), ed. by J. Rule, pp. 74–97.
4. J.V. Orth, 'The legal status of English trade unions, 1799–1871', *Law Making and the Law-Makers in British History* (1980), ed. by A. Harding (Royal Historical Society, 1980), pp. 195–207.
5. Foster, *op.cit.*
6. A.E. Musson, 'Class Struggle and the Labour Aristocracy, 1830–1860', *Social History*, 3,(1976), pp. 340–3.
7. I.J. Prothero, 'London Chartism and the trades', *Economic History Review*, xxxiv, no. 2 (1971), pp. 202–18; R. Fyson, 'Unionism, Class and Community in the 1830s: Aspects of the National Union of Operative Potters', *British Trade Unionism 1750–1850* (Longman, 1988), ed. by J. Rule, pp. 200–19.

8. S. and B. Webb, *The History of Trade Unionism* (1894); T. Lane, *The Union Makes Us Strong* (Arrow Books, 1971), and also supported by the views of J. Foster, *op. cit.*, and many other sources.
9. Bob Holton, *British Syndicalism 1900–1914* (Pluto, 1976).
10. H.A. Clegg, *A History of British Trade Unions since 1889: Vol. II, 1911–1933* (Clarendon Press, Oxford, 1985), chapter 2.
11. J. Foster, 'British Imperialism and the Labour Aristocracy', *1926: The General Strike* (Lawrence and Wishart, 1976), ed. by J. Skelley, pp. 3–57.
12. G.A. Phillips, *The General Strike: the Politics of Industrial Conflict* (Weidenfeld and Nicolson, 1976), chapter 13, particularly pp. 293–5.
13. Clegg, *op.cit.*, chapter 10.
14. A. Sked, *Britain's Decline* (Historical Association, 1987).

CHAPTER ONE

EARLY TRADE UNIONISM c. 1770–1850

The organization of workers into trade unions began well before the occurrence of the rising pace of industrial development of the late eighteenth and early nineteenth centuries. Already by the seventeenth century groups of artisans had organized themselves on both a permanent and temporary basis and, by the eighteenth century, industrial conflict was not an unusual feature of British industrial life, a fact testified to by the large body of legislation, of both a general and trade-specific nature, which emerged throughout the eighteenth century to restrict their activities. Employers were never very happy about the independent economic actions of their employees and often used the law to ensure that the workers remained dutiful and obedient to their wishes. The law, in any case, was hostile to workers' organizations, although the forty or so acts which existed to forbid workers' combinations were clearly neither effectively nor consistently applied. Trade unions and workers' combinations were obviously more clearly established and widespread in the seventeenth and eighteenth centuries than is commonly supposed, although one must always reflect that trade union membership up to the 1850s was generally confined to the few and to the skilled.

Historians, attempting to analyse the emergence of trade unions in this period have focused upon four main debates. The first has been a discussion of the extent to which trade unions existed: how pervasive was trade union organization and how frequent was strike action? The second has been very much associated with the controversy about the introduction of the Combination Acts: how effective were they in limiting trade union activity? The subsidiary question has often been: to what extent were these laws evidence of class legislation? Thirdly, there has been great attention paid to the Repeal of the Combination Acts. This has produced a multitude of questions. For instance, to what extent was the legislation the product of the work of Francis Place as opposed to other influences? Alternatively, how effective was trade unionism during the ten years between 1824 and 1834, and why did it fail to continue developing as a national movement? Emerging from this type of question is a fourth debate which has occupied the attentions of many, particularly Marxist, historians. The question is to what extent there was a class consciousness among the British working class between 1830 and 1850? Marxist historians, such as John Foster and Neville Kirk, maintain that there was a strong element of revolutionary working-class unity in this period, of which trade unionism was a part.[1] Indeed, Foster saw trade unions in Oldham as 'schools of war' fostering labour consciousness and acting as training grounds for the rapidly emerging class consciousness which eventually challenged the control of the state in the 1830s and 1840s.[2] Also, E.P. Thompson stressed that trade unionism was just one side of the coin of class consciousness.[3] They have, on the whole, supported the contention of the Webbs that the years between 1829 and 1842 were ones of revolutionary trade unionism.[4] In contrast, some historians have pointed to the relatively limited, sectional and moderate trade unionism which existed in this period, paving the way for the mid-Victorian period when trade unionism appears to have come to some type of agreement and accommodation with capitalism. Others, such as A.E. Musson, argue that there was no particular change in trade unionism in the 1850s from that which had developed in the 1830s and 1840s.[5]

The various explanations to these questions and debates are often presented in stark terms by historians of extremely divergent schools of thought. The reality is, however, usually rather less extreme and dramatic. Trade unionism has existed since the seventeenth century, was present in most trades and industries and, in the end, exhibited relatively little revolutionary potential up to, and including, the 1840s. Rather, the major feature of trade union growth was its steady and continuous development even in the face of adversity.

Trade Unions in the Eighteenth Century

By the mid- and late eighteenth century, British trade unionism was already commonplace, even if its membership was still very restricted and impermanent. Although the records of these trade union organizations do not survive, the evidence of newspapers and Home Office papers suggest that many trades had formed some type of workers' organization which might fairly be described as trade unions. C.R. Dobson, *Masters and Journeymen: A prehistory of industrial relations 1717–1800*, suggests that he has already counted 353 (333 in England) disputes for the years of his study and the local press will undoubtedly reveal more.[6] Other historians have also concurred that industrial conflict was more common than has often been supposed.[7] The fact is that strikes and disputes were frequent in many trades, and particularly evident among the skilled artisans. This is not to suggest that trade unions were, in any sense, permanent organizations – a characteristic which the Webbs ascribed to them in their pioneering work, *The History of Trade Unionism*. Most organizations, such as the Black Lamp among miners in South Yorkshire and the Institution among the textile workers of the West Riding of Yorkshire, seem to have led a broken existence although they survived over lengthy periods of time and their resilience was remarkable. Although there were many unions which did not seem to have endured much beyond the dispute, some organizations enjoyed a semi-permanent existence. The Journeymen Feltmakers were involved in negotiations and dispute with their masters from 1696, and by the 1720s there were organizations among the London tailors. As early as 1720 combinations in the tailoring trades of London and Westminster were prohibited, and wages were to be fixed by statute, but the tailors' organizations kept resurfacing, as in their conflicts over wages in 1744/5, 1752, 1764, 1768 and 1778. Indeed, Francis Place described the organization of the tailors as a 'perfect and perpetual combination' in which orders from an 'executive' reached upwards of twenty delegate-sending 'houses of call'.[8]

In recent years there has been substantial research into other groups of workers. Adrian Randall has noted that:

> The West Country shearmen [croppers] for example were certainly organized on a parochial basis from at least the 1740s, but their unions' presence was felt only on the odd occasions, as in 1769 when a country-wide Wiltshire and Somerset federation was involved in a dispute over incomings. Certainly they left no rule books or written agreements to evidence their 'continuous association'. And in 1802 it was discovered they had joined these parochial branches into a union which embraced all cloth workers in both the West of England and the West Riding and which issued common membership tickets and co-ordinated resistance to machinery. This 'Brief Institution' only came to the notice of the authorities because of the Wiltshire Outrages of 1802.[9]

The Gloucestershire weavers were well-established by 1755–6, when they petitioned Parliament to enact new legislation authorizing magistrates to fix wages annually.[10]

These various organizations emerged and disappeared from the official record throughout the course of the eighteenth and early nineteenth centuries – as economic and political situations dictated. It is not always easy to identify such organizations in the official record, much less to obtain direct evidence of their existence. Even in London, where there was always a substantial trade union presence, the record of trade union association is slight. In the 1830s and 1840s there were over four hundred handicraft trades in London, most of which had at least one society, 'but nearly all of these are unknown'.[11] I. Prothero suggests the difficulties of tracing these organizations:

> Contemporaries often found it difficult to track down the often small and local clubs. In the early 1840s the secretary of the proposed Trades' Hall located 189, the *English Chartist Circular* knew of 114 societies; in 1838 the trades' Combination Committee was supported by 58 London societies. On most of these we are ignorant. Many were lodges or societies in the same trade. Thus 17 London trades were represented at a national trade union conference in 1845, including 8 societies of boot and shoemakers, 10 of carpenters, 2 of carvers, and gilders, 3 of engineers; several had only 50 or 60 members. In 1825 the carpenters had 12 houses. In 1832 it was estimated that there were 7 societies of shoemakers, 27 of tailors, 2 of hatters, 12 of carpenters and joiners, 20 of cabinetmakers. In 1844 the carpenters' committee represented 21 houses.[12]

Notwithstanding such comments, Thomas Large, a Leicester stocking-weaver who took part in a deputation to London in 1812, found it easy to contact trade unionists at their 'houses of call':

> We have engaged the same Room, where the carpinter committee sat when they brought on the late Trail on the sistom of colting. We have had an opportunity of speaking to them on the subject, they thought we possessed a fund on a permanent principle to answer any demand, at any time, and if that had been the case would have lent us two or three thousand pounds (for there is £20,000 in the fund belonging to that Trade). . . [13]

The problem of establishing trade unions was obviously complicated by the fact that in some cases the details offered are for 'houses of call', normally public houses where contributions were collected and information disseminated, rather than trade unions, and it is quite obvious that some skilled workers, as in the case of the London coopers, had both a trade union and a friendly society.

There were active and powerful organizations among the west of England clothing workers, the West Riding weavers, the Newcastle keelmen, the Lancashire textile workers between 1769 and 1779, in the Liverpool seamen's strike in 1775 and also among the Spitalfield weavers, the hatters, bookbinders, printers and other groups. In some cases, there is evidence of links, as between the Institution in the textile areas of the West Riding and south Yorkshire miners, but this was often for limited strike purposes and the evidence is slight. Although by no means ubiquitous, trade unions were far more common than has often been supposed.

These organizations of workmen emerged for many different reasons. Historians generally discount any link between the medieval guilds and workers' organizations but they recognize in their decline the need for workers' organizations. And the seventeenth-century decline in the use of the Statute of Artificers (1563), whereby justices had the right to fix wages of both artisans and labourers, may have also encouraged similar developments. One obvious response was the emergence of friendly societies and box clubs throughout the eighteenth century. The Newcastle keelmen organized such a society against sickness, old age and the cost of death in 1699. Box clubs, where money was collected by the workers and placed for safe keeping and checking in a box, were one form of this friendly society arrangement. It was but a short step for some of these social responses to become involved in strike activity. The Friendly Society of Ironfounders (formed in 1809), the Friendly and Benevolent Society of Vicemen and Turners (London, 1818), the Mechanics Friendly Union Institution (Bradford, 1822), Steam Engine Makers' Society (Liverpool, 1824), and the Friendly Union of Mechanics (Manchester, 1826) are some examples of the gradual mutation of a friendly society into a trade union, which saw them assume the willingness to take strike action. Others workers' organizations simply emerged from groups of artisans and labourers who felt aggrieved at wage levels and working conditions, even if their commitment was short-lived. But there are also grounds for arguing that workers' organizations were part of a wider community response.

About twenty years ago, E.P. Thompson wrote about the 'moral economy' of the English crowd, whereby the crowd or the community exercised some controls over the markets through riots and related behaviour.[14] More recently, this notion has been applied to industrial conflict.[15] It seems possible that one aspect of the eighteenth-century industrial economy was the defence of customary wages. Such a view has been expressed in a recent article on the Gloucestershire weavers in the eighteenth century. It argues that:

> In the eighteenth century such assaults [the suspension of the weavers' protecting laws] provoked protest everywhere but some communities were particularly inclined to protest. Weavers in the West Country were. So were the Cornish miners and many others. In such areas a tradition of protest grew up; here that 'rebellious plebeian culture' to which Thompson refers was forged; here the moral economy was reinvoked and reinforced. Protest therefore fostered protest. But protest also fostered concessions. The authorities' and the clothiers' awareness of the readiness to protest influenced their handling of problems and perhaps made them a little more willing to arbitrate or negotiate. Even in defeat protest could be seen to pay dividends. The strike of 1756 failed to secure annual rating for long and in 1757 the machinery for arbitration was repealed. But the clothiers did not follow up their victory and begin a wholesale reduction of wage rates, which in fact stayed fairly stable in the second half of the century. Their victory had been too costly to want such another. It was because protest did offer such dividends therefore that the Gloucestershire weavers, as did many others, continued to invoke the moral economy not only as consumers but also as producers in times of crisis throughout the eighteenth century.[16]

Industrial action could equally be connected with the protection of wages, the improvement of conditions and a whole variety of activities which might, or might not, be considered to be part of the moral economy of the eighteenth century.

The variety of industrial activity was similarly diverse. It could take the form of strike activity, but was as equally likely to include a wide range of other activities. Strikes did occur in many cases, as among the West Country weavers in 1764 who were threatened with wage reductions, and rolling strikes were employed by calico printers, papermakers and compositors well before the end of the eighteenth century. However, in some cases the action was aimed against machinery – sometimes against those machines which were threatening a continued way of life but also against machines simply because they were the property of the master. Although Maxine Berg at one time argued that there was 'no machinery question' in the eighteenth century,[17] she now accepts that in areas of regional decline there was resistance to machinery:

> In Essex a major woollen weavers' revolt in 1715 extinguished any idea of
> a factory system there. In Barking in 1759 weavers fought the
> introduction of a mill for cleaning and loosening wool. . . . Spinning
> remained backward, and there were no jennies until 1794, whereas they
> had been in use in Yorkshire since the 1790s. In the West Country a
> jenny set up in Shepton Mallet in 1776 was destroyed by the
> mob. . . .[18]

In addition, it appears that the extent to which there were distinctions and barriers between the workforce and the employers may have contributed to the opposition to machinery – such feelings being greater in areas where the possibilities of social mobility were less. Evidently some opposition also emerged where machinery threatened the possibility of female labour:

> In the 1730s engine looms in the silk manufacture dispossessed the
> buttonworkers of their needlework. In 1737 the women of Macclesfield
> 'rose in a mob and burnt some looms'.[19]

Trade union organizations were, of course, restricted by a whole series of laws which forbade their existence. Many specifically declared against unlawful organization, such as the 1726 Act to prevent unlawful combinations in woollen manufacture where:

> great numbers of weavers and others concerned in the woollen
> manufactures in several towns and parishes in this kingdom have lately

formed themselves into unlawful clubs and societies, and have presumed, contrary to the law, to enter into combinations . . . .[20]

Nevertheless, the existence of such legislation does not appear to have prevented, although it might have restricted, the existence of trade union organizations.

The Combination Acts, 1799 and 1800

The Combination Acts of 1799 and 1800 were, in many ways, an acknowledgement of the growth of trade unionism during the late eighteenth century. What contemporary writers and historians have been uncertain about is their precise significance. Initially, on their repeal, it was argued that they had been largely ineffective; the clerk to the investigating committee of 1824 reflecting that the Acts had 'in general been a dead letter upon those artisans upon whom *it was intended to have an effect*: namely, the shoemakers, printers, paper-makers, shipbuilders, tailors, etc., who have had their regular societies and houses of call, as though no such act was in existence.'[21] However, historians of the late nineteenth and early twentieth centuries, particularly the Hammonds in their book *The Skilled Labourer*, rejected this assessment seeing the Combination Acts as a new departure by which the state forged an effective instrument of repression against the workers: 'the workpeople were at the mercy of their masters.'[22] In turn, this view was challenged by Dorothy George in the 1930s when she suggested that the Acts were limited in their effectiveness.[23] Recent writings have, on the whole, revived some of the views of the Hammonds. Both Professor J.V. Orth and Professor John Rule claim that the Combination Acts marked a departure in the State's attitude towards trade unionism and Rule, in particular, feels that there is sufficient evidence to suggest that they were being used, with some effect, by several employers.[24] James Moher, on the other hand, is far more dismissive, suggesting that the Combination Acts were ineffective.[25] What then do we make of the Combination Acts? Were they restrictive class legislation or so ridden with social and cultural difficulties as to be ineffective?

The story of the emergence of the Acts is well known. In 1795, during a period of disturbance and uncertainty, the master mill-wrights of London petitioned Parliament to take action against the combination of their employees. Out of subsequent debates a bill was prepared by Parliament but, on the suggestion of William Wilberforce, it was turned into a general measure. The result was the Combination Act of 1799, which was replaced by an amending Act in 1800. Trade unions were already treated as illegal in England in common law and under existing statutes but the new legislation did by-pass the lengthy procedure of preferring an indictment at the sessions or assizes, during which period the offenders had often moved to another part of the country, by allowing for immediate summary jurisdiction before two magistrates. However, if justice was to be administered quickly the sentences were, at a maximum of three months' imprisonment or two months' hard labour, very light by the standards of the day. In addition, the Acts also forbade combinations among employers.

There is little evidence that legal proceedings were ever taken against the employers and there has been no serious debate upon that point. The real differences between historians emerge as to the extent to which the Acts were effectively used to curb combinations. There is no doubt that the Acts were used. The 1800 Act was invoked in 1801 to threaten with punishment the workers of Messrs Bulmer's shipyard at South Shields; the workers subsequently apologizing to the employer for their threatened actions.[26] It was also used in 1802 when James Read, the chief Bow Street magistrate, was sent to Wiltshire to deal with disturbances and to arrest the shearmen's committee. Six men were gaoled for offences under the Act – although in this case the problem was one of social unrest rather than industrial activity.[27] John Foster also argues that although in Lancashire, excluding Wigan and Liverpool, there were in fact only seven convictions at the Quarter Sessions in the five years between 1818 and 1822, the Combination Acts were a serious challenge to trade unionism.[28] There is thus ample evidence that the Acts were used and John Rule argues, forcefully, that they were used in an effective manner against workers' combinations in Lancashire.

In 1818 there were four major cotton strikes in Lancashire: among both the jenny spinners and power-loom weavers of Stockport, the mule spinners at Manchester and among the handloom weavers ranged throughout Lancashire. In all but the first, the Combination Acts were used to break the strikes. The law was used against the power-loom weavers of Stockport and against the mule spinners of Manchester, who struck for a restoration of wage rates between June and September. Some of the leaders of the latter group, including John Doherty, were prosecuted under the Combination Acts and imprisoned. In the case of the handloom weavers they had, from the turn of the century been demanding state regulation of wages in order to protect their living. As their earnings diminished rapidly, and their plight increased, handloom weavers struck in Bolton, Manchester and elsewhere. In their attempts to raise money from the public, the president and the two secretaries of the weavers' union were committed for conspiracy under the Combination Acts on 16 September. In February 1819 they received two sentences of two years and one of a year. It is, perhaps, not surprising that John Rule should conclude that 'The tendency of modern historians to play down the effect of the Combination Laws as of little practical consequence gains small support from there.'[29]

Three years later, in 1822, the Blaenavon miners were also defeated in a strike by the use of the Combination Acts. As the Revd Powell stated in a letter to Henry Hobhouse:

> The triumph of the law is at this moment of unspeakable consequence, because if the men had been able to hold out for another month or six weeks, I fear the masters would have felt obliged to give way, the trade being certainly in an improving state, with almost certain prospect of a rise in price next quarter, which will enable the masters to give an advance in wages. . . .[30]

Nevertheless, there is a body of opinion which plays down the importance of the Combination Laws. James Moher, in a wide-ranging survey of the Acts, suggests that there were in fact very few examples in which the Combination Acts were taken up, that the Home Secretary was reluctant to proceed with prosecution, and that the effectiveness of the legislation was clearly blunted by the fact that many workers' combinations were clearly masters of obfuscation, claiming to be friendly clubs rather than trade unions.

The very occurrence of numerous industrial disputes is further proof to Moher that the Acts were effete. He instances the case of the London millwrights who were in dispute with their masters in 1801, 1805 and 1812 but were not faced with prosecution under the Combination Acts.[31] The suggestion is that the masters were reluctant to use the Acts since it was felt that such action might make trade relations worse and was in any case of limited value:

Judicial hostility to the extension of the magistrates' powers also seems to have made prosecution under the 1800 Act an uncertain venture, and the higher courts seemed to have been strict over the procedural requirements of the Act, so that obtaining a conviction before the justices came to be viewed by some masters as of doubtful value. . . . The ability of the journeyman's clubs to evade prosecution and conviction by various means has to be considered a most significant factor in rendering the Act of 1800, like so many before it, ineffective in suppressing trade union activity.[32]

Such a view is supported by the activities of the croppers of Yorkshire in 1802, who, before their ill-fated ventures into Luddism, struck at Benjamin Gott's mill near Leeds, in protest against the taking on of irregular apprentices. Gott complained of the croppers: 'Their power and influence has grown out of their high wages, which enable them to make deposits, that puts them beyond all fear of inconvenience and misconduct.'[33] In the end, the croppers won and the Combination Acts were ignored. The occurrence of the Lancashire weavers' strike of 1808, the London dock strike of 1810, and the strike by the Sheffield scissor grinders all provide further evidence of the ways in which the laws were ineffective in curbing industrial activities by aggrieved workers.

How does one reconcile these two contrasting views and, indeed, are they reconcilable? Clearly, much of the evidence is a matter of emphasis. There were obviously some prosecutions under the Combination Laws, but there were not that many and they did not prevent industrial activities by workers' combinations, although industrial action was blighted in some trades where the authorities took action against the strike leaders. As yet, there is no clear picture of the full extent of the use of the Combination Laws but the current state of knowledge suggests that there may have been regional differences – perhaps, for instance, the authorities taking tougher action in Lancashire than in London. What cannot be denied is that in some, perhaps only a few cases, the Combination Acts were used to destroy trade union activities in a few industries and trades. Equally, it also has to be accepted that employers in areas where industrial relations were better, and where groups of workers felt less threatened, were able to ride out industrial conflict without recourse to the law and without disturbing good industrial relations. The picture is thus much less clear and marked than some historians have suggested, and there appears to have been a patchwork of responses in the use of the Combination Acts.

If the application of the Combination Acts depended upon employer employee relations, occupational and regional variation, it is none the less clear that the Acts were class-orientated in nature. Employers were not prosecuted, even though their combinations were also made illegal, and the Acts introduced a new class element into English law. As Professor Orth has recently suggested that in 1799 the penalties were for the first time prescribed for workmen and not, as in previous legislation, directed against particular crafts. Something approaching a class dimension was being applied.[34]

The Repeal of the Combination Acts, 1824 and 1825

Although the Combination Acts may have been of variable impact and introduced elements of class legislation, it is clear that the government was persuaded, by 1824, that they were no longer required. But why did Parliament repeal the legislation? It has been normal to suggest that Francis Place played a vital contribution in the repeal of the Combination Acts, although there have been some reservations on this account which suggest that his campaign operated in an increasingly favourable climate for repeal. Indeed, without that atmosphere of reform undoubtedly his campaign would have failed.

Place was a somewhat unlikely leader of the repeal movement. He was a London Radical who had risen from being a member of the Breech-makers' Society to become a master tailor. He began his campaign in 1814, at the time when the statutory law requiring a seven-year apprenticeship before a skilled craft could be exercised was repealed. Place, himself, favoured such a repeal, wished to see the free operation of supply and demand and felt that workers' combinations would disappear if the Combination Acts were repealed, believing that they only existed because they were banned and because working men saw them as their only safeguard. He later wrote that:

> In 1814, therefore, I began to work seriously to procure a repeal of the laws against combinations of workmen. . . . As often as any dispute arose between masters and men . . . I interfered, sometimes with the masters, sometimes with the men . . . always pushing for the one purpose, the repeal of the laws.[35]

He also worked closely with economists such as J.R. McCulloch and Joseph Hume, who was also a Radical MP, and had his case publicized through the *Edinburgh Review*. His essential argument was that the repeal of the Combination Acts would bring about the demise of trade unionism. It was a view shared by others, including many employers, and as a result a sympathetic Select Committee was set up in February 1824. It was originally formed to look at a range of labour laws but was eventually given the duty of examining the laws of combination.

Outlining the events leading to the formation of the Select Committee and its activities, Place claimed a major part in the repeal of the Combination Acts:

> On the 12th February [1824] Mr. Hume made his motion and obtained his Committee. . . . Mr. Hume wrote a circular letter announcing the appointment of the Committee, and inviting persons to come and give evidence. . . . Meetings were held in many places; and both masters and men sent up deputations to give evidence. The delegates from the working people had reference to me, and I opened my house to them. Thus I had all the town and country delegates under my care. I heard the story every one of these men had to tell. I examined and cross-examined them; took down the leading particulars in each case, and then arranged the matter as briefs for Mr. Hume; and, as a rule, for the guidance of the witnesses a copy was given to each . . . Thus he was enabled to go on with considerable ease, and to anticipate and rebut objections.[36]

Obviously, then, Place could make some legitimate claim to stage managing the evidence and the activities of the Select Committee. However, Moher feels that Place was operating in a favourable climate in which he was assisted by the open-mindedness at Westminster, where William Huskisson at the Board of Trade and Robert Peel as Home Secretary appeared favourable to the new legislation.

For a variety of reasons, then, the Combination Acts were repealed in 1824. The new Act gave immediate immunity from prosecution in common law to 'combinations of masters and workmen' but reiterated that violence and malicious picketing would be punishable by imprisonment and hard labour for up to two months. But the consequence of this legislation, along with a boom in trade, was an outbreak of industrial unrest throughout the country. As a result the government set up a new Select Committee, which included Hume aided by Place, to investigate the seamen, papermakers, shipwrights, coachmakers and cotton spinners. Resisting the demand of the employers to re-impose the

Combination Acts, it recommended that the common law of conspiracy should be re-introduced although some trade union objectives, such as the regulation of work and hours, would be free from prosecution. The sentences for molestation, intimidation and obstruction were increased to three months and the courts were left to define these offences, a situation which has normally pertained ever since. In addition, the 1825 Act also deprived workmen of the right, granted by the 1824 Act, to combine to induce other workers to break their contract of service by striking.

Moher has suggested that the repeal of the Combination Acts acknowledged a place for trade unions within a framework of wage negotiations.[37] Rule, on the other hand, suggests that while the repeal of the Combination Acts did establish such rights one should not lose sight of the fact that those rights were limited and that employers 'made hardly any move towards incorporating unions into their management strategies'.[38] But how well did trade unions do between 1825 and 1850? To what extent is it possible to suggest that there was a 'revolutionary period' between 1825 and 1834, or between 1829 and 1842? To what degree were trade unions incorporated into the working 'class consciousness' of the years between 1830 and 1850? To what extent were trade unions involved in Chartist activity? And, can one talk justifiably about different periods and stages of trade union history as the Webbs did for the years up to 1850, or indeed beyond?

Conflict and General Unionism 1825–34

From 1824 the trade unions which came out into the open were a mixture of those already established and new ones which emerged to meet the exigent needs of the workmen at a particular period in time. There has been a temptation to compartmentalize these unions, and their organization, into periods of expansion and contraction. Trade unions apparently flourished from 1825 to 1834, until the affair of the Tolpuddle Martyrs and the collapse of the Grand National Consolidated Trade Union. Alternatively, as the Webbs suggested, trade unionism could be regarded as revolutionary between the formation of John Doherty's General Union of Spinners in 1829 and the plug plots and general strike of 1842. Such divisions might be convenient but they do not represent what really happened. They tend, on the whole, to exaggerate the importance of rapid change in trade union development. While some Marxist writers might hold to a belief in periods of revolutionary trade union activity, it is becoming increasingly evident, particularly through the writings of A.E. Musson, W.H. Oliver and R.A. Leeson, that, although there was change, trade unionism developed more steadily than the Webbs first suggested through patient organization and the improvement in working and social conditions.[39] The state also acted in a repressive manner when it needed to do so. And, as Musson has stressed, it is difficult to see what was distinctive or new in the 'New Model' unionism, which the Webbs saw as beginning with the formation of the Amalgamated Society of Engineers in 1851, given that many of their characteristics had emerged by the 1830s and 1840s.

To what extent can the years between 1825 and 1834, or between 1829 and 1842, be seen as periods of heightened, not to say, revolutionary trade unionism? There is no doubt that the repeal of the Combination Acts did provide an increased opportunity for open trade union activity, the threat of which forced the government to set up a second Select Committee to modify the 1824 legislation. Even in the wake of the 1825 legislation trade unionism continued to be more open and overt. Throughout the country, industrial activity continued apace. In June 1825, under the leadership of John Tester, the Bradford woolcombers and weavers' strike began, to win the 'equalisation of wages' throughout the textile districts of Yorkshire. The Saddleworth weavers fought for a similar cause in 1828 and 1829. John Doherty formed the General Union of Spinners in 1829, which organized strikes throughout Lancashire. There were the Swing Riots in 1830, the Operative Builders, organized in 1833; the Grand National Consolidated Trade Union, formed mainly around London trade union organizations, in 1833 and 1834; the Committee of United Weavers and many other similar organizations also emerged. There was the case of the Dorchester Labourers or Tolpuddle Martyrs, the disturbances in Oldham in 1834 and the plug plots of 1842. Yet these events, often presented as highlights of trade union history, were distinguished by their tendency to controversy and failure. The more bread and butter development of trade unionism, which saw the steady and more significant growth of trade unionism, is less frequently commented upon.

In the immediate years following the repeal of the Combination Acts, trade unions were generally defeated in their industrial actions, often amid suggestions of lack of internal unity and rumours that unions had been misused by the union or strike committees. The Bradford woolcombers and weavers, seeking to improve their wage rates, were defeated in a strike which began in June 1825. John Tester, the strike leader, later pointed to the way in which he felt that the funds of the union were squandered by the committeemen who possessed an ability to consume beer: 'Their powers of deglutition were most prodigious.'[40] The London tailors were defeated, for the first time, in 1827 when they attempted to prevent an influx of cheap female labour into their trade. The carpet-makers of Kidderminster were defeated in 1828 after resisting a wage reduction of 17 per cent for six months. The Saddleworth weavers were defeated, collapsing when the employers locked them out at the beginning of January 1829. In this case, the lack of internal unity was evident and George Shaw, in his diary, accused the committee of misusing the strike fund; 'the money has been decamped, and who can have taken it? I say those through whose fingers it has passed.'[41] Similar fates faced the cotton spinners and other groups in the 1830s.

The various attempts to form national union organizations were similarly unnecessary. There had been attempts to form 'a union of trades', the 'Philanthropic Society', throughout Lancashire in 1818, and a similar body, the 'Philanthropic Hercules', in London during the same year, but they had come to nothing despite, in the latter's case, the sterling efforts made by John Gast and the shipwrights. It was not until John Doherty organized the cotton spinners in the late 1820s that the prospect of national unionism loomed large.

The Lancashire cotton spinners were frequently in dispute during the 1820s but did not have any notable successes until 1828. During that year, John Doherty organized the Manchester Spinners into a series of 'rolling strikes' against masters who were not paying the normal rates. There were also numerous other disputes in the surrounding areas, at Hyde, Stalybridge, Stockport and elsewhere. In many cases it was found that the employers were able to press upon their workforce the 'document' or the 'odious document', forcing workers to leave the unions. Consequently, Doherty decided to attempt to bring all the unions together into the Grand General Union of Operative Cotton Spinners throughout the whole of Great Britain and Ireland. At a meeting in the Isle of Man in December 1829 it was agreed that there would be a national strike pay level of

10s (50p) per week and that the approval of strike action should be sought from other districts. The Grand General Union, in an attempt to control the labour market, also instructed 'That no person be learned to spin after the 5th April 1830 except the son, brother, orphan, nephew of spinners. . . .'[42] But the ambition was greater than the achievement. In 1830 there were strike defeats for the union at Bolton, Chorley and Ashton and, in December 1830, it faced a showdown with fifty-two owners in Ashton and Stalybridge who reduced wage rates and forced two thousand spinners to take strike action. Eventually, after violence and amid strong anti-trade union feeling, the strike was defeated in February 1831.

Doherty's attempt to create general unionism through the National Association for the Protection of Labour [NAPL] was no more successful. Formed in 1830, initially confined to Lancashire and attracting about twenty trades, this body ran two newspapers, *The United Trades Co-operative Journal* and *The Voice of the People*. It held its delegate meetings in Manchester and its main purpose was to defend wages, 'the funds of the Society shall be applied only to prevent reductions of wages', and paid out of contributions made into a central fund.[43] It is claimed that it quickly attracted about seventy thousand workers, mainly connected with the textile trades and concentrated in Lancashire and Cheshire but it also attracted coal miners and had spread into Yorkshire, being active in Huddersfield and Leeds. However, once the Grand General Union of Operative Spinners collapsed in early 1831, the NAPL also withered away. Its secretary absconded with £160 of funds, it had failed to give sufficient help to the spinners in Ashton-under-Lyne in their attempt to defend their wages, and Doherty's attempt to revive it in London in 1832 came to nothing.

The building craftsmen did only a little better than the cotton spinners in forming a national and general trade union movement. There had been moves to organize a national organization among carpenters and bricklayers in 1827 with the formation of a General Union of Carpenters and Joiners. [Ten years later there was a national society of bricklayers known as the Manchester Unity.] In the early 1830s the building craftsmen expressed their discontent at the practice of allowing 'general contractors' to intervene between themselves and the architects and were concerned to prevent the general contractors forcing down wages. They were also worried about piecework and the increasing number of apprentices. The result was confrontation with the masters in June 1833, when the masters decided to break the union. Employers in Liverpool and Manchester pressed their campaign forward and the operative builders responded by holding a six-day conference in Manchester, where 270 delegates representing 30,000 builders decided, following an address by Robert Owen, to form a Grand National Guild of Builders. Among its many functions was that of being a co-operative organization prepared to compete with the contractors: 'We shall be enabled to erect all manner of dwelling and other architectural designs for the public more expeditiously, substantially and economically than any Masters can build them under the individual system of competition.'[44] The conflict also developed in Birmingham as well as Manchester, and Owenite ideas were well represented in the activities of the union in that area, which appeared to extend to the building of the Birmingham Guildhall.

The Builders' Union certainly had some success in increasing trade union membership among the masons, the carpenters and joiners and other sections, to the extent that its membership may have reached forty thousand at its height – despite its sectarian base which excluded building labourers. But it proved to be a short-lived union. It attempted to conduct strikes and lock-outs in Manchester, Liverpool, Preston, London, Leeds, Nottingham and other areas at the same time as it was beginning co-operative schemes. It lost the strikes in Manchester and Liverpool towards the end of 1833. In Birmingham, the financing of the Guildhall failed and there were various problems in maintaining trade union unity. The 'Exclusive' section of the union, led by Angus McGregor, moved to avoid any development of the union along more general lines and, in about 1834 or 1835 the Builders' Union collapsed.

Neither the cotton workers nor the builders were able to create effective national or general unions and Robert Owen's famous attempt to form an alternative and more effective Grand National Consolidated Trades Union (GNCTU) was no more successful. The history of this union is almost legendary. Owen attempted to organize his new union in London, along the general lines suggested for the 'Philanthropic Hercules' in 1818. In addition, he wished to make his new organization a co-operative organization and a labour-exchange movement.

Owen's choice of London was encouraged by the improvement of trade union organizations in London during 1833, when the

26

carpenters, the shoemakers and the tailors were increasingly active. The Grand Lodge of Operative Tailors was formed towards the end of 1833 as an open or general union committed to reducing the hours of work and ensuring that a newcomer to the trade could work his 'stint', that is to produce a given quality and quantity of work. In effect this was partly an attempt to prevent newcomers entering the trade and consequent creation of sweated conditions. As a result, in April 1834 the union fought an unsuccessful strike against the employers. The shoemakers also attempted to control the influx of labour into their trade. They formed themselves into the United Trade Association in October 1833 and formed a Grand Lodge of Operative Cordwainers in order to encourage the creation of labour exchanges. The Federated Society of Carpenters also grew rapidly in London, and attempted to end task work, sub-contracting and overtime in order to prevent wage cutting and unemployment. These organizations, and many others, were active in industrial conflict in London throughout 1833 and 1834.

What appears to have welded these groups into Owen's GNCTU was the Derby lock-out of 1833/4. In November 1833 a 'turn-out' of workers in several trades took place in Derby and the employers decided that they would not take back any men who belonged to the trades' union. In the wake of this decision, the Derby men called for support throughout the country and, on the initiative of the London tailors, the GNCTU was formed in mid-February 1834. Ostensibly, its aim was to support the strikers in Derby but it also put forward a fanciful scheme for setting up its own factory in Derby. That scheme came to a halt in April when the Derby strike failed.

Much has been written about the GNCTU and the extent of its influence. The Webbs gave it undue emphasis and argued, and Henry Pelling still does, that its membership might have temporarily reached half a million.[45] Such a claim was dismissed many years ago by W.H. Oliver who suggested that the subscribing membership was about 16,000, 11,000 of whom came from London: 4,000 tailors, 3,000 shoemakers, 1,000 silk weavers and several thousand others.[46] What thus emerges is that it failed to act as a truly national organization. Although, as has often been pointed out, the original delegates who drew up the charter were drawn from Birmingham, Wolverhampton, Derby, Worcester and Bradford as well as London, it is clear that after the return to work it became an essentially London-based organization.

In its short history the GNCTU focused upon a number of issues. It attempted to establish mutual support in strikes, to provide friendly society benefits, and it also made efforts to organize women workers. It organized the Great Meeting at Copenhagen Fields, on 21 April, at which Robert Owen was present, in protest at the sentencing of the Dorchester labourers and it supported, apparently rather grudgingly, the London tailors in their strike in April 1834. Owen, by this time, had moved the GNCTU firmly towards a co-operative production in newly-acquired workshops and was becoming increasingly disdainful of industrial action. It was this factor which helped to precipitate the decline of the GNCTU in 1834, and its demise in 1835. The failure to adequately support the tailors, and the annoyance of the shoemakers who felt that they had a prior claim to strike action helped to ensure the practical collapse of the GNCTU in the summer of 1834. The tailors, defeated in their strike action by the end of June, withdrew from the organization and were soon followed in their decision by the shoemakers. The GNCTU was effectively dead, even though the last rites were not performed until August 1835.

Obviously the first major period of open, national and general unionism had not been the success which trade union leaders, such as Doherty, had hoped for. Professor Musson certainly feels that the importance of the whole period has been greatly exaggerated. On the other hand, John Rule maintains that the years between 1825 and 1834 were ones of some significance in the development of trade unionism and Dr Hunt has also maintained that the years between 1829 and 1834 saw moves in the direction of working-class consciousness.[47] In the final analysis, Professor Rule may have got the period and the events right. Here was a period when artisans used the rhetoric of 'labour' in an attempt to defend themselves against the threat of being driven down socially to the ranks of the unskilled.[48] There is certainly strong evidence that it was the skilled rather than the unskilled and semi-skilled workers who were active in trade union organization at this time. The problem they faced, however, was their continued sectionalism, which was a block to the development of any working-class consciousness in this period. Indeed, it is clear that the GNCTU lost some of its impetus due to such sectionalism.

One should not forget, however, that the state continued to play its part in limiting the power of trade unions at this time. J.A. Jaffe has recently argued that the powerfully-entrenched North-East Pitmen's Union, which was particularly active in 1831 and 1832, was destroyed by the coordinated power of the state and capital — troops for evictions, and loans from the Newcastle bankers to finance the import of blackleg labour.[49] Such action occurred fairly regularly, but the direct intervention of the state is most emphatically illustrated by the famous case of the Tolpuddle Martyrs.

The Tolpuddle Martyrs, 1834, and the Reaction of Trade Unions

The events which led to the sentencing and transportation of the Tolpuddle Martyrs have been repeated many times. In outline, six Dorsetshire farm labourers, from Tolpuddle, were prosecuted because of their attempts to form a union due to the zeal of a magistracy and government who were determined to stamp out potential industrial unrest in the countryside. Receiving a wage of only 7s (35p) per week, the labourers formed a union to resist a reduction to 6s (30p) per week. George Loveless, and his fellow labourers, had not planned a strike or intimidated anyone and their only crime, a minor one at common law, was to administer an oath of secrecy. As a result they were tried, as George Loveless recorded in his pamphlet *The Victims of Whiggery*, under 'the act 37 Geo III, cap. 123, for the suppression of mutiny and conspiracy against by the marines and seamen, a number of years ago at the Nore.'[50] Although they had no intention of committing sedition they were sentenced to transportation for seven years.

There was much protest and violent reaction to their sentencing. The trade unionists of London marched to Copenhagen Fields, with Robert Owen at their head, on 21 April 1834 to present a petition to the government protesting at the treatment of the Dorsetshire labourers. The London Dorchester Committee was formed to develop their case inside, and outside of Parliament, and there were meetings throughout the country, protesting at their treatment. The Oldham disturbances, which saw the impounding of trade union books and the arrest of two trade union leaders, attacks on the police by the crowd, attacks upon mills, and the shooting of James Bentley by those defending one of the mills, heightened tensions further. Although the Oldham disturbances stemmed from different causes, they collated into the events and concerns which surrounded the arrest, sentencing and transportation of the Dorsetshire labourers. Elsewhere, similar attempts were made to suppress trade union activity in Northamptonshire, Cheshire and Dublin.

The Webbs assumed that the militant trade unionism of this period came to an end in the mid-1830s with the failure of general unionism and the oppression which arose following the case of the 'Tolpuddle Martyrs'. But more recent assessments tend to suggest that the importance of the events of the early 1830s was exaggerated by the Webbs, that the campaign to release the 'Tolpuddle Martyrs' helped to unify trade unionism, and that there was success – the sentences of the Dorchester labourers being remitted in 1836 and they being returned home in 1838. Even more to the point, it has been argued, by R.A. Leeson, that trade unions were in no way halted by the events of 1834 and that 'Business as usual' continued between then and the 1850s.

'Business as Usual': Trade Union Developments 1834–50

Leeson suggested that as far as craft unions were concerned the events of 1834 and 1835 made little impact upon their development. Indeed, he argues that during the mid-1830s the craft unions moved to another stage of their development. From the late eighteenth century separate trade societies in different towns had begun to 'put themselves in a state of union', and that seventeen trades had achieved this by 1800, rising to forty by the mid-1830s. From then onwards:

> . . . most of these trades had embarked or were about to embark on a difficult, often contentious but remorseless process of achieving one single union, by the method known as 'amalgamation'. There were some 14 amalgamations or attempts at such, during the late 1830s and 1840s. The 1851 Amalgamated Society of Engineers and the Boilermakers and Iron Shipbuilders's amalgamation which followed in 1852 thus in a way crowned a development, rather than gave rise to one in an exemplary fashion. During this second period, the basis elements of the more highly centralised more solidly financed and more cautiously acting unions were brought into being, by internal and external pressures.[51]

Most of the 'amalgamations' which emerged consisted of between 20 and 80 member societies and contained between 500 and 2,000 members, thus suggesting that the average local society, or branch as it became in the 1840s, numbered between 15 and 50 members.

Leeson's view contrasts sharply with that presented by the Webbs. They argued that the defeat of general and national unionism led to a retreat back to the small local trades clubs and imply little trade union development. Leeson's evidence suggests that while the grand schemes for national and general unions did not work in the 1830s there were more stealthy moves to create amalgamations within the craft unions which were overlooked by the Webbs in their desire to establish the characteristic of the 'new model' unions.

This difference of interpretation and argument can, in part, be explained by the fact that trade unions were clearly less militant and more careful in their activities between 1835 and 1850. Discounting the 'general strike of 1842' and a few protracted strikes, there was less militant, violent and class conscious behaviour in the years between 1835 and 1850 than there had been before. Clearly there were still many incidents of conflict and one should not accept too readily the official trade union line of the typographers, the flint glass bottle-makers and other skilled groups, disowning unnecessary industrial action. In 1845 the National Typographers Association, which had just been formed, had forty-five strikes reported to it. Also, there were strong moves to establish the sectional rights of trade unions. Even though statutory apprenticeship had been abolished in 1814 many trades continued to impose apprenticeship rules in an attempt to enforce a 'closed shop' on the trade. The Sheffield cutlery trades, the typographers, the flint glass bottle-makers and many other trade unions were active in enforcing rules demanding both apprenticeship and a maximum number or ratio of apprentices that would be allowed in the works. For those who broke the rules in the Sheffield trades, sabotaging of equipment, known as 'rattening' frequently occurred. For the persistent offenders, intimidation in the form of blowing up houses and similar violent actions, was used as became obvious at the time of the revelations of the 'Sheffield Outrages' in the 1860s.

Craft unions clearly developed in a cautious manner and built up their funds, their amalgamations, their craft practices and their means of punishment for offenders during the 1830s and 1840s. Many of the features of craft unionism, dubbed as 'new model unionism' by the Webbs, were already developing and in place before the 1850s. As part of this process unions did begin to acquire funds – sometimes held locally and sometimes at the head branch –

not all centralized as the Webbs suggested of their 'new model unionism'. In the case of the Potters, for instance, this process was reversed. *The Potters' Examiner and Workman's Advocate* noted, in 1844, that:

> It will be recollected that the former union of our trade was grounded on the principle of one general fund, subscribed to by every branch of the trade and placed in the hands of a single individual and one General Board of Management in who were invested the Government of the Society both local and general.
>
> This gave rise to various events, among others . . . dishonesty from the accumulation of large funds in the hands of a few individuals, and the Society not being entrusted under the hands of a few individuals.
>
> The concentration of power in the hands of a few.
>
> The inevitable destruction of the Society in the event of the disturbance of its General Executive.
>
> This is now all altered in the present Union. The Society is now governed on the same principle as the U. S. of America. Each branch is a separate state, and each branch Board a State's Congress. All the funds and executive power of the branch is vested in its Board. A Central Committee, a General Board of Management is established . . . is invested with the general management of the United branches of the Operative Potters. This Committee controls all the branches, with the exception of $\frac{1}{2}$d per member subscription to defray all incidental expenses.[52]

In addition, the movable head office, whereby various branches shared the role of running the union in order to avoid cliquism, began to be replaced in the 1830s and 1840s, by the appointment of permanent national officers. In the late 1840s, the masons appointed a paid general secretary and in 1845 the boilermakers also elected their first full-time general secretary.

On balance then, the impact of the affair of the Tolpuddle Martyrs and the collapse of general unionism did not prevent the development of trade unionism. The grandiose schemes for general unions may have ended but there were significant developments in the growth of craft unionism and, despite their lower profile trade unions did not lack the militancy and commitment to taking strike action when necessary. The real casualty of these years was probably a commitment to general unionism, which did not reappear until the 1880s. Nevertheless, trade unionism, even in its more sectional mood, does not appear to have cut itself off from all other popular movements.

EARLY TRADE UNIONISM

The Trade Union Movement and Chartism

There has been considerable debate as to the extent of the involvement of the trade union movement in Chartism. The Webbs argued that the contacts between the two movements were of a limited nature.[53] Henry Pelling has concurred, arguing that the links between trade unionism and Chartism are 'tenuous'.[54] On the basis of current evidence, this view would appear to be in need of serious modification. The recent work of John Rule, I. Prothero, F.C. Mather, R.C. Challinor and Brian Ripley, make the views of earlier historians untenable.[55] The trade union connection with Chartism was clearly much more evident than has been suggested.

In his work on London Chartism and trade unionism, Dr Prothero suggests that some trades, such as tailors, shoemakers, carpenters and masons, were well represented in the activities of the London Chartists while others, most notably engineers, bookbinders and printers, were less in evidence. The reason for this split appears to be that those trade unionists in trades which were being threatened by an influx of unskilled labour, for example, in tailoring and shoemaking where 'sweated' conditions were occurring, gave their support to Chartist action. The engineers in Manchester and Glasgow were deeply involved in Chartist activities in 1842 and in Bradford, the Woolcombers Protective Society, which organized about 30 per cent of the increasingly threatened and structurally unemployed handcombers, was active in the violent events which occurred in Bradford Chartism in the summer of 1848.

Trade union action was also evident in the 'general strike' of 1842, although trade union support for the 'Plug plots risings', as they were popularly known, was far from universal. The strike occurred between July and August 1842 and spread throughout fifteen counties in England and Wales and eight in Scotland. The events began with a strike in the North Staffordshire coalfield in July 1842, in which production was stopped by the raking of boiler fires and by the drawing of drain plugs from the boilers. Such activities spread to the Lancashire cotton industry in August, as well as to Cheshire, the West Riding of Yorkshire, the Staffordshire potteries and other areas. In these regions there was some obvious trade union support for the action, particularly among the cotton spinners of Manchester and Oldham and the pottery trade unionists of Staffordshire. But such support was by no means universal. The cotton workers in many other areas, such as Stalybridge, Stockport and Bury, were less obvious in their support and it is fair to point out that many workers in the textile factories only walked out of work once the plugs had been drawn. And there is also considerable difference of opinion as to whether or not it was the economic conditions of the time, opportunism or a genuine commitment to the strike which united both trade unionists and Chartists. Notwithstanding such differences, there was a clear association with trade unions which is even more evident in the connections between Chartism and the miners.

The Miners' Association of Great Britain and Ireland was established at a conference in Wakefield towards the end of 1842 and united sixty thousand miners, from every coalfield in Britain, at its peak in 1844 – about 30 per cent of the mining workforce. Although Pelling argues that it wanted little to do with Chartism it is clear, from the work of Challinor and Ripley, that its Chartist credentials were unimpeachable.[56] Martin Jude, its treasurer, Thomas Hepburn, one of its leaders, and W.P. Roberts, the lawyer who became known as 'the Pitmen's Attorney-General', were active Chartists who encouraged the miners' support of Chartism before, but also particularly after, the four-month long strike in Northumberland and Durham which saw its defeat and paved the way for its gradual, but eventual demise as more strikes occurred, and failed, and as coal owners victimized trade union leaders. It is true that the main focus of the union was to raise wages, to reduce hours, and to get rid of the yearly contract or bond system which tied workers and saw them taken to court and imprisoned if they broke their bond. However, there is no doubt that the union had good Chartist credentials although it always fought strikes for economic issues, not for the Charter.

The problem in estimating the extent of trade union commitment to Chartism is that trade unions normally exist to represent the economic interests of their members and political interests are marginal, not central, to their cause. But quite clearly, there was widespread trade union support for Chartism, much focused upon particular periods of depression and the connection was more than a tenuous one.

Conclusion

Even if they were not ubiquitous, trade unions were common in most of the leading trades in the eighteenth century. Many societies sprang up to defend the wages and conditions of their members, and strike action was quite clearly a common activity. And, the Combination Acts of 1799 and 1800 did not seem to greatly affect the development of trade unionism. There was already restrictive legislation against many craft workers, much of which seems to have been ineffective, and the Combination Acts seem to have only been applied in those trades where employers decided to pursue trade unionists through the courts and where they were not intent upon maintaining good relations through traditional bargaining arrangements. That is not to say that the Combination Acts were not different, for, as Professor Orth has suggested, they brought a new class dimension to legislation by directing the legislation against *workmen*. However, recognizing the weakness of the legislation, there was a movement in favour of their repeal into which Francis Place's campaign for repeal fitted well. And the repeal of the Combination Acts in 1824 and 1825 did reveal, in the most overt form, the extent to which trade unionism was present in every trade. And the repeal did encourage the movement towards general and national unionism as never before. But it would be unwise to suggest that these movements and the Grand National Consolidated Trades Union had much success or that their failure led to the virtual demise of trade unionism, since it is clear that craft unionism developed its organization – appointed full-time officials and amalgamated in the 1830s and 1840s – and that trade unions gave significant support to Chartism. It also seems doubtful that trade unions became Foster's 'schools of war' although they may well have contributed to the growth of class consciousness, if not revolutionary class consciousness, in the years between the 1830s and 1850.

NOTES

1. J. Foster, *Class Struggle and the Industrial Revolution* (Weidenfeld and Nicolson, 1974).
2. Foster, *op.cit.*, p. 43.
3. E.P. Thompson, *The Making of the English Working Class* (Harmondsworth, Penguin, 1968 edition).
4. S. and B. Webb, *The History of Trade Unionism* (1894).
5. A.E. Musson, *British Trade Unions 1800–1870* (Macmillan, 1972).
6. C.R. Dobson, *Masters and Journeymen: A prehistory of industrial relations 1717–1800* (Croom Helm, 1980), pp. 22, 24–5.

7. J. Rule, *The Experience of Labour in Eighteenth-Century Industry* (Croom Helm, 1981); J. Rule, *The Labouring Classes in Early Industrial England 1750–1850* (Longman, 1986), p. 286; R.W. Malcolmson, 'Workers' combinations in eighteenth-century England', in M. and J. Jacob (eds), *The Origins of Anglo-American Radicalism* (Allen & Unwin, 1984), pp. 149–61.

8. Dobson, *op.cit.*, pp. 39–40, 60, 69–73.

9. A. Randall, 'The Industrial Moral Economy of the Gloucestershire Weavers in the Eighteenth Century' in J. Rule (ed.), *British Trade Unions 1750–1850: The Formative Years* (Longman, 1988), pp. 32–3.

10. *Ibid.*, p. 33.

11. I. Prothero, quoted in the *Bulletin of the Society for the Study of Labour History*, no. 36, Spring 1978, p. 10.

12. *Ibid.*, p. 11.

13. *Records of the Borough of Nottingham 1800–1835 (1952), VIII, Thomas Large to Thos. Roper and the Framework Knitters Committee*, 24 April 1812.

14. E.P. Thompson, 'The moral economy of the English crowd in the eighteenth century', *Past and Present*, 50 (1971), pp.76–136.

15. Randall, *op. cit.*

16. *Ibid.*, pp. 48–9.

17. M. Berg, *The Machinery Question and the Making of Political Economy 1815–1848* (Cambridge, CUP, 1980).

18. M. Berg, 'Workers and Machinery in Eighteenth-Century England', in J. Rule (ed.), *British Trade Unions 1750–1850*, p. 58.

19. *Ibid.*, p. 66.

20. 12 Geo, c. 34.

21. Rule (ed.), *British Trade Unions*, p. 11.

22. J.L. and B. Hammond, *The Skilled Labourer*, ed. by J.G. Rule (Longman, 1979), pp. 80, 89.

23. M.D. George, 'The Combination Laws', *Economic History Review*, 1st series, vi (1935/6), p. 177.

24. J.V. Orth, 'M. Dorothy George and the Combination Laws', presented to a Conference on the History of Law, Labour and Crime at the University of Warwick, 15–18 Sept. 1983; J. Rule, *The Labouring Classes*, p. 274.

25. J. Moher, 'From Suppression to Containment: Roots of Trade Union Law to 1825', in J. Rule (ed.), *British Trade Unionism 1750–1850*, pp. 74–97.

26. H. Pelling, *A History of British Trade Unionism* (Harmondsworth, Penguin, 4th edn., 1988 reprint), pp. 16–17.

27. Moher, *op.cit.*, p. 85.

28. Foster, *op. cit.*, pp. 49–50.

29. Rule, *The Labouring Classes*, p. 274.

30. Letter from Revd W. Powell to Henry Hobhouse, April [May], 18, 1822, HO 40/17/47.

31. Moher, *op.cit.*, pp. 89–90.

32. *Ibid.*, p. 89.

33. A. Aspinall, *The Early English Trade Unions* (Batchworth, 1949), p. 62.

34. J.V. Orth, 'The legal status of English trade unions, 1799–1871', in A. Harding (ed.), *Law-Making and Law-Makers in British History* (Royal Historical Society, 1980), pp. 205–6.

35. Francis Place Mss, 27,798ff, pp. 12–14.
36. *Ibid.*, 27,798ff, pp. 20–4.
37. Moher, *op.cit.*
38. Rule, *British Trade Unionism 1750–1850*, p. 13.
39. A.E. Musson, *British Trade Unions 1800–1875* (Macmillan, 1972); W.H. Oliver, 'The Consolidated Trades Union of 1834', *Economic History Review*, xvii, No. 1, 1964; R.A. Leeson, 'Business as usual – craft union development 1834–1851', *Bulletin of the Society for the Study of Labour History*, no. 49, 1984, pp. 15–17.
40. J. Tester, 'History of the Bradford Contest', mss, Bradford branch of the West Yorkshire Archives; J. James, *History of Worsted Manufacture* (1857), p. 402.
41. George Shaw Dairy, records of the Saddleworth Weavers' Union.
42. Resolutions of the Delegates from the Operative Cotton Spinners who met at the Isle of Man (December 1829), PRO, Home Office, 40/27 [1829].
43. *The United Trades Co-operative Journal*, 10 July 1830.
44. R.W. Postgate, *Builders' History*, p. 467.
45. H. Pelling, *A History of British Trade Unionism* (Harmondsworth, Penguin, 4th ed., 1988), pp. 29–30.
46. Oliver, *op.cit.*
47. E.H. Hunt, *British Labour History 1815–1914* (Weidenfeld and Nicolson, 1981).
48. Rule, *The Labouring Classes in Early Industrial England 1750–1850*, pp. 288–307.
49. J.A. Jaffe, 'The state, capital and workmen's control during the industrial revolution: the rise and fall of the North-East Pitmen's Union, 1830–1', *Journal of Social History*, 21, 1988.
50. George Loveless, *The Victims of Whiggery being a statement of the Prosecution Experienced by the Dorchester Labourers in 1834* (Blandford, National Agricultural Labourers' Union, 1875, being a reprint of the pamphlet produced in 1837.)
51. Leeson, *op.cit.*, p. 16.
52. Loc. cit., 6 July 1844.
53. B. and S. Webb, *History of Trade Unionism*, p. 158.
54. Pelling, *op.cit.*, p. 33.
55. Rule, *The Labouring Classes in Early Industrial England 1750–1850*, pp. 329–44; F.C. Mather, 'The general strike of 1842: a study of leadership organization and the threat of revolution during the plug plot disturbances' in R. Quinault and J. Stevenson (eds), *Popular Protest and Public Order* (Allen & Unwin, 1974); R.C. Challinor and B. Ripley, *The Miners' Association: A Trade Union in the Age of the Chartists* (Lawrence and Wishart, 1968).
56. Challinor and Ripley, *op.cit.*

CHAPTER TWO

'NEW MODEL' UNIONS AND CRAFT UNIONISM
c. 1850–87

The Webbs referred to the years between the 1850s and 1880s as the period of 'new model' unionism.[1] They considered the starting point of this period to be the formation of the Amalgamated Society of Engineers in 1851 and argued that the establishment of the amalgamation with its central funds, its headquarters in London, and its craft exclusiveness, provided an example which other union organizations followed. From the early 1860s until 1871 the secretaries of the leading amalgamateds met weekly in London as the 'Conference of Amalgamated Trades', referred to as the 'Junta' by the Webbs. The five-man Junta consisted of Robert Applegarth, of the Amalgamated Carpenters, William Allan of the Amalgamated Society of Engineers, Edwin Coulson of the Operative Bricklayers' Society, George Odger who was active in the London West-end Ladies' Shoemakers' Society and whose real power derived from being secretary of the London Trades Council between 1862 and 1872, and Daniel Guile of the Friendly Society of Ironfounders.[2] It was this body of men who, according to the Webbs, shaped the temper of British trade unionism between the 1850s and 1870s – although the Webbs recognized that other developments were also occurring. The Junta, apparently, encouraged trade unionism to eschew industrial action, fostered friendly society benefits and centralized union funds in an attempt to control strike action. It was the Junta who shaped the whole trade union movement into a pressure group to extend trade union rights. The views of the Webbs went largely unchallenged until the 1930s when G.D.H. Cole, and other historians, argued that the trade unionism of this period was dominated by the Junta and the amalgamateds. And, indeed, during the last thirty years the views of the Webbs on the 'New Model' have been largely revised – there being many unions outside the traditional craft amalgamateds, more strikes than supposed and overwhelming evidence that the 'new model' was not new. Trade unionism was clearly far more varied than the Webbs supposed although there still remains a debate about the extent to which trade unionism became integrated into mid-Victorian society.

Trade Union Growth, Structure and Policies Between the 1850s and the 1880s

Because British trade unionism was still in the early stages of its development and still subject to a wide range of legal restrictions, historians are still unsure of the precise number of trade unionists. Nevertheless, it is clear that their numbers increased and their organization improved substantially during this period. From perhaps a couple of hundred thousand by the early 1850s their membership had increased to possibly 500,000 by the 1860s and 1,600,000 by 1876.[3] Thereafter there was some decline, with Trades Union Congress membership, which represented about 70 per cent of trade unionists, falling to 379,000 in 1884 before rising to 568,000 in 1888. Such growth was obviously uneven and highly volatile – affected by trade depressions and immense regional variations. The 'Great Depression' of the 1870s and 1880s clearly reduced the number of trade unions and trade union members and it was only in London and the major industrial areas that effective trade union action persisted. In rural areas and in some industrial areas trade union membership was patchy. In the woollen and worsted textile district of Yorkshire, for instance, the almost endemically weak trade unionism of the 1850s and 1860s was further reduced in membership. Indeed, in Bradford, a community which – with its neighbourhood – exceeded a quarter of a million people, there were fewer than two thousand trade unionists organized in the Trades Council during the mid-1880s.[4] By 1850, as before that date, the typical trade society was small in size and displayed a multitude of varying structures. Some organized skilled workers, such as engineers, while others organized semi-skilled and unskilled workers, such as miners. Some had full-time officials whereas others relied upon part-time and temporary officials. Some had extensive friendly society benefits, which encouraged central control of the union, while others had nothing of the kind. Some based their executive on a 'governing branch', normally one in London, while others revolved the 'governing branch' between the largest branches. Some were open to all members of a trade or industry while others were extremely restrictive in their admittance of members. What unions lacked was a uniformity of style, although some characteristics did begin to emerge.

The Amalgamated Society of Engineers was thus merely an example of one type of trade union structure and no more typical than many others of the trade union movement, although the Webbs used it as the stereotype for their 'new model'. The ASE had centralized funds, a strong leader in William Allan, was committed to solving strikes peaceably and offered out of work, sickness and superannuation benefits to its members. Indeed, it provided an out of work benefit of 10s [50p] per week for twenty-six weeks and 5s [25p] per week sickness benefits thereafter, £12 funeral expenses, £100 on permanent disablement, as well as a variety of other benefits. Some of the features of the ASE had previously emerged in the Journeymen Steam Engine Makers' Society, which had been formed at Manchester in 1826, subsequently being known as the 'Old Mechanics'.[5] But few unions deliberately modelled themselves on the ASE, although it did provide the structure for Amalgamated Society of Carpenters and Joiners, which grew from 1,000 to 10,000 members, under Robert Applegarth's leadership between 1862 and 1871, and was committed to controlling the use of the strike weapon and developing a wide range of benefits.[6]

The majority of craft and non-craft unions did not follow the example of the 'new model'. In the Operative Stonemason's Society, the trade and sickness benefits were kept quite separate. The London Order of Operative Bricklayers' Society had no sickness fund until the 1870s while the National Association of Plasterers was a loose federation where subscriptions and benefits varied from area to area. In the Provincial Typographical Association the individual branches paid benefits, which varied greatly from branch to branch.

Many trade unions were simply not as centralized as the Webbs maintained. The Amalgamated Society of Cotton Spinners, formed in 1853, was a tightly federated society which did not centralize funds in the classic style of the amalgamateds. In the mining industry there were two major union organizations which attempted to bring the various district unions together, the National Association and the Amalgamated Association. The National Association of Coal, Lime and Ironstone Miners was formed in 1863 by Alexander MacDonald, and brought together the Scottish miners, the Yorkshire miners' unions formed in 1858, and many other district groups throughout the country. It was a federated body which, under MacDonald's leadership, attempted to control strike action. In 1869, however, those trade unionists in Lancashire and Wales, who desired a more centralized trade union, formed the Amalgamated Society of Miners which, in 1873, claimed 99,145 members compared with the National Association's 123,406.[7]

The Webbs' suggestions do not seem to be supported by the events among mining trade unions. Alexander MacDonald's union was a federated organization which sought to avoid strike action. On the other hand the Amalgamated Society was a centralized body which adopted an aggressive strike policy. Indeed, it was the defeat of several strikes which it supported that led to the collapse of the union in 1875.[8] The centralization of a union and its funds does not seem to have reduced strike action any more than a federal arrangement seems to have promoted it.

Clearly one of the central issues of recent debates has been the extent to which the trade unions of these years were moderate and pacific in their industrial relations and prepared to forego strike action. The Webbs maintained that strikes were deprecated by the trade union leaders, and, quoting the *Flint Glass Makers' Magazine*, wrote that:

> 'We believe' writes the editor, 'that strikes have been the bane of Trade Unionism.' In 1854 the Flint Glass Makers, on the proposition of the Central Committee abolished the allowance of 'strike money' by a vote of the whole of the members.[9]

And subsequently they noted the Flint Glass Makers' acceptance of capitalist society:

> Flint Glass Makers declare that 'the scarcity of labour was one of the
> fundamental principles laid down at our first conference held in
> Manchester in 1849. It is simply a question of supply and demand, and
> we all know if we supply a greater quantity of an article than we actually
> demanded that the cheapening of that article, whether it be labour or any
> other commodity is a natural result.' In this application of the doctrine of
> Supply and Demand the Flint Glass Makers were joined by the
> Compositors, Bookbinders, Ironmoulders, Potters, and, as we shall
> presently see, the Engineers.[10]

But such views have been the subject of intense debate between those who recognize the qualities of respectability and moderation which permeated this period and those who maintain that the emphasis upon the rejection of strikes has been exaggerated.

In recent years, W. Hamish Fraser has given qualified support to the view that trade union leaders, and to a large extent their rank and file, were presenting their moderation in industrial relations as part of a process of winning respectability in mid-Victorian society and within the overall strategy of obtaining trade union objectives. He does not take the Marxist line of depicting trade union leaders as having 'fob-watched' respectability and hob-nobbing with the employers, an image presented by Tony Lane in his polemical piece *The Union Makes Us Strong*.[11] Nevertheless, Fraser argues that conciliation became the main policy of British trade unions in their struggle for acceptance maintaining that:

> A third essential that unions had to get across to the middle class was their
> moderation and to do this they had to refute accusations that they were
> strike organizations. This the union leaders tried to do constantly, repeating
> time and time again the refrain 'we are averse to strikes', the 'executive
> council does all it possibly can to prevent any strike', 'the members are
> generally opposed to strikes'. 'Strikes are to the social world' declared George
> Odger in a much quoted statement, 'what wars are to the political world.
> They become crimes unless they are prompted by absolute necessity.'[12]

Elsewhere, he asserts that 'Between 1850 and 1880 the main policy adopted by trade unions, both socially and industrially, was a conciliatory one', later adding that 'It was a pragmatism that made the dominant strategy of the 1850s, 1860s and 1870s a policy of conciliation, a struggle for acceptance.'[13]

Fraser's views bend the stick towards the Webbs' view, while recognising that there were some trade unionists who had reservations about the policy of conciliation and others who were outright critics of such a strategy. And recently his general line of argument has found considerable support from E.F. Biagini, who has attempted to explain how trade union rights to negotiate over wages were encouraged by the changing attitude of classical economists to the role of trade unions and the recognition by trade unions of the reasonable limits of their power.[14] Biagini's main argument is that there was much support from classical economic thinking for the existence and the extension of combinations among working men and that public opinion came to accept this, the response being seen in the legislative improvement of the position of trade unions between 1871 and 1876. He particularly notes that J.S. Mill, in his *Principles of Political Economy* (1862), argued that 'trade unions, far from being a hindrance to a free market of labour, are the necessary instrumentality of that free market; the indispensable means of enabling the sellers of labour to take due care of their own interests under a system of competition.'[15] This 'Millian recantation', as he calls it, suggested that, unlike the old wage fund theory which denied that wages could be affected by anything other than supply and demand, trade unions had a role to play in determining the level of wages. Biagini argues that these ideas became more widespread within the trade union movement between the 1860s and 1880s, were encouraged by A.J. Mundella MP, spread by George Howell, and became standard currency within the popular press. Indeed, the *Leeds Mercury*, the most important provincial newspaper of the day, was able to accept that trade unions had a wage bargaining role by the mid-1860s. Effectively then, trade unions were legitimized in the eyes of the nation and it was, therefore, essential that they be recognized in a legal framework. For this reason the charge that trade unions were 'in restraint of trade', became less relevant. Almost in response to this changing position, it is maintained that trade unions began to recognize that they could only push wage levels up to a limited degree. For instance, T.J. Dunning, the secretary of the London Consolidated Lodge of Journeymen Bookbinders, wrote, in 1867, that:

> Beyond . . . the obtaining . . . [of] a fair demand and supply rate of wages, a trades' union can never go. . . . No legal enactment ever succeeded in preventing wages from approaching this rate, and no trades'

union ever succeeded in forcing them above it. . . . the action of trades'
unions is inseparable from and governed by the demand for labour. The
employers' class denounced trades' unions for their pernicious tyranny in
forcing up wages' when in reality it is the demand for labour . . . that
causes rises.[16]

Biagini's central point is that the classical economists began to
develop a new theory of wages which acknowledged the role which
Mill had anticipated trade unions playing in the establishment of
wage levels. This new approach, he argues, began to emerge in the
1860s and encouraged the legalisation of trade unions and the
development of a more pervasive pattern of conciliation and
arbitration. Such a machinery did not mean that trade unions
accepted their limited powers but meant that they were prepared to
defend their wage levels within a more regulated framework and
with less likelihood of strikes.

This view certainly fits in with the contemporary views expressed
by G.P. Bevan, who counted the number of strikes recorded in some
newspapers in the 1870s, and the more recent writings of J.H.
Porter and James E. Cronin.[17] Bevan's information, presented to the
Royal Statistical Society in 1880, suggests that strike activity fell to
a low level in the early 1870s before an explosion of activity
throughout the rest of the decade – and particularly in 1872 and
1873. He records that there were 30 strikes in 1870 but that the
figure had risen to 343 in 1872 and 365 in 1873. Although the
numbers fell thereafter, they remained high and 308 were recorded
for 1879. The point being made is that there was an increased level
of strike activity from about 1872, after a period of low strike
activity. Porter, in various works, has also suggested that the
development of conciliation, arbitration and sliding-scale
agreements reached its peak in the late 1860s and early 1870s but
that such arrangements could not survive the onset of depression and
falling prices – which, for instance, put paid to the attempts of
many mining unions, such as those in Yorkshire, to operate
sliding-scale agreements. He reflects that such agreements were
bound to fail if a protracted depression meant that there was only the
inevitability of wage reductions.[18] Cronin also acknowledges that
there appears to have been a strike explosion in the 1870s and that
between 1870 and 1920 strikes were more common than they had
been before.[19] Indeed, he argues that 'the strike truly came into its
own as workers' preferred form of action in the 1870s'.[20] It is thus

implied that strikes were less common before and that the 1850s and 1860s were periods of industrial calm.

Notwithstanding such endorsement, the views of the Webbs have been under attack for many years. In an important article written in 1937, G.D.H. Cole challenged the views of the Webbs that the trade unions of the 'New Model' period were not strike prone, and a succession of articles since the 1960s written by R.V. Clements, C.G. Hanson and G.R. Boyer, have suggested that trade unions did not accept the classical economics of supply and demand and were prepared to strike.[21] Indeed, Boyer argues that while insurance schemes attracted and kept members they did not enhance trade union discipline or bargaining power.

Cole attacked the importance which the Webbs placed upon the pacific policy of the 'Amalgamated Societies', writing that:

> I do not, of course, deny that the Amalgamated Societies did endeavour to follow a pacific policy, and to come to terms with the employers wherever they found this possible. But I deny that the Amalgamated Societies can be regarded as representative of the entire Trade Union movement, or even most of it, during this period, and that even the Amalgamated Societies were nearly as 'capitalist minded' as historians of the Trade Union movement commonly suggest.[22]

Clements presented very much the same argument, stressing that the British trade union movement did not suddenly relapse into an acceptance and acquiescence to capitalist conditions of employment, did not accept the political economy of the day, and always asserted the strength and value of trade unions. If they were less militant than they had previously been then that was because, in the period of mid-Victorian prosperity employers were more ready to concede wage increases. Trade union leaders were, evidently, aware of the conditions of the trade and quite willing to strike if they felt that that course of action was justified. Hanson, focusing particularly on the evidence presented to the Royal Commission on Trade Unions, 1867–9, amplifies the point by suggesting that the leaders of the 'Amalgamateds' were attempting to deliberately engineer the impression that trade unions were responsible and passive organizations and that, supported by Professor Beesly and Frederic Harrison, they were attempting to get trade unions legal recognition; Beesly, Harrison and the Positivists saw trade unions as the way to achieve progress in society. At the end of the day, as

Applegarth had to admit, when faced with the fact that the benefit schemes of the Carpenters and the Engineers were not actuarially sound:

> In the first place I am afraid that there has been so much said about the social aspect of our societies, that is their benevolent purposes, that the main purposes for which they are established have been somewhat lost sight of, and therefore I take this opportunity of stating that pure and simple ours is a trade society, and as such I wish it to be regarded, although we have a number of excellent benefits in connexion with it about which this gentleman [actuary] has been consulted.[23]

He adds that:

> A careful study of the evidence as a whole given to the 1867 Commission suggests that there had been no real change in the nature of trade unionists, or even in the nature of certain craft unions, in the 1850s and 1860s, although it suited the interests of the trade union lobby to imply that there had been such a change.[24]

The problem, of course, is to separate the intent from the reality. Was the trade unionism of the 'Amalgamateds' pacific in intent and action, as the Webbs, Fraser and Biagini imply, or was this simply a sedulously nurtured myth as Clements and Hanson argue? In other words, what actually happened?

It is true that the secretaries of the large societies were open in their hostility to strikes and attempted to control them. Robert Applegarth struggled valiantly to restrict strike action, as he did with the case of the Birmingham joiners who refused to return to work in 1865 despite the fact that employers agreed to withdraw the use of the 'discharge note'. Other members of the 'Junta' did the same. Nevertheless, their intent does not appear to have been supported by the actions of trade unions.

Many of the major trade unions seem to have emerged out of industrial disputes or to have been baptized by such action. This was true of the West Yorkshire Miners' Association and the South Yorkshire Miners' Association, both formed in 1858 at a time of strike action, and the Amalgamated Society of Engineers formed in 1851, which was faced with strikes and an engineering lock-out in 1852 arising from the use of unskilled, or 'illegal men' on the planing and boring machinery. The ASE dispute began at Messrs

Hibbert and Platt of Oldham in 1851 and became the basis of a national lock-out throughout Lancashire and in London where the employers locked out those men who refused to accept an increase in the number of unskilled men in the shops. And, despite raising £12,000 within the union and £12,000 from other unions and individuals, the ASE was defeated and the 'odious document' was forced upon many engineers. In addition, the following year saw the protracted Preston lock-out, which lasted from 24 November 1853 to 24 June 1854, during which the power-loom weavers of Preston, led by James Whalley, fought against an attempted wage reduction of 10 per cent, the importation of blackleg labour, and the arrest of the strike leaders on charges of 'molesting and obstructing' some of the blackleg labourers.[25]

The conflict within the London building trades in 1859 and 1860 also gave rise to militant industrial action. It began with the demand of a nine-hour, rather than a ten-hour, working day by the masons working at Messrs Trollope of Pimlico and led on to a general lock-out by employers against the trade unions in the building trade who responded to the demand for a nine-hour day by attempting to impose 'the document' upon the workers. Eventually, in February 1860, a compromise was arranged whereby the employers dropped their attempt to force the men out of their unions in return for the unions dropping their demands for the nine-hour day. It was as a result of this conflict that Applegarth's union, the Amalgamated Society of Carpenters and Joiners, was formed in June 1860 and that the London Trades Council was formed in May 1860. George Howell, Secretary, writing the Second Annual Report for 1861/2 noted the reasons for the foundation of the Trades Council:

. . . Most of you are aware that during the winter of 1859–1860 delegate meetings were held weekly for the purpose of aiding the Operative Builders of London in defending what is popularly termed the 'odious document'. That document was a blow aimed at the Trades' Unions of this country . . .

At the termination of the struggle it was felt that something should be done to establish a general trade committee, so as to be able, on emergency, to call the trades together with dispatch, for the purpose of rendering each other advise and assistance, as circumstances required. A Committee was therefore elected to draw up a code of rules, which was done, and after being amended at a delegate meeting was adopted and the Trades Council established.[26]

Trade unions were immensely aware of the need to settle industrial disputes, and none more so than the London Trades Council, but were equally committed to fighting disputes if the need arose.[27] And while Cronin and others argue that the mid-Victorian period was one of relative industrial quiescence it is simply speculation to maintain that point of view for there are no accurate strike figures for that period. Reasonably accurate strike figures did not appear for the first time until the late 1880s, and then were subject to many changes in definition. G.P. Bevan's survey of strike activity, based upon newspaper reports, can hardly be considered as an accurate indication of strike levels and, in any case, only covers the 1870s. The mid-Victorian period saw more trade unionism in Britain than had ever occurred before and that fact alone would tend to suggest that a higher level of industrial conflict ensued than was the case before.

In addition, as already suggested in the previous chapter, strikes were by no means the only form of industrial conflict available. The sabotage of equipment and intimidation were not uncommon. Indeed, the events of the early 1860s provide some of the strongest evidence of the way in which trade unions were prepared to be aggressive in their pursuit of control of the labour market. The Sheffield Outrages of the 1860s, which culminated in a Royal Commission, and a report in 1867, are part of the folklore of nineteenth-century trade unionism and reflect the willingness of trade unions to use a variety of techniques to control those who would not follow union policies. 'Rattening', the practice of removing wheel-bands from grinding machines or other tools of workmen was a common method of disciplining workers and there was other more violent activity, such as the Hereford Street outrage of 8 October 1866, when the house of Thomas Fearnehough was blown up. Only the offer of indemnity from prosecution to those who were guilty of this, and other offences, revealed the extent to which William Broadhead, of the Grinders' Union, had been prepared to go to enforce the unions' will. Broadhead had employed Samuel Crooks to enforce the union's power on several occasions for a sum of £15, 'that was about the regular sum'.[28]

The trade union movement of the mid-Victorian period may well have been selective and exclusive, and largely skilled and semi-skilled in the members it organized, but it does not appear to have been particularly quiescent in industrial matters nor necessarily inclined to provide benefits. Indeed, one should not forget that behind the mirage of order and respectability which the amalgamateds presented before the Royal Commission on Trade Unions, 1867–9, there was in fact a very diverse trade union movement which not only did not reflect the characteristics of the amalgamateds but which fundamentally opposed their domination. This was true of London, as well as the provinces, where George Potter became the main opponent of the amalgamateds.

Potter was a joiner who had shot to fame during the building trade disputes in London and had been secretary of the committee of London building trades' workers from 1859 to 1861. His fame spread as a result of the fact that he was manager, editor and owner of *The Bee-Hive*, a working class and trade union newspaper, at various times between 1861 and 1877 and could project his beliefs in the need to reject the ideas of the Junta and his demand for an independent political party for the working class to a relatively wide audience. He formed the London Working Mens' Association as a counter to the London Trades Council, which was for a time dominated by the amalgamateds, and was active in the National Reform League.[29] The main point is that Potter, who held a personal resentment against Applegarth, constantly challenged him on the London Trades Council throughout 1864–5, drew support from many of the small London societies who had lost members to the Amalgamated Carpenters, and presented an alternative to the rule of the amalgamateds.

One should, however, exercise caution in presenting the conflict between the two sides. Not all the leaders of the amalgamateds were present at any one time and Potter was often able to get his own supporters returned to the Council. But Potter's support was widespread. Apart from the London trades, many of the provincial trade unions supported him. Potter's supporters called a Conference of Trades which met in London in March 1867 and, briefly, had a representative on the Royal Commission on Trade Unions. In addition, the formation of the Trades Union Congress, which was initially more influenced by Potter than the amalgamateds, did much to undermine and replace the influence of the Junta.

A TUC-like body had long been the objective of many trade unions and it came into existence very largely as a result of the work of William Dronfield, a journeyman printer who was secretary of the Sheffield Association of Organized Trades, and Sam Nicholson,

President of the Manchester and Salford Trades Council. In 1866, they set up the United Kingdom Alliance of Organized Trades in order to raise funds to help unions resist lock-outs but it had collapsed by the end of 1867. In 1868 Sam Nicholson and William Wood, who was the secretary of the Manchester Trades Council, invited trades councils and, later, trade unions to meet in Manchester. Meeting in Whit-week 1868 it attracted thirty-four delegates from trades councils and some of the national societies from the provinces, but only attracted two delegates from London, one of whom was Potter, and the London Trades Council was not represented. There was at that time no formal organization, although it became an annual gathering and formed a parliamentary committee in order to pressure Parliament over the need to give legislative protection to the trade union movement.[30]

The fact is that there was much aggressive trade union action in London, influenced by George Potter, and significant trade union activity in the provinces and that it was not until the early 1870s that the amalgamateds began to participate in the wider movement, at a time, in 1871, when the Junta was breaking up and its main figure, Robert Applegarth, had resigned his post as secretary of the Amalgamated Carpenters. Equally obvious is the fact that trade unions were prepared to take aggressive industrial action, of many types, in order to secure their aims. Trade unions were not the acquiescent organizations that the Webbs portrayed them as being, but were quite willing to arrange industrial conflict without strikes if it appeared in their interests to do so. Nevertheless, although the role of the amalgamateds and the Junta has been exaggerated, it is clear that they did contribute significantly to the recognition of trade unions during the 1860s and the early 1870s and the views of Fraser and Biagini, which emphasize the increasing acceptance of trade unions by employers, classical economists and the press have some relevance – although even craft unions often faced a slow and painstaking struggle for acceptance.

The Problem of Trade Union Recognition: the Case of the Bradford Graphical Society

It is sobering to reflect that even the most skilled and exclusive of craft trade unionists could find it difficult to get recognition from their employers. For instance, the Bradford typographers were still having difficulties in negotiating with their employers in the mid-1860s. The Bradford Graphical Society claimed that it was founded in 1820 and it is first mentioned in 1845 in the records of the Northern Typographical Union, an association of local societies formed in 1830, which the Bradford Society appears to have joined in 1844. It was also a member of the National Typographical Association, founded in 1844, but was independent of that organization on its effective collapse in 1848. It remained so until 1859 when it became a branch of the Provincial Typographical Association, formed in 1849 in replacement of the National Association.[31]

In 1866, when the first remaining minute book opens, the Bradford Society was a small union of sixty or seventy skilled compositors and pressmen, led by a part-time secretary, Tetley Hustler, who remained in office until 1899. There was no systematic pattern of meetings but when it did meet the society used a room at the 'Shoulder of Mutton' in Kirkgate, Bradford. The members were men who could earn 24 shillings per week (£1.20) for a normal 57-hour week and considerably more with overtime; £2 and more was not uncommon when overtime and night-work on papers was included. In terms of skill and income levels the typographers ranked alongside, if not above, the engineers. Here was a society whose members were highly paid, which attempted to enforce apprenticeship rules, provided 'insurance' benefits and offered a 'travelling allowance' of a night's subsistence and a one shilling (5p) allowance for those on the tramp – men who were looking for work and travelling from society to society, in a predetermined order.[32] The society was also strengthened by the tendency of members to allow apprentices in the trade to lodge with them, thus maintaining a social as well as economic control of the emerging workforce.

Yet the Bradford Graphical Society, despite its powerful position, still found difficulty gaining acceptance from its local employers. Negotiations between the society and the employers was still conducted at local level with reluctant employers and communications with them remained unsigned. On 17 August 1866 they circulated to employers to meet them at Laycock's Temperance Hotel, Old Manor Hall, Kirkgate, on 27 August 1866, whereupon the employers would not concede a rise in normal wage rates from 24s (£1.20) to 27s (£1.35) although they offered 2d (about 1p) extra for those working between 10 p.m. and midnight, and 3d extra (just over 1p) for those working between midnight and 5 a.m. The society accepted this, although there was much unease and negotia tions were renewed in 1867.[33]

Part of the problem was that employers were reluctant to accept the legality of trade union activity and preferred to deal with the union separately. A letter from William Byles, of the *Bradford Observer*, to the society, dated 18 March 1867, said of the Master Printers that they were:

> unwilling as a body to enter into any arrangements with the members of the society . . . [but were] *individually* prepared to concede the request for uniformity in the hours of labour . . . other matters must be left to the separate action of the various employers and their workmen.[34]

The society appears to have accepted this stance, met the employers again, and attempted to couch their request for a 55-hour week and 27s (£1.35), in their circular of the 27 November 1867, in moderate language, 'in the sincere hope and expectation that a more satisfactory result may be arrived at.'[35] It appears the request for reduced hours and increased pay was settled amicably, although the precise arrangements were the subject of separate 'house', 'shop' or 'chapel' arrangements with the individual employers.

In the fashion of many of the societies of the skilled, the over-arching emphasis of the Bradford Graphical Society was the need for conciliation and accommodation. Reasonable employers, who conceded wage increases and reductions in hours, were often allowed to employ non-society men against the rules of the society. As a result, there were rarely major disputes which convulsed the whole industry in Bradford, but rather a set of limited and on-going disputes whereby the society refused union recognition to a specific printing shop. This was particularly evident in the case of the struggle with George Harrison's, General Printers, of Bolton Road, Bradford. The office was opened in 1869 when the eight journeymen were admitted as members but disputes began in 1873 when the printers employed too many apprentices. The society, therefore, closed the office to union men, although union men were allowed to take up jobs with Harrison's in the economic depression between 1877 and 1885, before the employers themselves dismissed their known society men without giving them a fortnight's notice. The men's case was fought in the law court and lost.[36]

This society of skilled workers also found it difficult to win concessions among the Bradford newspapers, and was constantly in a situation of closing or blacking union shops connected with uncooperative newspapers. Frequently, the problem was not one of controlling the employment of apprentices and non-society men but of controlling the introduction of new machines. The Bradford Graphical Society had to decide upon the introduction of the Hattersley composing machine into Bradford on 27 January 1868.[37] The Hattersley machines were often operated by four boys, one composing and three distributing, and the society adopted a policy of accepting the machines while trying to reduce the number of boys employed in printing shops.[38] Only gradually did it win concessions from employers on this policy and in 1878, a bad year for employment in Bradford, the society passed a resolution at a quarterly meeting:

> That this branch believes that any opposition to the introduction of composing machinery would be impolitic, but urges that all peaceful efforts be used to induce employers to utilise the labour of journeymen in working them.[39]

The experience of the Bradford Graphical Society was probably not untypical of many other craft societies throughout the country – with the proviso that the society was probably more powerful than many in that it represented workers whose wages rose above the ordinary for even craft workers. Groups of workers, such as the miners, might, temporarily, have wielded more power and the centralized amalgamateds might have been more powerful than the operation of essentially local societies, but it is difficult to suggest that most societies would have been in a stronger position to determine the pattern of industrial activity in their own trade. What their experience shows is the vulnerability which even craft workers had in dealing with their employers and the threat of new machinery.[40] It was of no small account then, that the amalgamateds, the trade councils that emerged throughout the country and the trade unions should win, in the 1860s and 1870s, a more permanent position for trade unions through the shaping and influencing of new parliamentary legislation.

The Fight for Legal Status

While historians have questioned the influence of the amalgamateds, they have not disagreed, except in matters of fine detail, upon the influence which the amalgamateds and other unions exerted upon Parliament in the attempt to strengthen the legal position of trade unions. There were, in fact, four areas in which they exerted influence: the protection of trade union funds, the treatment of workers and employers before the law, legality of trade unions and the issue of picketing, which had been a constant problem since 1825. Success was not achieved fully on all fronts, but between the late 1860s and 1875 it is clear that the position of trade unions had been transformed, both socially and economically, within Victorian society, and that this was in no small part due to the efforts of some of the amalgamateds.

The Amendment Act, the Combination of Workmen Act of 1825, had left trade unions in rather a precarious legal position. Most actions of trade unions could be interpreted as being illegal and the great concern for most trade unionists was Section 3 which penalized any action by workers that involved violence, threats, intimidation, molestation or obstruction. All these terms led to judicial interpretation but the last two were particularly malleable to varying interpretations and during the next few decades courts maintained that it was punishable to give an employer notice that his workmen would strike unless he dismissed a particular work-man; to tell a workman that he had been 'blacked'; or to shout 'Black' or similar words at a workman. It was not at all clear whether such actions were actionable in their own right or only if ac-companied by acts of violence. By 1851 courts were accepting that even peaceful persuasion to induce others to leave their employment was illegal. This position was altered and clarified by the Molestation of Workmen Act of 1859 which allowed workmen 'peaceably' and 'in a reasonable manner' to persuade workers to strike. But even these terms were open to judicial interpretation and in 1868 Baron Bramwell, trying the leaders of the London Operative Tailors' Society, declared that even watching non-strikers and giving of 'black looks' was to intimidate.

There were many other difficulties of law and it should be remembered that up to 1846, as a result of legislation in 1799 and 1817 designed to restrict political clubs, it was illegal for trade unions to organize themselves into branches. That issue had been clarified but as larger union organizations emerged and increased their funds, there was the problem of protecting those funds. Under common law a trade union was a voluntary association and its funds were held jointly by its members, and no member could be found guilty of stealing joint property. As a result, the trade union funds were usually held by someone outside the trade union, normally the publican at the public house where the trade union held its meetings. In 1855 a campaign led by the ASE won the right of trade unions to protect their funds by depositing their rules with the Registrar of Friendly Societies as long as, under Section 44, their purposes were not illegal. Unlike a friendly society their rules were not certified. However, the Scottish Registrar of Friendly Societies refused to receive the rules of trade unions and a court case in 1866 concluded that the actions of trade unions might be illegal since unions were in restraint of trade. It was at this point that the famous Hornby v. Close case occurred in 1866.

In this case, Hornby, the president of the Leeds, not the Bradford branch as normally suggested, of the United Society of Boilermakers and Iron Shipbuilders of Great Britain and Ireland, sued Close for the return of £24 of the branch funds, but the Bradford magistrates claimed that the union's funds could not be protected under the Friendly Societies' Act since some of its registered rules, including those forbidding piecework, were in restraint of trade and, therefore, illegal at common law. In January 1867 the Council of the Queen's bench upheld the ruling of the Bradford magistrates, the Lord Chief Justice stating that:

> We cannot hesitate for a moment in saying that we thought the
> magistrates were right in holding that a society did not come within the
> operation of the Friendly Societies Act. . . . I am far from saying that a
> trade union constituted for such purposes would bring the members
> within the criminal law, but the rules are certainly such as would operate
> in restraint of trade, and would therefore, in that sense, be unlawful.[41]

This judgement produced a round of feverish activities by the Conference of the Amalgamated Trades and, although bills to protect union funds were rejected, the unions found that they were able to take errant treasurers to court under other legislation introduced in 1868. Nevertheless, this was not a substitute for legislation which would legalize trade unions.

The whole issue of the legality of trade unions came to a head at this time. The 'Sheffield Outrages', the Hornby v. Close case, and a variety of other legal cases connected with trade unions led to the formation of a Royal Commission on Trade Unions. It met to consider the rules and organization of trade unions and to suggest improvements in the law. It was subjected, as Hanson and many others have argued, to intense pressure from the Junta and their associates. Robert Applegarth, William Allan and Edwin Coulson gave evidence, Applegarth acted as the Junta's expert trade unionist in attendance, Frederic Harrison acted as the Junta's nominee and Thomas Hughes, MP and a friend to the trade union movement, was also on the commission.

Applegarth and Harrison attempted to focus the attention of the commission on the activities of the amalgamateds and, as Hanson has ably demonstrated, they presented themselves as friendly societies rather than as strike-mongering trade unions – a ploy which failed when J.A. Roebuck, MP for Sheffield, called in actuarial experts to show the unsound basis of the union benefits. In the end, amalgamateds were able to demonstrate their responsibility and power, the ASE being particularly impressive with its 33,000 members and £140,000 funds, but the restrictive nature of trade unionism also emerged. As a result, the commission's Majority Report, partly due to the efforts of Harrison and Hughes, was less condemnatory than it might have been and suggested that trade unions, whose clauses were not objectionable, should register with the Registrar of Friendly Societies and that unions should separate their strike and benefit funds. However, the objectionable clauses included restrictions on the employment of apprentices and opposition to piece-work. The Minority Report, signed by Harrison, Hughes and the Earl of Lichfield, simply urged the legalization of trade unions and that the registrar should not have the right to refuse any set of rules. If this had been accepted unions would have been able to protect their funds and would not have been subject to legal action.

Within a month of the publication of the Minority Report, Frederic Harrison had produced a bill, which was introduced into the Commons by Thomas Hughes and A.J. Mundella, suggesting the removal of statutory restrictions on combinations, the protection of union funds under the Friendly Societies' Act and the abolition of special offences in trade disputes. Immediately, the Conference of Amalgamated Trades, the London Trades Council and George Potter and his supporters organized a vigorous campaign to support the bill. The measure was withdrawn on the promise of further government legislation.

'NEW MODEL' UNIONS AND CRAFT UNIONISM

A temporary Trades Unions' Funds Protection Act was passed in 1869, followed by a government bill on trade unions in February 1871. It protected the funds of registered unions, without limiting the content of their rules other than if they had criminal intent, and freed unions from criminal conspiracy because they were in restraint of trade. Yet it retained the special offences of 'molestation', 'obstruction', 'intimidation' and 'threat' by workmen during strikes, which led to a trade union campaign to protest at the retention of these criminal provisions. The Trades Union Congress convened in London to protest but succeeded only in persuading the government to divide the bill into two parts, with the criminal clauses contained within the Criminal Law Amendment Bill. This was stiffened in the House of Lords, due to the events surrounding the formation of the Commune in Paris, by the addition of 'persistently following' and 'watching and besetting' to the list of offences and making these criminal if done by 'one or more persons' rather than 'two or more' as in the original bill. This was held up in the Commons.

In 1871 the trade unions had obtained the Trade Union Act, which allowed them to protect their funds, but the Criminal Law Amendment Act was a great disappointment since it kept as criminal the special offences which had been established, in less vague terms, in 1825. At a time when the public mood was becoming more emollient towards trade unions, the Criminal Law Amendment Act provided a basis for a level of trade union unity which had never previously existed. Throughout the country trades councils moved into action to organize agitation against the act, and some were formed or reformed to lead local agitation; the Bradford Trades and Labour Council was reformed in 1872, having initially been formed in 1868, in order to oppose the act at the local level. Almost every trade union expressed its opposition to the new legislation. Their antagonism increased when, in December 1872, five leaders of the London gas stokers who had gone on strike and caused a black-out in parts of London, were sentenced to a year's hard labour by Mr Justice Brett. Brett went beyond the definition of 'molestation' set out within the Act and defined it as:

> anything done with improper intent which the jury would think as an unjustifiable annoyance and interference with the masters in their conduct of their business . . . and which would be likely to have a deterring effect upon masters or ordinary nerve.[42]

He had returned to the common law of conspiracy and now defined a strike to be not simply the conspiracy to restrain trade but could also be a conspiracy to coerce. The outcry, particularly against the men being sentenced to a period four times as long as permitted under the Criminal Law Amendment Act, eventually led to the sentence being commuted to four months. But the campaign continued because many other magistrates interpreted the act more widely than intended; shouting and catcalling was interpreted as 'coercion'.

Trade unionists continued to demand the repeal of the act and all legislation which discriminated against workers and trade unionists. In this respect, the case of the London gas stokers had revived concern about the use of the Master and Servant Act of 1867. The gas stokers had also been found guilty of breaking their contract of employment, a criminal offence, by not giving notice of their intent to leave employment. The law relating to breach of contract had been a contentious one since the eighteenth and early nineteenth centuries. In England workers could be summoned but in Scotland a warrant had to be issued for arrest. As a result the Scottish unions, and particularly the Glasgow Trades Council, campaigned to change the law. They were successful in 1867, by taking away arrest by warrant, demanding that the case should be examined by more than one magistrate, and by allowing a fine to be paid as an alternative to imprisonment. But even the Master and Servant Act of 1867 left the relationship between master and servant unequal, for a breach of contract by a workman remained a criminal offence while that by a master was a civil offence.

The grievances of trade unionists were revived to a new pitch by the actions of the courts. There was a mammoth demonstration of trade unionists in Hyde Park on 2 June 1873 and further agitation when sixteen farm labourers' wives, from Chipping Norton, were sentenced under the Criminal Law Amendment Act for hooting at, and, therefore, 'intimidating' blacklegs. In this climate the Liberal government, and then the Conservative one after its return to office in 1874, felt obliged to reconsider the law relating to trade unions. Indeed, in 1874 Disraeli's Conservative government set up a Royal Commission of the Labour Laws, which despite the fact that it included Alexander MacDonald as a trade union representative was made less effective than it might have been because it was boycotted by Frederic Harrison and the Parliamentary Committee of the TUC.

Its report was rather disappointing, advocating only minor modifications of the Master and Servant Act, the Criminal Law Amendment Act and of the law of conspiracy. In the end the government had to present its own legislation. There was the Conspiracy and Protection of Property Act, introduced in June 1875, which reversed the decision in the gas stokers case by removing criminal conspiracy from acts done 'in contemplation of furtherance of a trade dispute' unless the acts themselves were criminal offences.[43] On picketing, the controversial terms 'threats', 'molestation' and 'obstruction' were dropped, and it was established that to be at a place in order to communicate information was not the same as 'watching and besetting'. The second act, introduced at the same time, was the Employers and Workmen Act which removed the penal provision, made breach of contract a civil matter, and thus made employer and workman equal before the law.

In 1876, the new trade union legislation was completed by the Trade Union Act Amendment Act which re-defined 'trade union'. The 1871 Act had given protection to combinations which would have been unlawful combinations by being in restraint of trade without that act. This meant that certain unions, such as the ASE, could not register because they were not deemed to be illegal and, therefore, did not need the protection of the 1871 Act. The 1876 Act now made the term trade union applicable to any combination of workmen, whether it was in restraint of trade or not.

On the big issues of trade union recognition and rights, as well as many smaller and less controversial issues, it is clear that the trade unions had learned to use Parliament in order to obtain the type of legislation which it favoured. Both Fraser and Pelling write of the formation of 'pressure groups' which influenced Parliament as well as public opinion. Effectively, an eight-year campaign by trade union leaders against existing trade union legislation had created a measure of unity between unions which had not previously emerged, and had successfully won for trade unions all the demands put forward in the Minority Report of the Royal Commission of 1869. There were now no special offences for workers and equality at law was allowed. An action carried out by workers in a union was, apparently, no longer indictable if the same action done by an individual was lawful.

BRITISH TRADE UNIONISM

The Politics of Trade Unionism

Apart from their concern for more liberal legislation regarding trade unions, it is clear that trade union leaders also exhibited a deep concern to become involved in political action. This was evident in the 1860s when George Howell, a bricklayer and secretary of the London Trades Council between 1860 and 1862, became secretary in the National Reform League, which was demanding manhood suffrage. He was supported by many other prominent trade unionists: Robert Applegarth was on the Reform League's committee, Henry Broadhurst, a stonemason, was a member of the league, as was George Potter. When it became clear that the widened property franchise introduced by the 1867 Reform Bill made manhood suffrage a distant possibility these same trade unionists moved their attention towards gaining parliamentary representation for the working classes.

Their efforts were initially channelled through the Labour Representation League, which sought to come to some type of accommodation with the Liberal Party, although LRL candidates were generally shunned by local Liberal parties and often, if they stood, by Liberal voters. Nevertheless, many trade union leaders stood for Parliament in their own right or as LRL candidates. George Odger stood, unsuccessfully, on several occasions between 1868 and 1874, as did George Potter, who was defeated at Peterborough in 1868 and for Preston in 1886. Joseph Arch, who initially began his working life as an agricultural labourer and became chairman of the National Agricultural Labourers' Union, was Liberal MP for West Norfolk between 1855–6 and, again, from 1892–1900. In 1874 Thomas Burt, a Northumberland miner, was returned as Liberal MP for Morpeth, representing the seat until 1918. W.R. Cremer, a carpenter, was Liberal MP for Haggerston between 1885 and 1908. Thomas Halliday, secretary of the Lancashire Miners' Association, was defeated at Merthyr Tydfil in 1874. George Howell was Liberal MP for north-east Bethnal Green from 1885 to 1895. Alexander MacDonald was MP for Stafford from 1874 to 1881. William Pickard, miners' agent in Wigan and vice-president of the National Association of Miners in 1863, stood unsuccessfully for Wigan in 1874 and Benjamin Pickard, the leader of the Yorkshire Miners and the Miners' Federation of Great Britain, was Liberal MP for Normanton between 1885 and 1904. Henry Broadhurst, a stonemason and secretary of the parliamentary committee of the TUC, was Liberal MP for Stoke on Trent from 1880–5, for Bordesley Division of Birmingham 1885–6, for West Nottingham between 1886–92 and for Leicester 1894–1906.

Most of those who became MPs at this time were Liberals, and a preponderance of miners' leaders were returned to Parliament, helped by the large and organized standing army of miners who dominated some constituencies, making it impossible for the Liberals to contemplate any alternative candidates. Yet trade union parliamentary representation was still on a very small scale until the emergence of the Independent Labour Party and the Labour Party, at the end of the century, and limited outside mining, where the unions had often formed their own political funds, as did the Yorkshire Miners in the mid-1880s.

This connection with the Liberal Party was nurtured by the traditional link of Radical Liberals with the trade union movement, and encouraged by trade union leaders, such as Henry Broadhurst. He became secretary of the Parliamentary Committee of the TUC between 1875 and 1890, and was appointed under-secretary of the Home Office in the Liberal government of 1886 – thus becoming the first working man to be appointed to a ministerial post. But Lib-Labism was under attack almost before it was forged. The emergence of socialist groups in the 1880s, such as the Social Democratic Federation, the Socialist League and the Fabians challenged the validity of the trade union connection with the Liberals, even if not all those organizations favoured working with trade unions in order to pave the way to socialism. However, it was not until the emergence of the Independent Labour Party in the 1890s and the Labour Representation Committee in 1900 that the link between the Liberal Party and the trade unions was severed. In the meantime, the Liberals continued to enjoy substantial trade union support, particularly among the miners, and continued to ignore the demands of trade unions other than the miners despite the attempt of some Liberal trade unionists to create bodies such as the Labour Electoral Association, formed in 1887, which aimed to ensure that trade unionists gained Liberal approval both at the local and parliamentary level. The failure of the Liberals to respond helped to ensure their eventual demise as a major political party.

Depression and the Decline of Trade Union Industrial Power

While the mid-1870s saw trade unions obtain the legal recognition of their position and rights, they also saw the decline of their industrial power as industries faced the period of higher unemployment, falling prices and declining orders, the events of which have been subsumed under the title the 'Great Depression'. This, in fact, meant that many embryonic and established trade unions collapsed or experienced rapidly declining membership.

In several sectors of the economy trade unionism was only just beginning to develop in the early 1870s. In agriculture, for instance, it was not until the late 1860s and early 1870s that trade unionism began to develop. The highpoint of their activity occurred in 1872 when Joseph Arch, a Primitive Methodist lay preacher, formed the Warwickshire Agricultural Labourers' Union, which shortly afterwards became the National Agricultural Labourers' Union. By 1874 it had a membership of 86,214 and was selling 30,000 copies of the *Labourers' Chronicle*. Largely confined to the southern part of England, and buttressed by the existence of regional unions in Kent, Sussex and Lincolnshire, Arch's union looked set to organize most of the agricultural labourers along the lines of the industrial workers. However, the economic depression and the renewed opposition of landowners led to a rapid decline, the National Union falling to 40,000 members in 1875, 20,000 in 1879 and a mere 4,254 by 1889.[44] The fate of the railway unions followed a similar course. The Amalgamated Society of Railway Servants, formed in 1871, fared little better. Founded partly as a result of the efforts of M.T. Bass, a wealthy brewer and Liberal MP who appears to have influenced the union to accept a clause 'to prevent strikes', it failed to control strike activity and quickly suffered a loss of members as a result of the combined impact of inefficiency of the first secretary and the economic depression.

The depression also afflicted most of the established trade unions, whose membership normally declined – although the ASE and the Carpenters and Joiners, for a variety of reasons, survived better than most. The membership of many of these unions fell dramatically from the mid-1870s until the late 1880s – although most of the national unions survived. This was not necessarily the case with many of the small, skilled, regional unions which existed in the 1860s. Many of them led a chequered existence. This was particularly the case in the woollen and worsted industry of the West Riding of Yorkshire. The Bradford and District Amalgamated Society of Dyers collapsed in 1876 before being reformed in 1880, the Yorkshire Warp Dressers Society, formed in 1870, disappeared in the late 1870s, and the Huddersfield Cloth Dressers Society appears to have disappeared about 1874.[45] However, the impact of the depression should not be exaggerated for most unions survived, in their original or a modified form, although with a much reduced membership. Unemployment obviously accounted for a substantial part of that decline and was the cause of the unemployment agitation of the mid-1880s and the events which led to the development of a new stage and strategy in trade union development.

Conclusion

The mid-Victorian period has, quite rightly, been seen as the period in which trade unions established their legal and social recognition in Britain. Without doubt much of that change was the product of the work of many prominent and able leaders who organized the amalgamateds. But the British trade union movement was one of great variety in structure and objectives and it has long been clear that the views of the Webbs do not accurately reflect either the sentiments or the true aggressiveness of the new movement. The amalgamateds might well have encouraged society and employers to accept, albeit reluctantly, the need for trade union recognition in law, political economy and industrial relation but that does not mean that trade unions were reluctant to use the strike weapon – far from it. And, in any case, trade unions could and did use a battery of practices in order to protect their position – just as the 'new', apparently more aggressive, 'unionism' of the late 1880s and early 1890s was forced to do.

NOTES

1. S. and B. Webb, *History of Trade Unionism, 1666–1920* (1920 edn.).
2. W.H. Fraser, *Trade Unions and Society: The Struggle for Acceptance, 1850–1880* (Allen & Unwin, 1974), provides brief biographical sketches of all these leaders.
3. *Ibid.*, p. 16.
4. Bradford and District Trades Council, minutes and records of annual meetings 1880–5, West Yorkshire Archives, Bradford.
5. Fraser, *op.cit.*, pp. 29,31.

6. Alan R. Jones, 'Robert Applegarth', *Dictionary of Labour Biography*, vol. II (Macmillan, 1974).

7. Fraser, *op.cit.*, p. 22.

8. *Ibid.*, p. 22,33.

9. Webbs, *op.cit.*, p. 199.

10. *Ibid.*, p. 201.

11. Tony Lane, *The Union Makes Us Strong: The British Working Class, Its Politics and Trade Unionism* (Arrow Books, 1974).

12. Fraser, *op.cit.*, p. 58.

13. *Ibid.*, pp. 219, 225.

14. E.F. Biagini, 'British Trade Unions and Popular Political Economy, 1860–1880', *Historical Journal*, 30, 4 (1987), pp. 811–40.

15. *Ibid.*, p. 815.

16. *The Bee-Hive*, 1 June 1867, quoted in Biagini, *op.cit.*, p. 818.

17. G.P. Bevan, 'The Strikes of the Past Ten years', *Journal of the Royal Statistical Society*, XLIII (1980); James E. Cronin, 'Strikes and Power in Britain, 1870–1920', *International Review of Social History*, vol. 32, 1987; J.H. Porter, 'Wage Bargaining under Conciliation Agreements, 1870–1914', *Economic History Review*, Second Series, XXXIII (1970); J.H. Porter, 'Industrial Conciliation and Arbitration, 1860–1914', unpublished PhD, University of Leeds, 1968.

18. Porter, 'Industrial Conciliation and Arbitration'.

19. Cronin, *op.cit.*, p. 147.

20. *Ibid.*, p. 150.

21. G.D.H. Cole, 'Some Notes on British Trade Unionism in the Third Quarter of the Nineteenth Century', *International Review of Social History*, 1937, reprinted by E.M. Carus-Wilson (ed.), *Essays in Economic History*, vol. III (1962); R.V. Clements, 'British trade unions and popular political economy, 1850–1875', *Economic History Review*, second series, XIV (1961–2), pp. 93–104; C.G. Hanson, 'Craft Unions, Welfare Benefits, and the Case for Trade Union Law Reform, 1867–1875', *Economic History Review*, second series, XXVIII, May 1975; G.R. Boyer, 'What did unions do in nineteenth century Britain?', *Journal of Economic History*, 48, 1988.

22. Cole, *op.cit.*, Carus-Wilson collection, p. 202.

23. Hanson, *op.cit.*, p. 253.

24. *Ibid.*, p. 259.

25. H. Pelling, *A History of British Trade Unionism*, 4th edn. (Penguin Books, 1988), pp. 37–8.

26. Report of the Trades Council of London, Annual Report 1861.

27. This is made clear in the above and subsequent reports.

28. *Trade Union Commission: Sheffield Outrages*, 1867, Q. 13,545, evidence of Samuel Crooks.

29. Fraser, *op.cit.*, pp.47–8, 67–8, 154–8; S.W. Coltham, 'George Potter, the Junta, and the Beehive', *International Review of Social History*, IX (1964) and X (1965).

30. A.E. Musson, *The Congress of 1868: Its Origins and Establishment of the Trades Union Congress* (1955); B.C. Roberts, *The Trades Union Congress, 1868–1921* (1958).

31. A.E. Musson, *The Typographical Association: Origins and History to 1949* (Oxford University Press, 1954), pp. 69, 90–4.

32. J. Reynolds, *The Letter press printers of Bradford* (Bradford, University of Bradford, *c.* 1970–2).

33. Minutes and records of the Bradford Graphical Society, now deposited in the University of Bradford J.B. Priestley Library.

34. *Ibid.*

35. *Ibid.*

36. Reynolds, *op.cit.*, pp. 13–14.

37. *Ibid.*, p. 16.

38. *Ibid.*, pp. 16–17.

39. Bradford Graphical Society, Minutes, 1878.

40. J. Reynolds, *op.cit.*

41. *Bradford Observer*, 24 January 1867.

42. Fraser, *op.cit.*, pp. 192–3, 195.

43. *Conspiracy and Protection of Property Act, 1875* and Fraser, *op.cit.*, pp. 192–5.

44. P. Horn, *Joseph Arch*, (Kineton, Roundwood Press, 1971), p. 222.

45. K. Laybourn, 'The Attitude of Yorkshire Trade Unions to the Economic and Social Problems of the Great Depression, 1873–1896', unpublished PhD thesis, University of Lancaster, 1973.

CHAPTER THREE

'OLD UNIONISM' AND THE EMERGENCE OF 'NEW UNIONISM' *c.* 1888–1909

The Webbs referred to the resurgence of trade unionism of the late 1880s and early 1890s as the 'new unionism' and suggested that its main characteristic was not that unskilled workers organized but that many new groups of workers of all skills organized into trade unions for the first time. In addition they noted that there was a new attitude abroad which favoured state intervention and encouraged links between trade unionism and the emerging independent Labour movement, although many trade unions retained their links with the Liberals until the First World War. What the Webbs played down was the idea that a new trade union structure emerged and became dominant, although prominent general and all-grade unions, which brought workers of many different occupations and skills together, also emerged. In contrast to their views on the representative nature of the 'new model' trade unions, their observations of the 'new unionism' phase have generally received support from modern historians, although there has been some debate about the precise timing and impact of this 'new unionist' phase. And the exact extent of the influence of 'new unionism' on the wider trade union movement is still open to question – although its influence has often been greatly exaggerated and may be symptomatic of other developments within the trade union movement. Trade unionism did broaden out during the 1890s and early twentieth century and these developments might have had more to do with the changing structure of the British economy and society than with the impact of 'new unionism'.

Indeed, in recent years the debate about the impact and meaning of 'new unionism' has been somewhat overshadowed by, and absorbed into, one concerning the 'de-skilling' tendency of large-scale capitalism and the defensive reactions of trade unions in restricting such developments and maintaining apprenticeship. In 1974, Harry Braverman, a Marxist writer, produced his seminal work *Labor and Monopoly Capital*, in which he argued that the de-skilling of the workforce was the result of the demands of capital accumulation and technological developments that occurred in the early twentieth century.[1] His assumption was that technical developments led to gradual removal of skill as a factor and the creation of a more homogeneous working class, subject to the pressures of increasing monopoly capitalism. Although now generally rejected in its pure form, Braverman's work has encouraged the development of new ways of looking at trade unions, the working class and work experience. In particular, he has greatly influenced Professor R.J. Price, who, while rejecting the technological determinism of Braverman, has consistently argued that the control of the workplace has been a central aspect of class conflict.[2] Indeed, he asserts that the preservation of skill was the basis of industrial conflict in the late nineteenth century.

More recently, Patrick Joyce and John Benson have also emphasized the uneven development of capitalism, thus undermining the blanket approach of Braverman to the development of capitalism.[3] Indeed, Joyce maintains that:

> Far from the labour process producing the de-skilling and homogenisation of labour, skill and control were redefined and renegotiated in the process of industrial change, a situation especially marked in British industry.[4]

Charles More has also endorsed this approach, noting the survival of skill in many industries, often with the cooperation of employers and employees.[5] In other words, Joyce, More, and, to a lesser extent, Price, have challenged the Marxist notion of the de-skilling of the workforce as capitalism develops.

Such criticism has been partly rejected by William Knox, who has come to the rescue of Braverman with the suggestion that there is an 'inherent tendency within industrial capitalism . . . towards the specialisation of skill'.[6] What this means is that skills are narrowed to specific work processes. In addition, Knox argues that there are many factors reducing skill other than the exigencies of capital accumulation. In other words, there may be many reasons for the decline of skill, including the demands of capitalism, but it nevertheless survived in a very limited and truncated form due to technological changes.

Clearly, there remains a heated debate about the events that were taking place on the shop-floor and in the world of work in the late nineteenth and early twentieth centuries, with many shades of opinion emerging between the views of Marxist writers and those, such as Patrick Joyce, who reject, almost totally, their assumptions. In responding to these debates, the central argument of this chapter is that the challenge of foreign competition forced employers to speed up existing machinery, to reduce labour costs, to introduce new machinery, and to gain increasing control over their factories and mills. Woollen and worsted spinners in the West Riding of Yorkshire did, for instance, find their machines speeded up by 30 per cent between the 1860s and 1890s, with larger machines with more ends to attend to, for no more wages, and similar developments occurred in other industries. As a result of such action, the trade unions of the skilled recognized the need to broaden their trade union structures in order to admit more, semi-skilled, members in the desire to protect their skilled position. In this process skilled engineers, typographers, and others, increasingly found themselves in conflict with employers. The fight for workplace control, therefore, became central to this period of trade unionism. Indeed, the organization of the unskilled and semi-skilled was by no means the only feature of this period because the skilled trade unionist began to recognize, in a way he had not recognized in the mid-Victorian period, that he needed to broaden the basis of his own union, and the trade union movement as a whole, in order to more effectively protect and cushion his skilled and privileged position. There was also a political dimension to this for in protecting their positions, many skilled, as well as semi-skilled and unskilled, trade unionists began to identify with socialist groups and the Labour Representation Committee/Labour Party, not because they believed in socialism or political independence but because these bodies were prepared to act as the vehicles of working-class aspirations. Nevertheless, one should not assume that the trade unions of the skilled abandoned their defence of wage gaps between themselves and the less skilled. It is true that the growth of the semi-skilled workers in the late nineteenth century began to bridge the gap between the skilled and the unskilled, but there remained the view, expressed by Robert Knight in 1893, that 'The helper ought to be subservient, and do as the mechanics tells him.'[7] There may have been a narrowing of differences between trade unionists and workers between the 1890s and the First World War but often it was a narrowing within the ranks of skilled and semi-skilled workers and, as was evident in the case of the shop stewards' movement of the First World War, demarcation lines remained a potent force in the work situation. In the end, it is argued that Braverman's thesis appears to exaggerate the impact of technology upon skills, for while the capitalist challenge led to conflict, there were immense variations within industry, and an uneven pattern of work and life experience which Joyce and, more recently, John Benson have pointed to.[8] In the final analysis, trade unionism found itself broadening out to meet the challenge of capitalism faced with industrial and economic change but the contention that, somehow, trade unionism narrowed in structure and that the working class became far more homogeneous seems dubious.

The Challenge of New Ideas in the 1880s

The 1880s proved to be a decade of thought, reflection and change for the working classes. Many of the trade unions of the skilled faced a rapidly declining membership, resulting from the trade depression of the late 1870s and early 1880s, which made their reliance upon the defensive mechanism of arbitration, conciliation and strike activity less effective; socialist groups such as the Social Democratic Federation, the Socialist League and the Fabians emerged to encourage the working man, if not always trade unions, to challenge the existing political system; and there was rising social concern for the unemployed and the poor, partly represented in the work of Charles Booth on the life and labour of the London poor.[9] This was a decade of uncertainty in every aspect of society, a period when many erstwhile socialists began to question their role and position in society. Yet, it was the rising levels of unemployment, which led to riots and disturbances in the mid-1880s, which began to produce a change in the attitudes of trade unionists to their organization, aims and activities.

The key figure in this change was Tom Mann, a member of the Amalgamated Society of Engineers, who in 1886 published a pamphlet entitled *What a Compulsory Eight-Hour Working Day Means to the Workers*. Forged by the depression it offered a new conception of the role of trade unionism which went out to organize all workers in an aggressive manner rather than to simply defend, in a sectarian way, the wage levels of workers. Mann wrote that:

> None of the important societies have any policy other than endeavouring to keep wages from falling. The true Unionist policy of *aggression* seems entirely lost sight of; in fact the average unionist of today is a man with a fossilized intellect, either hopelessly apathetic, or supporting a policy that plays directly into the hands of the capitalist exploiter.[10]

His views found favour among a group of socialist activists, including John Burns, who like Mann had gained some grounding in the Social Democratic Federation, H.H. Champion, an ex-army officer who owned a printing press and introduced the eight-hour day for his employees and published Mann's pamphlet, and James Keir Hardie, who was struggling to organize the Ayrshire miners during the 1880s.

Mann's message had a powerful appeal. In the first place, it offered a solution to unemployment since it was maintained that the reduction of working hours would increase the demand for labour. Secondly, it made trade unions think about their position on the question of working hours. Some, like the miners, became committed to the eight-hour day for miners, others supported the view that the state should impose an eight-hour day on all workers, while others opted for trade exemptions, trade options and a variety of other schemes.

There were many disagreements and divergences of opinion. At first, the Amalgamated Society of Cotton Spinners was reluctant to support the eight-hour day fearing that it might raise costs and increase unemployment, while the cotton weaving unions favoured the movement. Nevertheless, the demand for the eight-hour day ultimately provided a programme for the international labour movement and May Day celebrations, and, as A.E.P. Duffy has argued, helped to unite many trade unions and socialist groups on one common platform.[11]

The link was forged with events such as the unemployment demonstration in Trafalgar Square on 13 November 1887, better known as 'Bloody Sunday', which saw conflict between the police and the demonstrators, and was evident in an upwelling of feeling towards it in the conferences of the Trades Union Congress. In 1889 Henry Broadhurst and the Parliamentary Committee of the TUC had been instructed to take action on the issue of the eight-hour day by the new groups of trade unionists, represented by James Keir Hardie. Broadhurst's failure to take action led to his departure, allegedly on grounds of ill-health, after the TUC conference of 1890. It is, therefore, not surprising that many trade unionists came to accept the views of James Bartley, a skilled typographer, who maintained that 'Those who accept the eight-hour day are new trade unionists, and those who do not are old unionists.'[12] The importance of this observation is that attitude, not skill, was to be the basis of the differences between old and new trade unionists.

Nevertheless, it is clear that unskilled and semi-skilled workers were beginning to organize into trade unions from the mid-1880s. The Knights of Labour, an American organization, fleetingly stimulated the formation of 'mixed assemblies' of workers in the Black Country and could claim about ten thousand members in 1887, although it had effectively disappeared by 1894. Nevertheless, its activities appear to have done much to have encouraged the formation of the Stove Grate Workers, formed in Rotherham, and may have influenced the creation of the dockers' organizations at Liverpool and Glasgow. The activities of the Knights of Labour also coincided with the organization of other groups of unskilled workers. The National Federation of Labour, for instance, came into existence in 1886 with the help of Edward Pease, a London Fabian socialist. But the real move towards mass unionism, and the organization of the previously badly organized groups of workers did not begin until 1888.

BRITISH TRADE UNIONISM

The 'New Unionism' of 1889 to 1893

The story of the explosion of trade unionism at this period has been told many times. The successful strike of the match girls at Bryant and May in London, led by Annie Besant and her journal the *Link*, in 1888, the activities of Will Thorne, a Birmingham-born Irishman in organizing the gasworkers at Beckton gasworks in London in March 1889 in winning the eight-hour day, and the work of Ben Tillett and Tom Mann in organizing the London dockers to strike for increased wages in August 1889 are legendary events. Without retelling well-known stories the main point is that for a brief period of time groups of workers who had been difficult to organize, were successful in winning industrial disputes. Even more surprising was the fact that this was achieved against relatively powerful employers and partly occasioned by a sense of unity which cut across different groups of workers. In the case of the London dock strike, for instance, stevedores, lightermen, coal porters and other groups of workers came out in support of the dockers' claim for 6d (2½p) per hour, 8d (3½p) per hour for overtime and a demand for a minimum employment of four hours. The fact that there was international recognition of the London dock strike, with £30,000 being sent to the dockers by the Australian trade unionists, helped to ensure the victory of the London dockers.[13]

This victory led to the development of the Dock, Wharf, Riverside, and General Labourers' Union – with Tillett as its secretary and Mann as its president, with John Burns in assistance – a union which quickly acquired more than thirty thousand members. It also encouraged similar industrial action in Hull, Bristol and many other ports throughout the country – although the dockers and port workers were often organized by different unions – the South Side Labour Protection League in the Thames basin, the National Union of Dock Labourers organized by James Sexton, a Liverpool docker of Irish origin, and both the National Federation of Labour and the National Amalgamated Union of Labour on Tyneside. The seamen in the ports were also being organized by Havelock Wilson. However, many of the improved conditions they won in 1889 and 1890 were rapidly won back by the port employers in the early 1890s. The Shipping Federation, formed in 1890, emerged to introduce its own register of seamen and to force union men to work alongside non-union men. As a result, the power of

Wilson's union was greatly reduced, and the onslaught of the employers reached its zenith in 1893 when thousands of labourers were brought into the Hull docks in 1893 to replace the men who were on strike.

A similar pattern of events occurred in the case of the gasworkers. During the autumn and winter of 1889 most large towns saw successful strikes, and threatened strikes, by gasworkers in order to obtain the eight-hour day. In many cases the employers struck back in the summer of 1890. In Leeds, for instance, blacklegs were brought in to work the Wortley gasworks. They were temporarily housed in Leeds Town Hall. However, the authorities were defeated fairly quickly since they had to march the blacklegs, under police escort, to Wortley gasworks, passing under a railway bridge from which they were stoned by the gasworkers whose jobs they were taking. The blacklegs were withdrawn and the gasworkers maintained their improved position.

Nevertheless, throughout the 1890s the gasworkers, like the dockers, began to lose power and influence as employers eroded their gains and undermined the strength of their union. Their situation was also threatened further by the formation of William Collison's National Free Labour Association in 1893, which supplied 'free' or blackleg labour to the Shipping Federation and, later, to the railway companies.

Out of these, and similar, events emerged a variety of 'general' organizations which attempted to unite all members of a class, regardless of skill. The main 'general' unions were the Gasworkers and General Labourers (formed in 1889), the Dock, Wharf, Riverside and General Labourers' Union (1889) and the Tyneside and General Labourers' Union (1889). All went through a variety of mutations before they coalesced into the two giant unions of the Transport and General Workers and the General and Municipal Workers. As Eric Hobsbawm made clear many years ago, these 'general' unions experienced mixed fortunes in their early days and were by no means as general as is often suggested:

> The General Unions, at any rate between 1892 and 1911, depended far more on their foothold in certain industries and large works than on their ability to recruit indiscriminately, hence (one may suppose) on the whole on a stabler and more regular type of worker than they had originally envisaged.[14]

Thus, in the Leeds district of the Gasworkers' Union, the dyers and the gasworkers made up 12 of the 18 branches in 1891 and 10 of the

23 branches in 1891–2. The Tyneside and General Labourers Union, which was later re-organized as the National Amalgamated Union of Labour was based upon the shipyard workers.

In addition there were a number of 'all-grade' trade unions, which sought to bring together workers in an industry regardless of skill. They included the London Carmen, the Amalgamated Tram and Vehicle Workers and a variety of others, including the Liverpool dockers. Initially, they were small in the number of members they organized, although by the eve of the First World War they were in excess of 100,000.[15]

The origins of this 'new unionist' phase may be partly sought in the trade revival at the end of the 1880s and the difficulties caused by the 'Great Depression'. But, in addition, it is clear that it can also be explained, in part, by the changes in technology within the various industries most affected. Professor R.J. Price, in fact, has outlined, in detail, the changes which occurred.[16] In gasworking it appears that the new retorts used in the 1880s changed the work pattern from one of intense work followed by lengthy periods of rest to more or less intense periods of activity. The result was that the number of charges required for each retort increased from two per shift in the 1860s to six in the 1880s, and the number of mouthpieces to be dealt with by each gang of labourers increased from forty-five to about ninety. As a result, the number of workers required tended to fall but those who remained often had more permanent employment opportunities than before, thus encouraging the collective action of the men and the formation of a gasworkers' union. A similar situation also existed in dock-work, where the demise of the sailing ships and the emergence of steam-driven ships which required larger berths and quicker turn-round times encouraged the retention of a larger core of workers and the possible emergence of a dockers' union. The technological changes in the newly-organized sectors of the British economy most certainly provided some impetus to the spurt of activity which has become known as 'new unionism'.

Yet, as already suggested, new unionism was far more than simply the organization of new members within unions. It also represented a partial change of attitude by the older more established trade unions. Tom Mann was a skilled engineer and a member of the Amalgamated Society of Engineers, and although he unsuccessfully contested for the leadership of his union in 1891, his campaign appears to have encouraged the ASE to increase its number of full-time officials from four to seventeen in 1892, to reduce the entrance barriers to the union 'that prevented or retarded the admission into our society of any workman, who in following the engineering trade, can claim to be a skilled artisan', and to encourage the holding of delegate meetings for the revision of rules every four years.[17]

New unionism was also about organizing workers together more effectively than before. The miners are a case in point. All mining areas, except for Northumberland and Durham and South Wales, joined together in 1889, under the leadership of Ben Pickard, to form the Miners' Federation of Great Britain with the ostensible aim of winning the eight-hour day for miners. As Pickard stated to the miners of Denaby Main, in 1890:

> The officials were empowered to go over Yorkshire and were pledged to this position whether they liked it or not — that a question must be put to the candidate on the eight hours question. They must not give the candidate their support if he would not support them — whether Liberal or Tory.[18]

This new, more assertive, policy by the miners might have endangered their long-established alliance with the Liberals, although Pickard felt that most Liberal candidates would support their stand, and eventually forced the federation into conflict with the coal owners in a nationwide lock-out towards the end of 1893 — the first truly national miners' strike and one which necessitated pressure from the government to force the employers to accept the *status quo* on wages.

It was, in essence then, the old craft and semi-skilled unions who did best out of the economic recovery of 1888 to 1893. By altering their rules and admitting more members, particularly from the ranks of the semi-skilled, the more skilled unions experienced a substantial growth in their membership figures. For instance, the Amalgamated Society of Engineers saw its membership rise from 53,740 members at the end of 1888 to 71,221 by the end of 1891. Other established unions prospered similarly.

They, like their semi-skilled and unskilled brethren, were conscious of the threat to their position presented by the introduction of new machinery. In engineering, new lathes allowed handymen to be promoted, and thus to enter the union, without the need for craft or apprenticeship training. As a result, the semi-skilled workers began to be absorbed into some skilled unions, whose position was thereby strengthened.

An Homogeneous Working Class?

The new unions and general unions which emerged in the late 1880s and early 1890s claimed a membership of upwards of one-third of a million in 1890, although this was greatly exaggerated, and had more like 130,000 members in 1892 and 80,000 in 1896. Against this must be set the fact that trade union membership had risen to about one and a half million in 1890 and to about 1,608,000 in 1896. The sustained growth among the established unions was far more impressive than that among the 'new' unions. After 1896 trade union membership lurched steadily towards two million by 1900, fluctuating at or about that level until 1906 when it reached 2,210,000, rising to 2,485,000 by 1908. The direct impact of 'new union' membership was, therefore, very restricted, and in some respects the indirect impact of 'new unionism' has also been exaggerated. Instead of seeing it as moving the trade union movement towards socialism and political independence it is, perhaps, more sensible to see this phase of trade union development in a wider framework. Trade unions had always taken advantage of good economic conditions, still remained essentially sectarian in their approach, continued to vary widely in their effective organization, and still, by and large, failed to organize female workers. The 'new unionist' phase may have instilled the trade union movement with a more aggressive image, no matter how short-lived and ill-founded, but it failed to create the more homogeneous working class which some authors have written about. Indeed, the lack of an homogeneous working class is evident at many levels.

As Patrick Joyce and John Benson have noted, class consciousness is subject to many factors which may inhibit or shape its development. Joyce, in fact, stresses that:

> Class consciousness and political choice themselves, are a product of a variety of contexts, ranging from work to family life, education and religion. These contests repress or express class feeling and form attitudes in a thousand subtle ways, by gesture and language, ritual and symbol. It is upon this ground that conscious manoeuvre is exercised. If work is not

the only ground upon which economics, class and politics are linked it is an important one.[19]

The fact is that the variety of experiences of work, education, housing, and other factors, ensured that throughout this period the working class continued to be divided in numerous ways. Indeed, during the 1890s the Independent Labour Party (ILP), attempting to organize areas where the working class lived in poverty, were unskilled and lacked a tradition of trade union activity, found their political activities to be ineffective. This contrasted sharply with those areas where skill, trade union membership, better housing and other social advantages were more apparent.[20]

In addition, it is evident that trade unions maintained both a general antipathy and hostility towards the employment of women. It is clear that women, a not insubstantial proportion of the workforce, failed to be effectively organized within unions. In 1901 women formed 30 per cent of the workforce but only 7.5 per cent of the total number of trade unionists. The nature of their employment was part of the reason for their poor organization, many being active in domestic service, agriculture and in industrial activities, such as woollen and worsted weaving, where all workers were badly organized. In the vast majority of trades women did not receive the training necessary to obtain skilled employment. In engineering, printing and cotton spinning there was almost institutional opposition to their employment, and thus recruitment to the appropriate union. Since women's wages were normally much lower than those of men, skilled unions were determined in their opposition to the admittance of women into their unions. If women did enter a specific employment area, which had normally been dominated by men, it was not unusual for the male trade unionists to demand that they were paid the same rate as men, not out of any enlightened attitude but in an attempt to discourage employers from recruiting them. Such an attitude often emerged in the newly-expanding service industries, and was most evident in the case of clerkship, a profession which was developing rapidly as banks, insurance companies, merchant houses and government activities expanded. The National Clerks' Association was formed in 1893 to organize these workers. Shortly afterwards, Walter J. Read began to edit *The Clerk*, and included in it 'The Clerks' Charter'. It asserted, under the title 'Women's Place is not in the Office', that:

Plenty of employers will agree to that principle, but women are cheaper, after all, 'Business is business' and there is competition to face.

What is just? Many thousands of women did not come into the clerical world for the love of it, but because they must earn their living, and support others dependent upon them. Men have no right to dictate to women how and where they shall earn their living. On the other hand, women should not cut salaries, for their own sakes as well as that of the men. Men are willing to meet competition on fair terms, and, if women prove themselves better clerks, to give way; but women should not compete unfairly. They should not make themselves too cheap.

The competition also decreases the chance of young women marrying. Few will marry on a wage that means certain misery, and if young women compete by cheapening themselves more and more will be left 'on the shelf. . . .'[21]

In other words, if women could not be kept out of the office they ought not to sell themselves too cheap.

Even more hostility was directed against married women who worked. Lady Dilke and Mrs Marsland were involved in campaigns against this trend in the textile district of the West Riding of Yorkshire in the mid-1890s, and it should be remembered that, partly as a result of such tactics, less than 10 per cent of married women were in paid employment in 1910.[22] Indeed, it should be remembered that many of the early women trade union activists were in fact middle-class women whose concept of trade unionism was extremely limited. The Women's Provident and Protection Society, formed in 1874, which became the Women's Trade Union League (WTUL), was organized by middle-class women who sought to set up unions for women, to encourage existing unions to take women, and aimed at protecting women by encouraging the introduction of improved parliamentary legislation. They were opposed to strike activity and did not get very far in organizing women, although the West Riding women weavers formed a Weavers' Union Committee in Dewsbury in 1875. Indeed, as James Hinton has noted, neither the WTUL nor its offshoot the National Federation of Women Workers, formed in 1906, were considered to be more than organs of middle-class charity and were largely ineffective in their impact upon established trade unions. Indeed, in 1914 the dominant view of trade unionists was reflected by Will Thorne, who stated that 'Women do not make good trade unionists and for this reason we believe that our energies are better used towards the organization of male workers.'[23]

The lack of homogeneity of the working class was further evidenced by many other obvious differences and divergences. There was, for instance, the slow change of the TUC which meant that it was not responsive to the increasing moves towards socialism and political independence. In addition, there was the continued sectional differences of the working class – most evident in the workplace.

The TUC dragged its heels on many issues. On the eight-hour day issue, for instance, the 1891 conference passed a motion calling for a bill with an optional clause, allowing trade unionists opposed to a compulsory eight-hour day to opt out. But officials did little on the matter until 1894. There was also continued conflict over the emergence of socialist opinion. Although the 1893 TUC conference urged unions to support only those parliamentary candidates committed to the collective ownership of the means of production, it is clear that the older, more Liberal-inclined, trade unionists continued to hold control. And it was not until 1900 that the TUC agreed to encourage a direct link between trade unions and the Labour Representation Committee/ILP, even though this was ultimately affected by the Osborne Judgement and the fact that only about half the trade union movement committed itself fully to the Labour Party before the First World War. There remained deep political divisions between many of the older trade unionists and of the newer more advanced elements within the movement.

This split was most apparent in the continued defence of the established workplace arrangement by the trade unions of the skilled. These unions still fought vigorously to maintain control over their workplace processes. Professor Price, for instance, notes the experience of the London engineering firm of Thorneycrofts which attempted to impose feed and speed charts, introduced time clocks, re-organized departments and changed the control of work in the early twentieth century but found their activities sabotaged by the old skilled craftsmen who eventually compromised by accepting some aspects of the new systematized approach to production but removed some of the repressive features of production.[24] This picture of trade union defence and compromise in the workplace, was common, if not necessarily universal, and joint arbitration structures, established in the 1860s, were used in the steel unions to resist significant changes in the workplace, just as the London boot and shoe trade unions used 'a highly restrictive piece list which impeded the ability of the industry to respond to the mass-market opportunities of the 1880s' [25]

Not all employers were happy to go along with these arrangements. Employers in the building trade tended to re-organize work through greater sub-division of labour. As Knox notes, between 1890 and 1914 the development of new semi-automatic machines in engineering, the increased use of semi-skilled and unskilled workers in what had been skilled areas of work, the introduction of standardization of parts, the emergence of factory over workshop and the introduction of a variety of incentive schemes to production did undermine the position of some unions. Although his argument could not be sustained for all parts of the British economy it is clear that in some industries, and particularly in engineering and shipbuilding, there is some evidence of such developments. Indeed, the introduction of the pneumatic riveter in shipbuilding could be done by apprentices just as much as a skilled man. [26]

In essence, the picture one gains of British industry is that it was immensely varied and that in some industries trade unions were successful in controlling change while in others employers largely determined and controlled the changes in the workplace situation. In some industries then, workers enhanced their position while in others their position was weakened. In many respects this meant that occupational distinctions could become marked and any moves towards occupational homogeneity in some areas were more than offset by quite opposite moves in others. While the trade union movement was more powerful than it had been before it remains doubtful whether or not there was much improvement in the unity of the working classes before the First World War.

Trade Union Developments 1893–1909

From what has already been suggested, it is clear that trade unionism underwent a period of steady expansion between 1893 and 1909. Throughout most of this time the national economy was either depressed or in a stable position, although individual sections did prosper. This situation obviously neutralized some of the militancy of the trade union movement. Yet, it was an exciting time of change for the trade union movement with at least four major developments in trade unionism during this period. First, there was the development of close links between the trade union movement and the politically independent Labour movement. Secondly, there was the fluctuating legal position of unions, which challenged both their economic and political activities. Thirdly, there was the continued rise of the semi-skilled worker. Fourthly, the structure of trade unionism began to change as the white-collar sections expanded and tentative moves were made to create greater unity between union organizations through the formation of federations, especially in the wake of the 1897 engineering dispute which saw the defeat of the Amalgamated Society of Engineers, the richest and most powerful of the unions of the skilled.

Many members of the Independent Labour Party were inclined to see themselves as the alternative side of the trade union coin. Clearly, in the 1890s that was not so, as the vast majority of trade unionists maintained an allegiance to the Liberal Party, and, to a lesser extent, the Conservative Party. Yet, from 1893 onwards, when the national ILP was formed, there were strong moves in some areas for it to capture trade union support. In areas where it was weak, such as the north-east and in parts of Lancashire and South Wales, the Liberals continued to retain significant trade union support. But in other areas, most notably in the textile area of the West Riding of Yorkshire, the ILP/trade union link became firmly established through the textile trade unions, the local trades councils and a variety of joint organizations between trade unions and the local ILP/Labour unions. That connection had been partly established through the famous Manningham Mills strike of 1890 and 1891, which galvanized trade union strength against Samuel Cunliffe Lister and the directors of Manningham Mills for their attempts to reduce the wages of their workforce. The strikers were defeated after a nineteen-week struggle but the actions of the Liberal-dominated Bradford Watch Committee in seeking to pre-vent the strikers holding meetings, and the events which led to the calling in of troops and the reading of the riot act, gave the strike the image of being a class conflict and demonstrated, to many working men, that the Liberal Party was against the economic interests of the mill workers. Towards the end of the strike, in April 1891, Charlie Glyde, a leading local socialist, stated to the strikers that 'We have had two parties in the past, the can't and the won'ts and it's time we had a party that will.'[27] About a month later moves were afoot to form the Bradford Labour Union, later to become the Bradford ILP, and in its wake emerged the Colne Valley Labour

81

Union, the Halifax Labour Union and many others.[28] As E.P. Thompson accurately observed, the defeat of the strikers speeded up the formation of the independent Labour movement, whereas victory might well have held back its progress.[29]

Very quickly the embryonic ILP captured the trades councils in the West Riding of Yorkshire and in some other areas of the country. And it was through the trades councils' delegates attending the TUC conferences, that socialist and independent labour views began to develop within the national trade union movement, supporting the views of Keir Hardie and others. They pressed on conference their demands for the eight-hour day and a commitment to advising unions to support only those parliamentary candidates committed to collective ownership of the means of production. But socialist and independent labour opinion was still a minority one in the TUC in the early 1890s and was reduced somewhat by the decision, made in 1894, to exclude trades councils' delegates from the TUC, to allow one delegate per thousand members, or part thereof, to trade unions and to restrict delegates to those working in the trade or acting as trade union officials. These new TUC Standing Orders reduced the power of the socialists and independents within the TUC from 1895.

It was as a result of this situation, combined with the poor showing of the ILP in the 1895 general election, which saw all the ILP candidates, including Keir Hardie, lose their contests, that the ILP leaders decided to move towards capturing greater support from the trade union movement. Such a move was not surprising, given that areas of ILP strength had always attracted significant trade union support and that some of the new unions, such as the Gasworkers and the Dockers, had collaborated with socialist groups from their formation. From the mid-1890s, Keir Hardie, faced with the prospect of unifying with the Social Democratic Federation or returning to the Liberal fold, pursued the trade union alternative with vigour – putting forward his views that there should be a working arrangement with the trade unions at the ILP conference of 1897. As a result the ILP approached the Parliamentary Committee of the TUC and the corresponding body of the Scottish TUC, a body formed by the Scottish trades councils in 1897. The Scottish TUC, which had a majority of ILP members on its Parliamentary Committee, agreed, in April 1899, to call a special conference of trade unions, socialist societies and cooperative societies in January

1900. At this meeting the Scottish Workers' Parliamentary Committee was set up.

Matters moved more slowly in the rest of the United Kingdom but in 1899, Thomas R. Steele, an ILP member of the Doncaster branch of the politically-aware Amalgamated Society of Railway Servants (ASRS), encouraged his branch to put forward a resolution to the TUC for the organization of a labour representation conference. The resolution was proposed at the 1899 TUC by John Holmes, the ASRS's west of England organizer. Despite the opposition of W.E. Harvey, of the Derbyshire miners, who felt that unions should organize their own political representation and Thomas Ashton of the Cotton Spinners, who was concerned at the deep political divisions which existed between the Lancashire spinners and the Lancashire weavers, the TUC approved of a voluntary arrangement whereby trade unions could decide themselves whether or not to attend a special conference with the ILP.

It was at that special conference, held at the Memorial Hall, London on 27 February 1900, attended by delegates from about half the trade union membership of the TUC, that the Labour Representation Committee was formed. As is well known, the progress of this alliance was, at first, slow. After the first year, the LRC had trade union and trades council support of only 353,070 members, and it returned only two of its fifteen candidates, Keir Hardie of the ILP and Richard Bell of the ASRS, at the 1900 General Election. After two years its trade union affiliated membership stood at 455,450, although it rose rapidly to almost 850,000 by early 1903 as a result of the final settlement in the Taff Vale case. Thereafter, having become the Labour Party in 1906, its membership increased fairly quickly, stimulated somewhat by the decision of the Miners' Federation of Great Britain to affiliate in 1909.[30]

The strength of the alliance between the trade unions and the emergent independent Labour movement was greatly challenged by the fluctuating legal position of the trade unions – both in an industrial and political sense. This link was particularly evident in the Edwardian age but was also apparent in the 1890s.

The resurgence of trade union militancy during the late 1880s revived the issue of the legal position of trade unions. The 1870s legislation had protected union funds from liability for damages in cases of tort, because trade unions were not considered to be corporations, and peaceful picketing was also guaranteed. In the late

1880s and throughout the 1890s, both these rights were challenged by judges who objected both to the increasing violence occurring in industrial disputes and to trade unions not being legally responsible for their actions. However, at first, the law seemed to deal sympathetically with trade unions. In 1891, for instance, the Queen's Bench overruled the Recorder of Plymouth who had judged guilty of intimidation those trade unionists who had threatened to strike if their employer did not dismiss non-union labour. In the Curran v. Treleaven case of 1891, the bench decided that intimidation must involve actual violence or damage.[31] Other cases tended to endorse this view.[32]

When that intimidation was related to picketing, however, the unions tended to do badly as in the case of Lyons v. Wilkins (1896–9). Lyons, a leather-goods manufacturer took action against Wilkins, the secretary of Amalgamated Trade Society of Fancy Leather Workers due to a strike and picketing against his premises in 1896. Although there was no violence involved, he applied for and gained an injunction, which was upheld by the Court of Appeal, by the High Court and the Court of Appeal again. Effectively, this meant that even peaceful picketing, made legal in the 1870s, was now illegal. Indeed, Mr Justice Byrne argued that picketing was only legal if confined to communicating information. Picketing to encourage strike action was illegal, a view upheld by the High Court in 1899.[33]

The legal position of unions was, however, much more confused where their actions appeared to inflict injury on a third party not involved in a dispute. In the Temperton v. Russell case of 1893 the Court of Appeal held that an action was maintainable against three unions involved in boycott action by the building unions of Hull. Other cases endorsed that position, although the Allen v. Flood case of 1898, when the House of Lords rejected the claims of two carpenters discharged from a shipyard dispute as a result of a demarcation dispute, appeared to reverse that position.

If the legal position of trade unions was rather confused, if tending to limit their action, there was no such confusion or lack of clarity in the case of the famous Taff Vale case. This arose as a result of the Taff Vale Railway Company taking action for damages against the Amalgamated Society of Railway Servants (ASRS). The ASRS had taken strike action against the company in order to secure union recognition at a time when prices were high, due to the shortage of labour resulting from the Boer War, and when the company might be expected to concede. Ammon Beasley, the company's general manager did not concede, entered litigation and won an injunction against the union. This was reversed by the Court of Appeal but later, in 1901, upheld by the House of Lords in 1901. The Taff Vale decision meant that unions could be sued, and that union funds, rather than those of the union officials, could be open to legal claims. As a result of this decision, the ASRS was forced, in a subsequent case, to pay £23,000 to the Taff Vale Railway Company in January 1903, as well as its own costs of £19,000.

Combined with the restrictions imposed upon unions by the Lyons v. Wilkins case and the decision of the Quinn v. Leathem case of 1901, which involved an attempt by the Belfast Butchers' Union to prevent meat being bought from an employer who had taken on non-unionists and re-emphasized the vulnerability of union funds, it is clear that the position of trade unions was extremely precarious. Many union leaders felt that the judges were biased against working men, and it is hardly surprising that many unions began to seek their future salvation through affiliation with the LRC/Labour Party. The Taff Vale case won trade union support for the political Labour movement on a scale that could never have been contemplated by LRC officials campaigning to gain grudging support from an essentially Liberal-dominated trade union movement. There is no doubt, as the LRC/Labour Party found, that it speeded up the process of union affiliation, although, as K.D. Brown suggests, there were some trade unionists, including Richard Bell, who maintained that the Taff Vale decision would strengthen the central control of the union over local branches and would force unions to accept responsibility for the actions of their agents.[34] Brown has a fair point to make, but it is clear, from the correspondence of the LRC, that many trade unions expressed their concern over the Taff Vale decision and that that was the reason for their affiliation.[35] That was equally evident in the case of trades councils, which often acted as local LRCs in the absence of the formation of separate organizations. In the West Yorkshire textile belt the trades councils at Bradford, Leeds and Todmorden had already joined the LRC before June 1901, when the Taff Vale decision was made, but six others, Halifax, Wakefield, Keighley, Dewsbury, Huddersfield and Shipley joined between 1902 and 1904, once they could afford the subscription fees.[36] Nevertheless, Brown correctly suggests that the

real impetus of the Taff Vale case occurred after the final settlement of
£23,000 in January 1903, the scale of which did increase trade union
affiliation enormously.[37] Thereafter, the TUC decided to seek a
parliamentary bill that would give the unions immunity against all
actions for damages. The Royal Commission, set up in 1903 to
investigate the laws relating to trade unions, reported to a new Liberal
government in 1906, suggesting that the Taff Vale decision was
consistent with existing trade union law. It recommended that trade
unions should be recognized as statutory legal entities and that their
benefit funds should be separated from their general and strike funds,
thus allowing benefit funds to be immune from action for damages.
The Liberal government intended to introduce legislation along the
lines of the Royal Commission report but, faced with a hostile reaction
from Labour MPs, and aware of the commitment which many Liberal
MPs had made to the legal immunity of trade unions, Campbell-
Bannerman, the Prime Minister, decided to introduce legislation
which would grant trade unions the total immunity they had fought
for. Ignoring the Royal Commission and his legal advisers, the Prime
Minister had, according to Brown, responded to the presence of John
Burns, an old socialist trade unionist, in his Cabinet, who acted 'for
several years as a sort of unofficial adviser to Campbell-Bannerman on
trade and labour affairs'.[38] As a result the Trade Disputes Act was
passed in 1906, legalizing picketing and actions which would not
have been illegal if carried out by an individual, and no trade union
activity could be illegal if it induced a breach of contract.

The Taff Vale case drove many trade unions to affiliate to the
LRC/Labour Party. In many cases, these unions raised a political levy
on members in order to sponsor a trade union/Labour candidate and to
pay for their presence and upkeep in Parliament. Such action was
challenged in the courts by W.V. Osborne, a member of the
Walthamstow branch of the ASRS, who decided to bring an action to
restrain the union from contributing to the upkeep of the Labour
Party. The case was heard and rejected in the High Court in 1908, but
was subsequently upheld in the Court of Appeal and, eventually, the
House of Lords in December 1909. The main attack against the ASRS
was that political activity was *ultra vires* for a trade union, since
political activity lay outside the purpose of trade unions as defined by
statute in the 1871 and 1876 trade union legislation.

The Osborne Judgement challenged the benefit funds of unions,
since they were not mentioned in the 1870s legislation, and deprived

sixteen Labour MPs of their salaries, with little prospect of them being maintained by voluntary support. Indeed, as Brown notes, only 5,000 of the 117,000 members of the ASE were willing to pay a voluntary levy of a shilling per head to maintain the union's MPs.[39] This problem was only resolved when the Liberal government decided to introduce payment for MPs and when, in 1913, a Trade Union Bill permitted unions to use their funds for political purposes as long as the majority of their members agreed and those who opposed it were allowed to contract out.

Regardless of the legal and political situation, trade union organization developed apace. The semi-skilled workers, who formed 45 per cent or so of the male workforce, benefited from both the introduction of new machinery, which enabled them to acquire some more narrowly defined skill than the old skilled workers, and the deflation in prices of the late nineteenth century. Their presence was particularly marked in the expanding transport sectors, such as railways. By acquiring skills over many years, often extending into adult life, the broadening semi-skilled sector found itself lapping on the boundaries of skill, to which some of its members were eventually admitted.

There were also other structural changes in the economy, most notably the development of the white-collar workers and the growth of service sectors. In the fifty years between 1861 and 1911, the number of men in commercial occupations increased from 130,000 to 739,000 and the numbers of women employed in clerical labour rose from almost none to 157,000.[40] This white-collar and 'white-blouse' revolution led to the formation of unions and associations, such as the National Clerks' Association, the National Union of Teachers, and the Post Office Workers' Union. They may not have exhibited the militancy of the blue-collar unions – although J.L. Mahon did threaten to make the Post Office workers into a militant body – but they became an increasingly important force within the trade union movement.[41]

The admittance of these new sectors into the trade union movement was, perhaps, a slow and grudging development but in many respects the whole period from 1893 to 1909 might be seen in that light. The trade union movement, faced with the introduction of new technology, more assertive employers and a changing pattern of employment structures, found that progress was slow and that gains in some areas were offset by losses in others. Steady, rather than spectacular, growth was the hallmark of this period. Indeed, after the peaks of the 1889 to 1893 period, the number of strikes, strikers and days lost declined dramatically, with some slight fluctuations, until about 1908/9, according to the evidence on strikes and lock-outs produced by the Labour Department of the Board of Trade. From a peak of 1,211 strikes in 1889 the numbers fell to 354 in 1904, rose to 601 in 1906, and fell back to 436 in 1908 before rising to 531 in 1910 and 903 in 1911. The number of strikers fell from a peak of 599,000 in 1893, largely as a result of the coal lock-out, to 56,000 in 1904 before rising again to 385,000 in 1910.[42]

Part of the reason for this relative passivity in industrial affairs was the increased concern of government to reduce the potential for industrial conflict. Governments always had an interest in maintaining law and order during industrial disputes but also developed a concern to avoid serious conflicts which could affect the whole nation. Hence, they became involved in settling the coal lock-out of 1893, in the threatened 1907 national rail strike and in the introduction of the Conciliation Act of 1896.

The coal lock-out of 1893 was the first time the government intervened to end an industrial dispute. Gladstone acted when the coal lock-out, which had lasted from July to November, appeared to have reached stalemate. He invited both parties to a conference, chaired by Lord Rosebery on 17 November 1893, at which a settlement was achieved. It was this settlement, along with the Majority Report of the Royal Commission on Labour which encouraged the introduction of the 1896 Conciliation Act, which allowed the Labour Department of the Board of Trade to offer conciliation if one party agreed and arbitration if both parties asked. The Conciliation Act enabled settlement of some disputes, though the Labour Department of the Board of Trade was rebuffed on many occasions, as in the case of Lord Penrhyn during the strikes of his quarrymen during 1896–7 and 1899–1903.[43]

Nevertheless, the action of the government in averting the 1907 national rail strike was a personal triumph for David Lloyd George, President of the Board of Trade from 1905–8. The threatened strike had been initiated by Richard Bell of the ASRS, who initiated an 'all-grades' movement and approached the various railway companies for a rise in wages. The North-Eastern Railway Company accepted the proposal but it was rejected by all the others and the union members voted for a national strike. Lloyd George intervened, and acted as a go-between, in order to bring the two sides together and it was finally agreed to set up Boards of Conciliation for each railway and every grade of employment on each railway, on which both company and employees would be represented. However, in no way did it represent the recognition of trade unions since the employees' representatives were to be elected by the direct vote of all railway workers and they might not be union officials – although there is no doubt that the ASRS would ultimately dominate the employees' side.[44]

Such a tendency to institutionalize industrial relations between the employers, the trade unions and the government did, however, tend to limit trade union support for rank-and-file action. Indeed, this increasing domination of trade union organization, often to the exclusion of the local interests, was to produce its own difficulties, particularly in the form of rank-and-file discontent which certainly came to dominate the years from 1910 to 1918.[45]

Furthermore, while governments worked to maintain industrial harmony, and trade unions worked with employers to do the same, it is clear that there was some unease within trade union ranks at some industrial developments. The employers' counter-attack in the 1890s produced a more cautious and protective attitude on the part of the British trade union movement – especially given that the employers did not only win back ground lost to the 'new unions' but also that lost to the well-established skilled unions. Indeed, it was the attack and defeat of one of these, the ASE, which provoked some considerable rethinking in the minds of trade unionists.

In recent years there has been substantial work on the organization of employers.[46] Although this area of research is still in its infancy, it is already clear that employers' organizations were only formed when the challenge of trade unions became serious, and that their interest in forming associations increased towards the end of the nineteenth century with the decline of sub-contracting and with the increasing need of employers to run their own businesses in a more direct manner. The formation of the Shipping Federation, designed to counter the influence of dockers and sailors, has already been referred to. Equally famous is the Employers' Federation of Engineering Associations formed in 1896 to counter the ASE, now under the influence of George Barnes, a member of the ILP. In 1897 some of the London engineers struck in favour of the eight-hour day and the federation ordered a national lock-out, which lasted from July 1897 to January 1898. The Federation maintained that the ASE had undermined the efficiency of British industry and could no longer be allowed to do so. With the aid of the National Free Labour Association, some of the employers kept their works going, but by and large most firms closed. During the six months of the dispute, the trade union movement rallied round the engineers, providing them with £169,000 in voluntary subscriptions to supplement the £489,000 spent by the ASE on the dispute. In the end, however, the union was forced to concede on the eight-hour day and had to accept the employers' right to determine what grade of workmen would be employed on new machinery.

The defeat of the ASE created immediate problems for ASE members in areas outside London, who, in any case, could not understand the reason for their involvement in the conflict. They lost some control over the introduction of new machinery and found themselves unable to improve wages. In Halifax, for instance, the ASE pressed the Halifax Branch Employers' Federation for an increase of wages in 1906, noting that:

> It is something like nine years since we had an advance in the rate of wages . . . there have been changes in several directions, and would point out that the cost of living to us has been increased.[47]

The issue of higher wages, combined with a concern that engineers in Halifax earned 33 shillings per week compared with 34 shillings for those in Bradford, and 38 shillings for those in Sheffield, and generally higher rates elsewhere, led to a protracted round of discussions which lasted several years and only occasioned minor changes.

If ASE branches were inhibited from taking industrial action, then the consequence of the defeat of one of the most powerful trade unions in the world was evident for all to see; any union could be defeated in the absence of wide trade union support. As a consequence, attempts were made to form federations of trade unions for mutual support. Indeed, there was an attempt to form a General Federation of Trade Unions, although this proved to be relatively unsuccessful. The TUC established a committee to form such a body in 1897, the committee recommended to the 1898 TUC that such a body be formed and the General Federation of Trade Unions was established at Manchester in 1899. It was a committee which controlled funds and attracted only forty-four unions with a total membership of 343,000, about a quarter of the TUC membership.

Nevertheless, there was a general movement in many trades to form some type of federation. The Labour Department of the Board of Trades' *Report on Trade Unions in 1908–1910* lists five pages of federations. Most were local, but there were thirteen besides the General Federation of Trade Unions, with more than 50,000 members. Some, such as the Miners' Federation of Great Britain, with 597,000 members, had come into existence before the 1897 engineering lock-out but many others had emerged in its wake. The list includes the Durham Miners' Federation (124,000), the British Metal Federation (204,000), the Federation of Engineering and Shipbuilding Trades (372,000), the Northern Counties Textile Trades' Federation (128,000), the United Textile Factory Workers' Association (144,000), the Printing and Kindred Trades' Federation (68,000), and the National Federation of Shop Workers and Clerks (58,000). Generally, they organized small and medium-sized unions together in an attempt to coordinate negotiations with employers. There was, indeed, a lively federation, if not amalgamation, movement afoot even before the emergence of syndicalist activities in the years between 1910 and 1914.

Conclusion

The years between 1888 and 1909 have been dominated by the exaggerated importance of the 'New Unionism', although it might be said to have been more important in encouraging skilled unionists to be less sectarian than it was in organizing the unskilled. Indeed, evidence of the occupational changes within the British economy and the increasing pressure that was placed upon employers by the intensification of foreign competition would in any case have led to significant changes within the trade union movement. In other words, 'New Unionism' may simply have been symptomatic of the changes that were occurring. The Webbs may have been right about the characteristics of 'New Unionism' but, in a sense, that is no longer the question or the issue, for current historical debate is far more concerned about the changing nature of the economy, the homogeneity of the working class and the world of work during these years. In the end, many of the changes that were occurring worked to maintain sharp, social and economic divides within the workforce rather than to blur those divisions. Technological developments may have challenged the skilled workers, yet there is no reason to assume that they de-skilled the workforce, and Professor Price may be correct in arguing that the control of the workplace was central to class conflict at this time, although political developments also played their part in this class conflict and the conflict may not have been as universal to all industries and sections. Indeed, the control of the workplace became, in its own way, a central issue in the trade union events which took place between 1910 and 1918.

NOTES

1. H. Braverman, *Labor and Monopoly Capital* (1974).
2. R.J. Price, *Masters, Unions and Men* (1980).
3. P. Joyce, 'Labour, Capital and Compromise: A Response to Richard Price', *Social History*, IX (1984); P. Joyce, 'Work', *The Cambridge Social History of Britain 1750–1950, Vol.2, People and their Environment*, edited by F.M.L. Thompson (CUP, 1990).
4. Joyce, 'Work', p. 151.
5. C. More, *Skill and the English Working Class 1870–1914* (1980); C. More, 'Skill and the Survival of Apprenticeship', *The Degradation of Work*, ed. by S. Wood (1982).
6. W. Knox, 'Apprenticeship and De-skilling in Britain 1850–1914', *International Review of Social History*, vol. 31, 1986, p. 169.
7. E.J. Hobsbawm, *Labour's Turning Point* (1948), p. 4.
8. J. Benson, *The Working Class in Britain 1850–1914* (Longman, 1989).
9. C. Booth, *Labour and life of the people*, vol. 1, *East London* (1889), vol. II, *London* (1891), which in the second edition in 1892 became *Life and Labour of the people in London*.
10. T. Mann, *What a Compulsory Eight-Hour Working Day Means to the Workers* (1886).
11. A.E.P. Duffy, 'The Eight-Hour Day Movement in Britain 1886–1893', two parts in *Manchester School of Economic and Social Studies*, XXXVI, 1968, pp. 202–22 and 345–63.
12. *Bradford Observer Budget*, April 1890; James Bartley, 'Early Days in Bradford', Bradford and District Trades and Labour Council, *Year Book 1912* (Bradford, 1912).
13. T. McCarthy, *The Great Dock Strike 1889* (Weidenfeld & Nicolson, 1988).
14. E.J. Hobsbawm, *Labouring Men* (Weidenfeld & Nicolson, 1964), p. 187, from the article on 'General Labour Unions in Britain, 1889–1914'.
15. *Ibid.*, p. 180.
16. R.J. Price, *Labour in British Society* (Croom Helm, 1986), pp. 114–27.

17. *To All Classes of Workmen in the Engineering Industry*, a recruiting leaflet.
18. *Barnsley Chronicle*, 8 November 1890.
19. Joyce,'Work', p. 183.
20. J. Reynolds and K. Laybourn, 'The Emergence of the Independent Labour Party in Bradford', *International Review of Social History*, vol. XX (1975), part 3, p. 319.
21. W.J. Read, *The Clerk's Charter*, copy in the Webb Collection, Coll. E, B, cviii, item 3, British Library of Political and Economic Science.
22. J. Hinton, 'The Rise of a Mass Labour Movement: Growth and Limits', *A History of British Industrial Relations 1875–1914*, edited by C. Wrigley (Brighton, Harvester Press, 1982), p. 29.
23. *Ibid.*, p. 30, quoting from T. Olcott, 'Dead Centre: the Women's Trade Union Movement in London, 1874–1914', *London Journal*, 2 (1976).
24. Price, *Labour in British Society*, p. 100.
25. *Ibid.*, p. 101.
26. Knox, *op.cit.*, p. 175.
27. *Bradford Observer*, 20 April 1891.
28. K. Laybourn and J. Reynolds, *Liberalism and the Rise of Labour* (Croom Helm, 1984), p. 106.
29. E.P. Thompson, 'Homage to Tom Maguire' in *Essays in Labour History* (Macmillan, 1960), edited by A. Briggs and J. Saville, pp. 276–316.
30. R. Gregory, *The Miners and British Politics 1906–14* (Oxford, Clarendon Press, 1968).
31. K.D. Brown, 'Trade Unions and the Law', *A History of British Industrial Relations 1875–1914* (Brighton, Harvester Press, 1982), edited by C.J. Wrigley, p. 120.
32. *Ibid.*, pp. 120–1.
33. *Ibid.*, p. 121.
34. *Ibid.*, pp. 124–5.
35. Labour Party Archive, Labour Representation Committee Correspondence, 1900–7, also microfilmed by Harvester Press, Brighton, 1981.
36. Laybourn and Reynolds, *op.cit.*, pp. 106–7.
37. Brown, *op.cit.*, pp. 126.
38. *Ibid.*, pp. 128–9.
39. *Ibid.*, p. 132.
40. G. Anderson, 'Some Aspects of the Labour Market in Britain *c.* 1870–1914', in *A History of British Industrial Relations 1875–1914*, edited by C.J. Wrigley, p. 10.
41. G.S. Bain, *The Growth of White-Collar Unionism* (1970).
42. J.E. Cronin, 'Strikes and Power in Britain 1870–1920, *International Review of Social History*, vol. 32, 1987, p. 148, which are gathered from the Board of Trade, *Reports on Strikes and Lockouts*, 1888–1914.
43. C. Wrigley, 'The Government and Industrial Relations', *A History of British Industrial Relations 1875–1914*, edited by C.J. Wrigley, pp. 135, 142.
44. *Ibid.*, pp. 143–4.
45. V. Gore, 'Rank-and-File Dissent', *A History of British Industrial Relations 1875–1914*, edited by C.J. Wrigley, pp. 47–73.

46. W.R. Garside, H.F. Gospel and A. McIvor have written, extensively, on this matter and a useful outline is provided by W R Garside and H.F. Gospel, 'Employers and Managers: Their Organizational Structure and Changing Industrial Strategies', *A History of British Industrial Relations 1875–1914*, edited by C.J. Wrigley, pp. 99–115.

47. Meeting between the Halifax Branch Engineering Employers' Federation and the Amalgamated Society of Engineers (Halifax Branch), 22 June 1906. Deposited in the Calderdale branch of West Yorkshire Archives (located at Halifax), TU 1/6.

CHAPTER FOUR

SYNDICALISM, MASS UNIONISM AND THE GREAT WAR 1910–18

Industrial conflict began to increase dramatically immediately prior to the First World War and continued apace throughout the wartime years. To many contemporaries, the rise in the strike activity which occurred at this time was associated with the rise of syndicalism and the emergence of the shop stewards' movement, but the balance of recent opinion has emphatically played down the importance of these events. Instead, recent research suggests that syndicalism was a minor and incidental occurrence to the wider developments within the trade union movement and that the shop stewards' movement represented a rather small element of protest against the suspension of trade union rights during the war years, despite some recent research to the contrary by Joseph Melling and John Foster. Indeed, the balance of more recent research also calls into question the wider issue of the stability of Edwardian, and immediate post-Edwardian, society. If the current view on the role of syndicalism and the shop stewards' movement is correct then it must follow that the instability of the late Edwardian period, and particularly the years between 1910 and 1914, has been exaggerated – although there remains the possibility that the wider developments within the trade union movement may well have created some instability.

Until the mid-1970s the traditional view about British syndicalism is that it was a rather limited movement which exerted a fitful impact upon British society between 1910 and the summer of 1912. Henry Pelling, for instance, concluded of syndicalism that 'we must not exaggerate the importance of the new ideas upon British trade unionism as a whole.'[1] This view was endorsed by James Hinton who wrote that:

> Lacking any systematic doctrine, entirely dependent on the momentum of industrial militancy, the syndicalist movement grew with meteoric speed during the great strike movement of 1910–1912 – and fell just as fast in the year before the war. After 1914 its influence was diffuse and difficult to trace, though the syndicalist-inspired Amalgamated Committee movement played an important role in the origins of the shop steward movement in England.[2]

Even Geoff Brown, a great supporter of the ideas of syndicalists, has linked the rise and fall of British syndicalism with the brief involvement of Tom Mann between 1910 and 1912.[3] Such views, which minimize the impact of syndicalism, were challenged by Bob Holton in the mid-1970s.[4] He maintained that its influence extended between 1910 and 1914, noting that many workers acted in a proto-syndicalist manner, that workers began to feel that they could change society through industrial rather than political action, and that British syndicalism was just as alive and vital as that on the Continent and in the United States. In addition, he suggested that syndicalism was developing in the Black Country and other regions throughout 1913 and 1914. More recently, however, Professor Clegg has noted that, apart from the Cambrian dispute of 1910–11 and the dockers and seamen's strike in Liverpool in the summer of 1911, there is little to suggest that syndicalism held much sway in the fourteen major industrial disputes that occurred between 1910 and 1914.[5]

The first shop stewards' movement has also evoked intense controversy. During the First World War and the inter-war years the radical and militant action which it took on 'Red Clydeside' were celebrated widely, with somewhat exaggerated importance, by Willie Gallacher in his book *Revolt on the Clyde*.[6] In more recent years, James Hinton has examined the events of Clydeside, in Sheffield and other engineering centres, and fitted the industrial militancy of the shop stewards' movement most firmly into the response of engineering craftsmen to the threat of the new technologies.[7] Apparently, faced with such a threat, and led by an able group of shop stewards, the rank and file ignored their moderate leaders and adopted other strategies, including opposition to dilution and the demand for workers' control, in a desire to protect their craft privileges. Imposed upon these events were subsidiary issues, such as hostility against conscription and anti-war sentiments. In addition, many of the shop stewards, through their radical actions, gradually associated themselves with the movement which eventually became the Communist Party of Great Britain. Although Hinton's work modified many of Gallacher's images of the 'Red Clyde' it did not go far enough for some writers, most particularly Iain McLean whose book, *Legend of Red Clydeside*, produced in 1983, suggests that our understanding of Scottish society has been distorted by the myth that there was a class struggle on the Clyde.[8] He suggests that the Clyde Workers' Committee were isolated and confused, that they represented a conservative strand in trade unionism, and that it was progressive, rather than reactionary, politicians who were attempting to bring about dilution and change on the Clyde through the Ministry of Munitions – contrasting Hinton's notion that the Ministry was dominated by politicians who were part of the long arm of the Servile State. McLean argues that Hinton, and indeed Middlemass in earlier years, gave too much credence to the views of the Clyde shop stewards and that, in effect, the marxist shop stewards were a marginal influence on the Clyde. In any case, the primary interest of the shop stewards was to defend the sectional interests of their members. Socialism, he argues, emerged from other factors on Clydeside, such as the rent strike and religion. However, while McLean clearly attacks some of Hinton's view on Clydeside it must be remembered that Hinton did note that the failure of the shop stewards' movement on Clydeside had a lot to do with the fact that the semi-skilled and unskilled workers did not identify with a craft group who were wishing to keep them, and their type, at bay.

Since McLean's book appeared, there have been many contributions to the debate about 'Red Clyde'. On the revisionist side, and generally supporting McLean, Alastair Reid has argued that Hinton has exaggerated the importance of the dilution campaign, has underplayed the crucial resistance of the shipyard workers to the Munitions Act, and that wartime industrial policies advanced popular politics.[9] Gerry Rubin's work on the Glasgow Munitions Tribunal also suggests that moderate and state-inclined policies emerged from the tribunals as trade union officials were converted by their experience of legal regulation under the munitions act to the need for state regulation.[10] In the end it appears that trade union leaders were converted to moderate state reconstruction which encouraged the evolution of the politics of the Labour Party.

These revisionist views have been challenged in two articles by Joseph Melling and John Foster.[11] Both articles accept some of the views of the revisionists but argue that the struggle of the skilled workers on Clydeside contributed to the growth of Labour politics on the Clyde. To Melling, the distinctive features of Clydeside are that the industrial conditions were varied and that there was much resistance against the state imposing state regulations. In addition, it appears that industrial and non-industrial actions overlapped in determining the politics of Clydeside. Melling is adamant that the shipyard workers, despite their different position to the engineers, shared a common interest in opposing dilution, and believes that the struggles on Clydeside exerted as much influence on the ILP, which came to dominate Clydeside, as they did on the Communist Party. In some senses, then, he builds upon his research on employer associations of a decade ago, which indicated the bitter determination with which the employers sought to exclude trade union organization from their works – a factor which gave a class dimension to some of the struggles on the Clyde.[12] Foster, in his article, criticizes the revisionists for ignoring the reality of what was occurring in Clydeside for the fact is that strike levels were rising dramatically in the west of Scotland throughout 1918 and 1919, particularly in shipbuilding, and that the vote for the Communist Party increased substantially in the immediate post-war years. In other words the 'Red Clyde' was a 'real phenomenon' caused by a variety of factors – the strength of the trade union organizations, the rapid expansion of the workforce, the use of state powers to enforce the will of capital – which were responsible for the limited but significant radicalization of the workers in the west of Scotland.

There is also a third, more general, debate for these years, connected with the development of syndicalism. It concerns the stability of British society on the eve of war. Contemporaries were certain that they were living through unusual times of disturbance between 1910 and 1914, and their views were captured in George Dangerfield's, *The Strange Death of Liberal England*, in the mid-1930s.[13] Dangerfield linked the syndicalist-inspired revolt with the difficulties posed by the suffrage movement, Ireland, the emergence of the Labour Party, and other issues, to produce an impression that Liberal England was collapsing due to its failure to deal with these problems. But by the 1950s and 1960s Henry Pelling and E.H. Phelps Brown were challenging this notion of instability,[14] and current opinion appears to be divided. On the one hand, there has been support for Dangerfield's view from Alan O'Day, Bob Holton and Richard Price. On the other, support for the views of Pelling and Phelps Brown has come from Professor Donald Read, who has emphasized the continuity of Edwardian institutions, despite the challenges they faced.[15] Even Joe White, who sympathizes with the message of syndicalism as a force for unrest, accepts that 'syndicalism was – and had to be – limited in its appeal and its successes.'[16]

These debates and issues raise four main questions. Has the impact of syndicalism been exaggerated? Did the challenge of the workers represent a threat to the industrial *status quo* before 1914? Why was there so much rank-and-file protest in the years before the war? And, how important was the shop stewards' movement as a reflection of the frustrations and demands of rank-and-file trade unionists during the First World War? And on the last question there are at least two subsidiary issues. First, how did the craftsmen react to new technology? Secondly, what was the position of the state regarding the control of the workforce?

Syndicalism

The industrial events of 1910 to 1914 have often been associated with the development of syndicalism in Britain, and the alarmist reaction of some contemporary writers. Sir Arthur Clay wrote that syndicalism was a dangerous foreign idea 'the object of which is the destruction by force of the existing organizations and the transfer of industrial capital from its present possessors to Syndicalists, or in other words to the revolutionary Trade Unions. The means by which this object is to be secured is the General Strike', adding that 'Syndicalism – like vice – is a Monster of such hideous mien, as to be hated need but to be seen'.[17] Yet this must be balanced by the more sober opinion of politicians, most notably those of Philip Snowden[18] and Ramsay MacDonald, who played down its importance. Indeed, MacDonald wrote that:

> As a matter of simple fact, nothing can be denied with more certainty, for Syndicalism in England is negligible, both as a school of thought and as an organisation for action.[19]

Contemporary opinion was clearly divided on the issue even more than current writers are.

The syndicalist movement owed part of its existence to the socialist activities in the United States which led to the formation of the Industrial Workers of the World in 1905, and the advocacy of its views through the work of Daniel De Leon. Disdainful of the craft trade unions of the United States, De Leon argued for 'dual unionism', whereby revolutionary trade unions were to be formed alongside the existing craft union in order to attract all workers to them, to create an industrial union and to ultimately, with other industrial unions, call a general strike which would bring about the downfall of capitalist society. This strand of opinion attracted some support among the miners of South Wales and in Scotland, and its views were pushed forward by the newly-formed Socialist Labour Party (1903), which had been formed in Scotland and, in 1906, by the British Advocates of Industrial Unionism.[20] This movement was dominated by George Yates and James Connolly, the Irish revolutionary who later became the leader of the 1916 Easter Uprising. The anarcho-syndicalist groups in Britain also contributed some syndicalist ideas, especially from 1903 when Sam Mainwaring launched a journal called *The General Strike*. Other anarchists, such as Guy Aldred, who formed the Industrial Union of Direct Actionists in August 1907, also contributed their part. But it was Tom Mann, returning from Australia in April 1910 who was, for a couple of years, to dominate the direction which the syndicalist movement took. Influenced by his industrial experiences in Australia, having read E.J.B. Allen's book, *Revolutionary Unionism* (1909), he was attracted to the ideas of winning industrial unionism by 'boring from within' the existing trade union structure, uniting the working class, and of using the general strike to win control of the state.

Allen, a gasworker who lived at New Street, Honley near Huddersfield, had set up the Industrial League, in 1908, to push

100

forward that type of view which Mann came to support, and later wrote out his views in *The Industrial Syndicalist*. He argued that the trade union movement was the only one capable of uniting the workers since working-class representatives on public bodies simply became absorbed into the system, that the workers had to take control of industries and services, and to create a 'state within a state' capable of challenging the capitalist oligarchy:

> We shall unite all the workers in any one industry, and unite all industries. We will build a 'State within a state', a workers' democracy in opposition to the capitalist oligarchy.
>
> The existing unions must be united, strengthened and enlightened as to the real purpose that a labour union should be formed for: to teach their members to think every time they enter the yard, mill or mine: 'This is the place where my fellow-workmen and I are robbed; this is the place that we keep going; this is the place *we* ought to own and control. . . .'
>
> *Let us think and Act as a Class*
> The industrial union is destined to become the most powerful instrument in the class struggle by showing the working class how to hold in check the rapacity of their masters and the tyrannies of the State by direct pressure of their collective economic strength which power reaches its highest expression in the complete paralysis of the whole of the normal functions of capitalist society by means of a general strike. The use of a general strike must be amplified and extended, embracing a larger number of workers in the actual combat; evolving that unity of action and sameness of inspiration which will make them *think and act as a class*, for the direct and forcible expropriation of the capitalists.[21]

It was Allen's ideas which greatly influenced Mann, although on his return to Britain he made a brief visit to France to discover more about the syndicalist movement. On returning, Mann began to publish, with Guy Bowman, the *Industrial Syndicalist*, and formed the Industrial Syndicalist Education League. He also established 'Amalgamation Committees' in various industries, to encourage the movement of craft unions into large industrial unions.

Clearly, under Mann, the syndicalist movement united along the French model of 'boring from within' and there were developments within trade unionism at this time which suggested that section-alism was being reduced. In addition, it is clear that in forming industrial unions and organizing a parliament of industrial unions to call a general strike, the philosophy of industrial unionism con-sidered the need to reject parliamentary control and substituted the idea of establishing some type of workers' control, working through the trade unions. In the end syndicalism envisaged trade unions being the agency of the transition to socialism and the basic structure of the socialist society. But how much influence did such views exert in Britain?

The years 1910 to 1914 certainly saw some significant industrial conflict. There was the famous Cambrian Combine dispute in the Rhondda Valley, South Wales, between September 1910 and August 1911, which, at its height, involved up to thirty thousand miners and was marked by the picketing and rioting against the safety men, who were there to prevent the mines from flooding, at Tonypandy on the 7 and 8 November 1910. These riots led to the death of one striker and the injury of five hundred others.[22] Throughout 1911 there was much industrial conflict. The seamen at Southampton held up the liner *Olympic* and quickly won a wage advance. There was a short, general strike in the London docks, brought to an end by the government conciliator G.R. Askwith, as a result of which the Shipping Federation was forced to recognize the Sailors' Union. There was a prolonged strike in the Liverpool docks, where the carters and dockers – the first, largely Protestant and the second, largely Catholic – organized effectively to stop the movement of essential food supplies without a special licence of the strike committee or a military escort. This strike led to conflict and the death of a policeman and the injury of many strikers on 'Bloody Sunday', 13 August 1911, when troops clashed with rioters. Two days later two rioters were shot dead as convicted rioters were being taken by van to Walton Gaol.[23] There was also a national railway strike on 18 August 1911, due to the frustration of railway workers with the slow processes of their conciliation board, although it was settled after only two days by the intervention of Lloyd George who arranged that a Royal Commission should be set up to examine the operation of conciliation boards. As a result, a new conciliation scheme was introduced into the railways which effectively recognized the trade unions, who normally supplied the secretary who was appointed on the men's side of each conciliation board. However, brief as it was, this dispute led to deaths, when, on 19 August, troops fired on a crowd in Llanelli killing two protestors. The resultant disturbances led to the deaths of five other people, killed when a van of gunpowder blew up in the local goods yards which had been looted and fired.

SYNDICALISM, MASS UNIONISM AND THE GREAT WAR

In February 1912 there was a strike by the Miners' Federation of Great Britain to secure a minimum wage of five shillings (25p) for men and two shillings (10p) per shift for boys, the government rushed through a bill to establish minimum district wage agreements, the miners rejected the move, struck, but very quickly accepted that this was the best that could be won. There was another London dock strike in May 1912, when the Port of London Authority, under the chairmanship of Lord Devonport, insisted upon its right to employ non-union men. Since this involved the National Transport Workers' Federation, a national strike was called, with little effect, and even the London strike collapsed in August as blackleg labour was brought into the port. Strikes were beginning to be less effective than before and in 1913, the struggle between the Irish Transport Workers' Union, led by Jim Larkin, and the Dublin employers, began. It lasted eight months but finally collapsed in January 1914.

These, and many other disputes, form the stuff of industrial conflict during these years. But to what extent were they influenced by syndicalist ideas? There were obviously some areas of success and influence. Mann played some part in encouraging Ben Tillett, of the dockers, and Havelock Wilson, secretary of the National Sailors' and Fireman's Union, into forming the National Transport Workers' Federation in November 1910. Mann, and several local syndicalists were active in the Cambrian Combine dispute, and Mann wrote an article entitled 'Hurrah! Gallant Little Wales', from the battle lines in Tonypandy.[24] Mann was also deeply involved, with about fifty local syndicalists, in organizing the strikers in Liverpool in 1911, writing, with some pride, that:

> Never in my experience did so many workers in such varied occupations show such thorough solidarity as on the occasion in Liverpool. I was chairman of the Strike Committee for the seventy-two days the strike lasted. . . . Further, the seven thousand carters of Liverpool have a very close relationship with the North of Ireland, and a much larger number of dockers in Liverpool are correspondingly identified with the South. The differences that arise between these are frequently of a very emphatic character, but I have pleasure in recalling that when we commenced the strike and began committee work, it was definitely agreed that neither political nor theological opinion were to find advocacy or expression on the committee. We were engaged purely on an industrial subject and that alone should receive attention.[25]

In addition, Mann and Bowman elicited some support when they were arrested and imprisoned in 1912 over the publication of the famous 'Don't Shoot Leaflet', the 'Open Letter to British Soldiers'. This had been written by Fred Bower, a syndicalist stonemason, and had first appeared in the *Irish Worker* in July 1911, and was then reprinted in *The Syndicalist* in January 1912. Both Mann and Bowman were arrested in March, under the Incitement to Mutiny Act of 1797, and Mann was sentenced to six months imprisonment and Bowman to nine months. In the end, trade union pressure ensured their release after only seven weeks.

Furthermore, one should not forget that the Reform Committee of the South Wales miners did produce *The Miners' Next Step* in early 1912. This is usually considered to have been the highest point of British syndicalism, and the definitive statement of syndicalist intent with its call for the Miners' Federation of Great Britain to force the South Wales Miners' Federation to take action to represent their members, to get the rank-and-file to take action, to make the leaders more militant and to build up a union structure which would be far more centralized than had ever existed before in mining. In outlining the objective of industrial democracy the pamphlet noted that:

> Our objective begins to take shape before your eyes. Every industry thoroughly organized, in the first place, to fight, to gain control of, and then administer, that industry. The co-ordination of all industries on a Central Production Board who, with a statistical department to ascertain the needs of the people, will issue its demands on the different departments of industry, leaving the men themselves to determine under what conditions and how, the work should be done. This would mean real democracy in real life, making for real manhood and womanhood. Any other form of democracy is a delusion and a snare.[26]

In effect this recognized the need for central direction from a co-ordinating body of trade unionism while allowing workers' control at the pit face, so to speak.

Obviously, there were also syndicalist activists in other areas. Leonard Hall was active among engineers, and other groups, in the Midlands, and Larkin was active in Ireland. But it is difficult, if not impossible, to believe that syndicalism was in any sense pervasive among the British working class.

Active syndicalists seemed to have established themselves in a few small areas, as in Liverpool and South Wales, but to have been rather thin on the ground elsewhere. There was scant support for syndicalists in coalfields outside South Wales.[27] It has also been pointed out that mining unions rejected the centralization contained in *The Miners' Next Step* in favour of local autonomy.[28] In other words, the philosophy and approach of syndicalism do not appear to have carried much force. And it is also illuminating that at the ballot of miners before the 1912 Miners' Strike the South Wales miners produced a two-to-one majority (62,538 votes to 31,127) in favour of accepting the government's Minimum Wages' Act, while all the other coalfields voted to reject the government's bill, thus committing themselves to strike action. Even Holton has to admit that:

> this undoubtedly represented a setback to the syndicalists of the Unofficial Reform Committee. . . . The most outspoken supporter of industrial militancy during the strike was in fact John Williams, miners' agent at Merthyr, a man with no record of syndicalist commitment. The overwhelming Welsh vote in favour of a return to work is best explained in terms of strike weariness and depletion of financial reserves. The effect of the almost two-year old Cambrian dispute undoubtedly undermined coalfield resistance during the subsequent national strike.[29]

In the end, syndicalist views seem to have carried little weight in South Wales, and much less in the rest of the British coalfields. And it is hard to escape the conclusion that, for the most part, industrial conflict in the coalfields at this period was little different from that at any stage between 1890 and 1914, a view supported by Roy Church who argues that coalfield and quarrying militancy affected, broadly, the same number of strikers annually in the 1890s as it did between 1901 and 1913.[30]

In addition, as Professor Clegg has noted, there is little evidence that the industrial disputes at this period had much to do with syndicalism – in the sense of challenging capitalism and the state in the way which syndicalists urged. While noting the impossibility of examining the four thousand strikes of 1911–14 he stresses that by examining the fourteen major disputes, which account for 51 million of the 70 million working days lost through strikes, a fair reflection of the events of this period can be gained. Examining each of these disputes and analysing the overall pattern of events, he notes that only four of the disputes involved syndicalists and that, apart from the Liverpool strike, they involved relatively small numbers of workers but contributed to a large number of days lost because of their protracted nature.[31] Clegg is at pains to stress that syndicalism was a relatively minor factor in the industrial conflict of the pre-war years and that nearly all the major strikes could be accounted for by two factors: firstly, the boom in union organization, and, secondly, the poor financial position of some groups of employers, mainly the coal owners and railway companies, who were forced to reject what might otherwise have been considered reasonable demands.

If there is little evidence that syndicalism exerted any impact upon structural union reforms or imposed a new trade union leadership upon the British trade union movement, and that it does not account for the rise of the general level of industrial militancy between 1910 and 1914, what other factors may explain the industrial developments of this period? Was there a general malaise throughout the nation, fuelled by the constitutional conflicts between the Liberal Government and the House of Lords? Was it the failure of the Labour Party to make an immediate impact? Or were there other events which account for the problems of this period?

Trade Union Developments and the Stability of British Society, 1910–14

Clearly, there is still some debate about the stability or the instability of the period 1910–14, and even more so about the factors which might have led to a crisis in society. There was, for instance, some frustration expressed at the failure of the Labour Party to make political headway at this time, and part of this frustration was channelled into the British Socialist Party. But there has never been a time when the Labour Party has failed to have a vocal and critical minority whose support is greatly outweighed by the vast majority of supporters who work quite contentedly within the party. The Liberal Party also may have faced serious political problems but that, by no means, suggests that there was a major political crisis which was threatening to tear it apart. Yet, whatever the disagreements between historians as to how deep-rooted the political and economic crisis of these years was, there is no doubting that there were developments within trade unionism which created an atmosphere of change and which altered the balance of re-lationships within the trade union movement and between unions, employers and government.

The most obvious point about this period was the rapid growth of trade union membership, from 2,477,000 in 1909 to 4,145,000 in 1914. This reflected similar bursts of trade union growth in the early 1870s and between 1888 and 1893 when economic conditions favoured their development; there was more demand for workers, better prospects for pay increases and more likelihood that workers would be able to pay trade union dues. This was also a period of price inflation following a period, from about 1901 onwards, when the real wages of workers had fallen. Obviously, there was some ground to be made up by the trade union movement and the prosperity from 1909 onwards provided the opportunity.

Nevertheless, although trade unionism was more aggressive within the economic and social conditions which operated at this time, it is also evident that they were locked into a widening structure of conciliation and arbitration, and that government was intervening with some regularity and effectiveness to prevent or end major disputes. Given these situations, it is hardly surprising that rank-and-file protest became increasingly evident during this period. Syndicalism, and so-called proto-syndicalism, may be regarded as part of this process but such rank-and-file action was something which was independent of mere syndicalism. Trade union members often took industrial action on their own account when their trade union leaders failed to respond to their requests. Indeed, there was an element of that in the Cambrian Combine dispute when the conciliation board, which included the former miners' leader, William Abraham (Mabon), recommended rates of pay for opening new seams which the miners refused to accept. Indeed, the message that came across in the early days of the dispute was the need to get the South Wales Miners' Federation (SWMF) to support the miners in this dispute. In essence, they eventually achieved this objective once the SWMF agreed to raise money to support the strikers, with the help of £3,000 per week from the Miners' Federation of Great Britain from the end of January 1911.[32] Trade unions often attempted to meet the concerns of their members but obviously found themselves facing difficulties in controlling them when faced with national or regional arbitration and conciliation exercises, and when faced with the problem of controlling their members.

Another dimension to this problem of union control has also been raised by Dr Roy Church who, noting that the industrial unrest of 1910–14 is not unique, offers evidence that the level of militancy and strike action varied from region to region in the mining industry, thus suggesting that there were marked regional problems and variations which meant that, even in mining, militancy could not be spread from one area to another, contrary to the view of James E. Cronin.[33] Church concludes that:

> Insofar as industrial unrest has been interpreted – and reinterpreted – as a mortal spasm which heralded the death of Liberal England our analysis reveals the extent to which traumas that may be identified in Edwardian England were mild by comparison with those which threatened the social equilibrium of Liberal south Wales. If we are to understand the origins of militancy in the coalfields then detailed comparative inter-regional research should be the historian's next step.[34]

In the end, then, it may be that national explanations of events are insufficient to explain the industrial conflict of this period.

It might well be the regional differences that persisted which inhibited the speeding up of the move towards amalgamations. There had been a fairly rapid development of federations in the first decade of the twentieth century but not a great deal of evidence of amalgamations or arrangements between unions in various industries. The National Transport Workers' Federation lacked consolidation and only the formation of the National Union of Railwaymen in 1913, bringing together the Amalgamated Society of Railway Servants, the General Railway Workers' Union and the United Pointsmen and Signalmen's Society, provided evidence of any significant movement towards amalgamation. Nevertheless, although its weakness was subsequently exposed in 1921, there was a move towards forming an alliance between the miners, the railwaymen and the National Transport Workers' Federation, which became known as the 'Triple Alliance'. Negotiations took place between the three bodies with the aim of coordinating their activities for mutual support during industrial conflict, the contracts of members of these organizations to terminate at the same time when in dispute. But the fact that the Miners' Federation membership was about twice that of the other two unions put together inhibited the smaller organizations from allowing a strike to be called by a ballot of all members. Instead, the support of any union in strike action had to be referred back to the executives and a decision taken within the other unions. Throughout 1914 and 1915 the three unions stumbled to an arrangement based upon mutual suspicion of the intent of others and which failed at the first hurdle, the miners' strike and lock-out of 1921. The 'Triple Alliance' was never to be a militant and revolutionary body which some believed it to be.

The First World War and the First Shop Stewards' Movement

Historians have seen the First World War as a crucial period of change and transition in British economic, social and political developments. It brought about a decline in British economic fortunes, divided the Liberal Party, and improved the economic and social position of the poorer sections of the working class. It also saw the strengthening of the status and position of the Labour Party, due to the fact that the party was drawn into Asquith's Coalition government in 1915 and the trade union leaders also acquiesced to the government requests to cooperate with it for the duration of the war. Indeed, Arthur Henderson, Labour's wartime leader, entered the Cabinet as President of the Board of Trade and George Barnes, the ex-secretary of the Engineers, was appointed Minister of Pensions. The leaders of the trade union movement cooperated with the government in order to produce the 'Shells and Fuses' agreement of March 1915 whereby 'dilution', the introduction of unskilled labour into jobs formerly reserved for skilled men, was permitted in return for a guarantee by the government and the employers that the suspended trade practices would be restored at the end of the war. Under this arrangement Sir George Askwith's Office of Industrial Commissioners was used to keep the industrial peace and any industrial problems in 'controlled establishments' that did munitions work were referred to legally binding courts of arbitration under Askwith's jurisdiction, following a voluntary agreement between the Treasury and the trade unions.[35]

The new industrial arrangements were generally accepted by trade unionists throughout the country, the vast majority of whom did well out of the improved economic conditions of wartime. Indeed, undue attention has tended to be placed upon the skilled engineering trade unionists of the Clyde, Sheffield and Manchester, who registered their protest at the new cosy relationship which had been engendered between the government, the employers and the trade unionists. Although detailed evidence is still slight, on balance it appears that most of the British workers were patriotic, accepted the industrial demands of the wartime government and posed no serious threat to the authorities.

Jonathan Schneer has emphasized this point in one of only a small number of articles conducted on workers, other than engineers, and their workplace relations. In his study of the British dockers, an unskilled section of the workforce, he notes that the war led to the improvement of some conditions and the deterioration of others, although the former exceeded the latter. He argues that the many dockers who volunteered for military service had created a labour shortage on the docks, and together with the government scheme to set up Transport Workers' Battalions, that this tended to bring to an end the casual employment of labour system which had prevailed before the war. In effect, the dilution of labour in the docks which had existed in the pre-war years practically disappeared. In addition, the war bonuses, given as lump sums rather than as percentages, tended to benefit the previously badly paid dock workers. Dockers might have been concerned about inflation, the preservation of skills and other matters, but, as Schneer concludes:

> Basically, the war improved labour conditions and thus helped keep the workers patriotic. Industrial militancy surfaced mainly after the sharp deterioration of conditions which followed the unprecedented improvements of 1914–17.[36]

War weariness, and the ending of the exemptions from conscription for dockers aged 18–25, which had extended from January 1916 to March 1918, created some tensions but in the end the dockers' leaders accepted the need to avoid strikes and to protect their improved position. Ben Tillett, having seen his Dock, Wharf, Riverside and General Labourers' Union increase from 38,000 to 85,000 members between 1914 and 1918 was anxious not to rock the boat and, fittingly reflected in 1919 that:

> Our own union has been able to command such improvements in the conditions of labour, such advantages in real wealth as to make me kick myself now and again to ascertain whether I am awake.[37]

Professor Chris Wrigley also confirms the general impression that most workers were doing well out of the war, noting that:

> During the First World War 4,970,000 men were enlisted in the Army, 407,000 in the Navy, and 293,000 in the Air Force out of a total male labour force of some 15 million. This left the remaining labour, especially skilled labour in essential war work in a very strong bargaining position.[38]

SYNDICALISM, MASS UNIONISM AND THE GREAT WAR

Such improvements for the unskilled and semi-skilled workers, which appear to have been fairly widespread, were not necessarily of comfort to the members of the skilled unions, for they saw their hard-won rights rapidly whittled away by the circumstances of war. The Defence of the Realm Act (DORA), the Munitions of War Acts and the Military Services Acts severely limited the freedom of craftsmen to operate traditional controls, even if there were some exemptions from industrial and military conscription. Indeed, several points of contention developed. There was some frustration at the Committee on Production becoming a statutory arbitration tribunal, the number of cases it dealt with increasing from 141 in 1915 to 2,298 in 1918. There were objections at the introduction of 'Leaving Certificates', imposed by the Munitions of War Act, which restricted the right of workers to leave their employment for a more highly paid job in the munitions or non-munitions sections of the economy – as a result of which they were eventually removed. The introduction of a munitions tribunal system, also a product of the Munitions of War Act, aggravated industrial relations. Ten general ones were set up throughout the country to deal with major offences, and fifty-five local munitions tribunals were set up to deal with lesser matters. The general ones dealt with strikes and prosecutions over leaving certificates, while the local ones dealt with the consideration of the granting of leaving certificates.

Even though such tensions affected workplace relations, by and large trade unions continued to work with the state in its new, more interventionist, activities. Despite some hesitations, they worked with the government's state control of mining, cotton, woollen and other industries and services. They also helped to form joint industrial councils, along the lines suggested by J.H. Whitley, as in the case of the Wool Textile Industrial Council which was formed at the end of 1918, with four regional councils for employers and employees. Indeed, these new arrangements increased the ability of the trade unions to extend trade unionism and enhanced their powers to force wage increases and to win war bonuses. There were problems in industries such as cotton, which lost export markets and was subject to fluctuating supplies of raw materials, and major strikes were threatened and occurred. A similar situation arose in mining, and shortly after the introduction of the Munitions of War Act, the South Wales Miners rejected a wage award decided upon by Sir George Askwith and 200,000 miners struck. Despite the illegality of their action, Lloyd George was forced to negotiate a settlement with these miners, accepting many of their demands in order to get the strikers back to work. However, on the whole, the miners reciprocated to the demands of the state, and the Miners' Federation of Great Britain, for instance, worked with it in shaping the military recruitment requirements for the war effort. Indeed, despite the mounting level of industrial unrest arising from the increased economic opportunity of wartime, there was relatively little dissent against the war effort and revolutionary intent was minimal within the trade union movement. The only major exception to that rule, the importance of which has been greatly exaggerated, occurred among the skilled engineers.

Willie Gallacher, in his book *Revolt on the Clyde*, and David Kirkwood, in *My Life of Revolt*, painted and embroidered a romantic picture of the events on Clydeside during the war but, as James Hinton has indicated, the reality was somewhat less romantic and the class warfare which Gallacher presented now appears much more sectional and reactionary.[39] Indeed, Hinton argues that 'the shop stewards' movement was a child of the war',[40] arising from the sudden and acute threat that was presented to the position of craftsmen who were determined that their status and privileges should be kept intact. It was, effectively, the response of a relatively small group of skilled engineers, working without the support of the unskilled and semi-skilled workers, who objected to the demand of Glasgow engineering employers that trade union rights should be suspended and that wages should be controlled or frozen. In the final analysis, their resistance was swept away quickly once the state acted to arrest the main shop stewards and to introduce dilution, during the early months of 1916, although the extent to which this evidence proved the failure of the movement has been hotly debated by Hinton, McLean, Reid, Melling and Foster.

The Glasgow engineering employers quickly recognized that the war, in creating a labour shortage, had given skilled trade unionists a strong bargaining position. Sir Hubert Llewelyn Smith, in a memorandum, wrote that:

> The shortage of labour directly delays production. It is, however, at the present time having direct effects perhaps even more serious. Practically any workman of any pretensions to skill at all in the engineering and shipbuilding trades has so little difficulty in finding work the moment he

wants it that he has little economic motive left for remaining with the
employer, if he is in any way dissatisfied, whether with good reason or
without.

On the other hand, the employers, constantly urged by the
Government to increase their output, do not feel themselves really in a
position to bargain with the men, and have, indeed, in many cases owing
to the terms of their contracts, little incentive to do so.

The ordinary economic control of the individual workman has
practically broken down. The result is that to a very considerable extent
men are out of the control of both employers and their own leaders.[41]

The Munitions of War Act of 3 July 1915 was an attempt to
re-establish control in the labour market and to prevent the
interruption of war work, introducing, as it did, the control of
munitions establishments, leaving certificates and the introduction
of a volunteer scheme. While this did redress the balance of
industrial bargaining in favour of the employer, it was not enough
for some Glasgow employers, most notably William Weir, the part
owner of the Cathcart engineering works which employed about two
thousand men, and Director of Munitions in Scotland. Weir disliked
the government negotiating with the trade unions and informed Dr
Christopher Addison, a Junior Minister attached to the Ministry of
Munitions and later to become Minister of Munitions, that:

The fallacy was the belief that bargaining was necessary . . . the
bargaining spirit was rife. The actual position was that the men would
have loyally done whatever the country required of them, if the position
had been clearly put to them, as they have done as soldiers.[42]

Given this type of attitude among the employers, testified to by
Melling's work on the employer organizations of Clydeside which
revealed their determination to exclude trade unions from their
works,[43] and an equal determination among skilled engineers to
protect their position, it is hardly surprising that bitter industrial
conflict ensued. The history of the conflict on the Clyde is
dominated by two major events – the wage demand which led to
strikes in February 1915 and the formation of the Clyde Workers'
Committee in October 1915, in response to the challenges posed by
the Munitions of War Act.

The first of these conflicts was anticipated in December 1914
when a three-year wage agreement came to an end and shop stewards
demanded a rise of 2d (1p) per hour in wages. When the employers

rejected this demand the workers imposed an overtime ban. There was no strike action, however, until 16 February 1915 when workers at Weir's Cathcart factory struck against the employment of a small number of American workers at ten shillings more per week than their British counterparts, with a £10 guaranteed bonus at the end of six months. There was no official trade union leadership for this strike but it soon spread to eighteen thousand workers in the twenty-six factories, forges and workshops. The lack of trade union leadership was compensated by the formation of a Central Labour Withholding Committee on 18 February, which drew together men of all unions under local shop stewards. By the beginning of March, after government intervention and threatened continued industrial unrest, the workers returned on the compromise arrangement of 1d (O.4p) per hour increase.

The conflict on Clydeside appeared to be defused until the Munitions' Act, because the introduction of leaving certificates and the victimization of shop stewards that action brought, weakened the bargaining position of the workers, fuelled unrest on the Clydeside, and led to the formation of the Clyde Trades Vigilance Committee, which became Clyde Workers' Committee in October 1915 – a body of shop stewards representing workers of all plants. The Committee has, inaccurately, been linked with the strike against higher rents that occurred on Clydeside but was, in fact, primarily concerned with the defence of craft traditions and the resistance to dilution of labour. What was significant about the organization is that the delegates did not represent the old trade union sections but workers from a variety of union groups within each workshop. It was composed of delegates from every shop and objected to the 'treachery' involved in trade union leaders accepting the Treasury agreement and the Munitions' Act without demur. In a circular addressed to all Clyde workers the committee declared that:

> Our purpose must not be misconstrued, we are not for unity and closer organization of all trades in the industry, one Union being the ultimate aim. We will support the officials just so long as they rightly represent the workers, but we will act independently immediately they misrepresent them. Being composed of Delegates for every shop, and untrammelled by obsolete rule or law, we claim to represent the true feeling of the workers. We can act immediately according to the merits of the case and the desire of the rank and file.[44]

SYNDICALISM, MASS UNIONISM AND THE GREAT WAR

Despite the impression of great control and industrial turbulence given by Willie Gallacher, and others, the events on the Clydeside were relatively restricted and swiftly dealt with by the government. The committee clearly, from its statement, did not espouse the syndicalist objective of a single industrial union in each industry, something which would have, in any case, been difficult in an organization which was concerned to protect the wages and conditions of the skilled workers against the threat of unskilled labour. The Clyde Workers' Committee was, indeed, a conservative organization despite the demand for workers' control which J.W. Muir made to David Lloyd George when he visited the Clyde at Christmas 1915, and despite being led by a group of socialists.[45] Nevertheless, it is fair to point out that the opposition against dilution was exerted with more effect elsewhere in Clydeside, particularly among the shipbuilding workers, and that the level of industrial conflict rose from fewer than 200,000 days lost each year in the west of Scotland in 1916 and 1917 to 300,000 days lost at the beginning of 1918 and one and a quarter million days lost, largely in shipbuilding, in January 1919.[46]

The government had acted swiftly to defuse the situation on Clydeside. In January 1916 it introduced the Military Service Bill, by which workers might be conscripted into the army and dilution imposed. In addition, it sent commissioners to the Clyde to negotiate dilution with the workers in individual plants and it decided to arrest and remove from the Clyde some of the leading members of the Clyde Workers' Committee. Indeed, the government appears to have followed the advice of Paterson, the Glasgow area munitions officer, when he wrote that:

> Below I give the names of the gentlemen whose removal from the Clyde district for an indefinite period would go a long way towards helping production, viz: [Kirkwood, Gallacher, Messer, McManus, Clark, McLean, Petroff].
>
> I am afraid the removal of almost any one of these men (with the possible exception of McLean and Petroff, who are not working men or officials of societies here) would at once cause a big strike.[47]

On 2 February 1916 Gallacher and two other shop stewards were arrested under the Defence of the Realm Act and charged with having published material likely to cause 'mutiny, sedition or disaffection'.

115

At first, there was some local resistance to these developments but the Dilution Commissioners began to win shop stewards' support for schemes which involved the formation of joint worker/management committees. These schemes soon restricted the activities of shop stewards and a number of strikes occurred, most notably the walk-out of one thousand workers from Parkhead on 17 March 1916. It was then decided that the whole of the Clyde Workers' Committee would be deported and, on 25 March, David Kirkwood and two others from Parkhead Forge were arrested. There were strikes in their defence but these collapsed quickly. On 14 April Gallacher and Muir, arrested in February, were sentenced to one year's imprisonment and, in due course, others like Maclean were arrested. The authorities had moved against the Clyde Workers' Committee in a most effective manner. Although, as Hinton suggests, the failure of the committee was also an internal one because the:

> Committee failed to become an effective vanguard for the local working class as a whole. Even the revolutionaries could not escape entanglement in the protective reflexes of the craftsmen, and it was a narrow and self-isolating path that they cut through the turmoil on the Clyde. The Committee was easy prey for the Government. In the dilution struggles the tortuous self-deceptions of the revolutionaries contrasted vividly with the actions of the Government. The Ministry of Munitions and the Dilution Commissioners directed an offensive remarkable in its clarity of aims, its flexibility, its ruthlessness, and for the careful planning of the means. [48]

Dilution was not going to be an issue which could easily sustain class struggle on the Clydeside, although it should not be ignored that it encouraged craft conservatism, since to gain dilution agreements the employers and the Dilution Commissioners had to guarantee the union leaders that workshop practices would be continued.[49] The general commitment to pay trade rates to all dilutees ensured that there would be no sense in employing a female dilutee rather than craftsmen after the war. In essence, then, the dilution issue saw the end of the CWC but strengthened the position of the skilled workers who effectively maintained control over the introduction of new machinery by establishing the primacy of the craftsman in dilution arrangements.

Outside the Clyde the shop stewards' movement met with varied success. In areas like the Midlands, where the new motor car

Robert Owen (1771–1858)

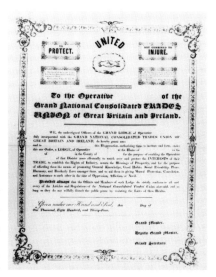

A dispensation authorizing the
formation of a lodge of Owen's
Grand National Consolidated Trade
Union in 1834

Cleaves Penny, *Gazette of Variety*, 12 May 1838. A contemporary drawing,
entitled *The Returned 'Convicts'*, of five of the six 'Tolpuddle Martyrs' who were
pardoned

An engraving of the Great Chartist Procession at Blackfriars in 1848 on the way to Kennington Common (*below*)

The Great Chartist Meeting on Kennington Common, 10 April 1848. Daguerreotype by William Edward Kilburn (*courtesy of Windsor Castle, Royal Archives* © *1992, Her Majesty The Queen*)

PROPOSED CONGRESS OF TRADES COUNCILS

AND OTHER

Federations of Trades Societies.

MANCHESTER, FEBRUARY 21st, 1868.

FELLOW-UNIONISTS,

The Manchester and Salford Trades Council having recently taken into their serious consideration the present aspect of Trades Unions, and the profound ignorance which prevails in the public mind with reference to their operations and principles, together with the probability of an attempt being made by the Legislature, during the present session of Parliament, to introduce a measure detrimental to the interests of such Societies, beg most respectfully to suggest the propriety of holding in Manchester, as the main centre of industry in the provinces, a Congress of the Representatives of Trades Councils and other similar Federations of Trades Societies. By confining the Congress to such bodies it is conceived that a deal of expense will be saved, as Trades will thus be represented collectively; whilst there will be a better opportunity afforded of selecting the most intelligent and efficient exponents of our principles.

It is proposed that the Congress shall assume the character of the annual meetings of the British Association for the Advancement of Science and the Social Science Association, in the transactions of which Societies the artizan class are almost entirely excluded; and that papers, previously carefully prepared, shall be laid before the Congress on the various subjects which at the present time affect Trades Societies, each paper to be followed by discussion upon the points advanced, with a view of the merits and demerits of each question being thoroughly ventilated through the medium of the public press. It is further suggested that the subjects treated upon shall include the following :—

    1.—Trades Unions an absolute necessity.
    2.—Trades Unions and Political Economy.
    3.—The Effect of Trades Unions on Foreign Competition.
    4.—Regulation of the Hours of Labour.
    5.—Limitation of Apprentices.
    6.—Technical Education.
    7.—Arbitration and Courts of Conciliation.
    8.—Co-operation.
    9.—The present Inequality of the Law in regard to Conspiracy, Intimidation, Picketing, Coercion, &c.
    10.—Factory Acts Extension Bill, 1867: the necessity of Compulsory Inspection, and its application
          to all places where Women and Children are employed.
    11.—The present Royal Commission on Trades Unions: how far worthy of the confidence of the
          Trades Union interest.
    12.—The necessity of an Annual Congress of Trade Representatives from the various centres of
          industry.

All Trades Councils and other Federations of Trades are respectfully solicited to intimate their adhesion to this project on or before the 6th of April next, together with a notification of the subject of the paper that each body will undertake to prepare; after which date all information as to place of meeting, &c., will be supplied.

It is also proposed that the Congress be held on the 4th of May next, and that all liabilities in connection therewith shall not extend beyond its sittings.

Communications to be addressed to MR. W. H. WOOD, Typographical Institute, 29, Water Street, Manchester.

By order of the Manchester and Salford Trades Council,

S. C. NICHOLSON, PRESIDENT.
W. H. WOOD, SECRETARY.

Circular calling the first Trades Union Congress. After the circular was issued, it was decided to postpone the Congress until 2 June 'in order to afford sufficient time for all the various trade organisations to send delegates and prepare papers'. It was also decided that the invitation should be extended to include individual unions as well as trades councils and other federations of unions.

Demonstration at Ham Hill, Yeovil, Whit-Monday 1877 (1) Joseph Arch,
(2) George Mitchell, (5) Mr King, London Trades Council, (7) Stephen
Price, (8) Revd W. Jubb, Bristol, (9) Mr Winter (Somerset delegate),
(11) T. Halliday, miners' leader

Heavy Woollen Weavers' Association, 1875. This was an organization dominated by women weavers. Normally known as the Dewsbury Woollen Operatives' Union, it was formed in 1875 and united with the Huddersfield Power-Loom Weavers' Association in 1883 to form the West Riding Power-Loom Weavers' Association

Demonstrators during the London dock strike of 1889

Ben Tillett, leader of the London
dock strike

John Burns, a labour leader in the
dock strike and, later, a prominent
Liberal working man and
parliamentarian

Tom Mann, a leader in the dock
strike, became one of the most
famous and important trade
unionists, leading the British
Syndicalists before the First World
War and acquiring an international
reputation for his trade union work

Finance Committee during the 1889 dock strike. *Left to right*: Tom Mann, Ben Tillett, John Burns, Charles Miller, Tim Walsh

Strikers' families outside Union relief centre during the 1889 dock strike

The National Union of Gasworkers and General Labourers, formed in London in 1889 by Will Thorne to reduce the hours of gasworkers from twelve to eight per day without wage reductions.

Will Thorne, General Secretary, National Union of Gasworkers and General Labourers, 1889

Gasworkers' meeting, Peckham Rye, 1889. From *Illustrated London News*, 12 October 1889

Parliamentary Committee and Trades Union Congress officials, Bristol, 1898 (taken after the fire at Colston Hall). Robert Knight (Boilermakers) is standing second from left in the back row, sixth from left is George Howell, MP and Will Thorne (Gasworkers) is sitting on the left in the front row

Dock pickets in 1926

Builders' march in Leamington Spa during the 1926 General Strike

Kellingley miners marching to their pit but not to work in support of the
NUM strike, March 1985 (*courtesy of the* Yorkshire Evening Press)

industry was developing, the newness of the industry and the lack of a traditional craft industry tended to lead to the quick submission and acceptance of the law. Indeed, as Steven Tolliday has suggested, the move to mass production and the semi-skilled nature of some of the new skills allowed management to control the work process more effectively than in many other industries.[50]

On the Tyne, at Barrow and in Woolwich, the shop stewards' movement led a chequered career for a number of years, and it was only in Sheffield that real advances were made, for here were an extremely privileged and exclusive set of workers who, due to the heavy nature of their work, were not easily replaced by women dilutees. Indeed, it was not the issue of dilution as much as that of conscription which emerged most effectively in Sheffield. Throughout 1916 there had been much debate about the issue of trade exemptions, especially in the light of the fact that the government was conscripting skilled engineers despite claiming to be short of such workers. It was in this climate of suspicion that the famous case of Leonard Hargreaves occurred to threaten industrial peace.

Hargreaves, a fitter from Sheffield, was taken into the army in October 1916. This provoked a stoppage in Sheffield on 16 November, and subsequently another at Barrow, which only ended when Hargreaves appeared at a meeting in Sheffield on Sunday 19 November. The situation appears to have speeded up the negotiations between the government and the Amalgamated Society of Engineers, leading to the Trade Card Agreement, agreed on 18 November, to the effect that skilled members of the ASE, and later other unions, would receive exemption from conscription. This situation favoured the skilled workers but, as Professor Chris Wrigley has noted, 'did nothing to enhance inter-union feelings' when semi-skilled and unskilled workers were losing their exemptions.[51] Indeed, a feature of the whole issue of dilution and exemption from conscription, as Hinton and Wrigley have implied, is that the pursuit of the sectarian interests of the skilled unions meant that other workers and their unions developed no sense of unity, trade or class consciousness with the engineers.

Loose exemption arrangements were never going to be ideal for a government which required to balance military manpower requirements against the problems of shortages of skilled workers. As a result, the government moved towards a rigorous Schedule of Protected Occupations. The decision to introduce this, combined with the extension of dilution to private engineering works, led to the May 1917 engineering strikes, which involved two hundred thousand workers and the loss of one and a half million working days. Begun in Manchester in April, it eventually spread to forty-eight towns and lasted for about four weeks. It was seen as a massive defence of craft privilege and for that reason the unskilled and semi-skilled workers who were affected had no sympathy with the strikers, whose craft views negated the more revolutionary ambitions of some of their leaders. The result can be seen in the parody of the craftsmen's slogan:

> Don't send me in the Army George,
> I'm in the ASE
> Take all the bloody labourers,
> But for God's sake don't take me.
> You want me for a soldier?
> Well, that can never be –
> A man of my ability,
> And in the ASE!

The arrest of some of the leading shop stewards and the collapse of the May strike combined with the tensions between the skilled and unskilled workers to ensure that the first shop stewards' movement's impact was limited.

Obviously, the revolutions in Russia in March and October 1917 heightened the sense of expectancy within the shop stewards' movement, as did the inaugural meeting of the Workers' and Soldiers' Council held at Leeds in June in order to give support to some of the developments emerging from the first Russian Revolution of 1917. But little of real significance emerged from these events in an industrial sense. The National Administrative Council of the Shop Stewards' and Workers' Committee was formed on the 18 and 19 August 1917, but gained only limited support which was largely focused upon Glasgow, Sheffield and Manchester. In aiming to be inspirational in encouraging the formation of rank-and-file organizations, and in attempting to encourage an anti-war stance, it was a remarkable failure. When it tested its strength against Sir Aukland Geddes' new Military Service Bill of January 1918, which effectively got rid of all trade exemptions, the national strike it called was remarkably ineffective – the only area of significant support being the Clyde. Ultimately, this movement found itself among that small rump of political parties and industrial organizations which formed the Communist Party of Great Britain in 1920.

Conclusion

The period 1910 to 1918 was marked by a rising level of trade union organization and industrial militancy, but there should be no illusion that the trade union movement was in any sense dominated by revolutionary ambitions or that British society was being seriously threatened. The fact is that the pre-war syndicalists carried little influence within the British trade union movement and that the shop stewards' movement was far too sectional in intent to command the support of the vast majority of organized labour. Edwardian and post-Edwardian society might have been under strain, as the issues of suffrage, Ireland, the Labour challenge and the war emerged, but in no sense did it appear that these factors threatened its stability.

Instead, these years of change saw an increasing tendency towards the development of a more orderly and institutionalized pattern of industrial relations which enhanced the position of the British trade union movement in its relation to employers and the government. An increasing number of negotiating arrangements were set up between employers and unions, culminating in the formation of numerous joint industrial councils during the war years. As far as the government was concerned, it was increasingly forced into working with the trade unions, ultimately to the mutual benefit of both during the First World War. Many of the government's actions were of an *ad hoc* nature but the ultimate consequence was to draw trade unions more firmly into the responsible decision-making structure of the nation.

In essence, then, the impact of syndicalism has been exaggerated. There was little threat to the industrial *status quo* before 1914, and the shop stewards' movement revealed the frustrations of a privileged section of engineers, who wished to protect their craft privileges, rather than the discontent of the vast majority of workers who benefited greatly as a result of the war and held few revolutionary intentions.

NOTES

1. H. Pelling, *A History of British Trade Unionism* (1987 edn., rep. 1988), p. 130.
2. J. Hinton, *The First Shop Stewards' Movement* (George Allen & Unwin, 1973), p. 278.
3. G. Brown, introduction to *Industrial Syndicalist*.
4. B. Holton, *British Syndicalism 1900–1914: Myths and Realities* (Pluto Press, 1976).
5. H.A. Clegg, *A History of British Trade Unionism, Vol. II 1911–1933* (Oxford, Clarendon Press, 1985.)
6. W. Gallacher, *Revolt on the Clyde* (1936), rep. 1978, and *Last Memoirs* (1966).
7. Hinton, *op.cit.*, particularly the conclusions pp. 330–7.
8. I. McLean, *The Legend of Red Clydeside* (Edinburgh, 1983).
9. A. Reid, 'Dilution, Trade Unionism and the State', in S. Tolliday and J. Zeitlin (eds), *Shop Floor Bargaining and the State* (Cambridge, 1985), pp. 46–74.
10. G. Rubin, *War, Law and Labour* (Oxford, 1987).
11. J. Melling, 'Whatever happened to Red Clydeside? Industrial Conflict and the Politics of Skill in the First World War', *International Review of Social History*, XXXV (1990), pp. 3–32; J. Foster, 'Strike Action and Working-Class Politics on Clydeside 1914–1919', *International Review of Social History*, XXXV (1990), pp. 33–70.
12. Melling, 'Clydeside'.
13. G. Dangerfield, *The Strange Death of Liberal England* (1935).
14. H. Pelling, *Popular politics and society in late Victorian Britain* (1969, 1979); E.H. Phelps Brown, *The Growth of British Industrial Relations* (1959).
15. D. Read (ed.), *Edwardian England* (1982); A. O'Day (ed.), *The Edwardian age: conflict and stability* (1979), pp. 3–5; Holton, *op.cit.*; R. Price, *Master, unions and men: work and control in building and the rise of Labour, 1830–1914* (Cambridge, CUP, 1980).
16. J. White, '1910–1914 Reconsidered', *Social Conflict and Political Order in Modern Britain* (Croom Helm, 1982), edited by James E. Cronin and Jonathan Schneer.
17. Sir A. Clay, *Syndicalism and Labour* (1911). W. McCartney, *Syndicalism: What is it?* (1912) and A.D. Lewis, *Syndicalism and the General Strike* (1912) commented similarly.
18. P. Snowden, *Socialism and Syndicalism* (1913).
19. R. MacDonald, *Syndicalism: A Critical Exposition* (1912), p. 39.
20. R.C. Challinor, *The Origins of British Bolshevism*.
21. E.J.B. Allen, 'Working-Class Socialism', *The Industrial Syndicalist*, November 1910.
22. Clegg, *op.cit.*, p. 29.
23. *Ibid.*, p. 37.
24. *The Industrial Syndicalist*, November 1910.
25. T. Mann, *Memoirs* (1923), pp. 212–13.
26. Reform Committee of the South Wales Miners, *The Miners' Next Step* (1912).

27. P. Davis, 'Syndicalism and the Yorkshire Miners, 1910–1914' (unpublished M.Phil. dissertation, University of Bradford, 1977).
28. White, *op.cit.*, p. 90.
29. Holton, *op.cit.*, p. 119.
30. R. Church, 'Edwardian Labour Unrest and Coalfield Militancy, 1890–1914', *Historical Journal* 30, 4 (1987), p. 848.
31. Clegg, *op.cit.*, chapter two, and particularly pages 71–4.
32. *Ibid.*, p. 30.
33. J.E. Cronin, *Industrial Conflict in Britain* (1979), pp. 106–7.
34. R. Church, 'Edwardian Labour Unrest and Coalfield Militancy, 1890–1914', *Historical Journal*, 30, 4 (1987), p. 857.
35. C. Wrigley, 'The First World War and State Intervention in Industrial Relations, 1914–18', *A History of British Industrial Relations, Vol. II, 1914–1939* (Brighton, Harvester Press, 1987).
36. J. Schneer, 'The War, the State and the Workplace: British Dockers during 1914–1918', *Social Conflict and the Political Order in Modern Britain* (Croom Helm, 1982), edited by J.E. Cronin and J. Schneer, p. 110.
37. *Ibid.*, p. 99, quoting from Dock, Wharf, Riverside and General Labourers' Union, *Triennial Meeting*, 1919, p. 10.
38. Wrigley, *op.cit.*, p. 23.
39. J. Hinton, *The First Shop Stewards' Movement* (George Allen & Unwin, 1973), chapter 13, conclusions.
40. *Ibid.*, p. 23.
41. Sir Hubert Llewelyn Smith, Memorandum of Labour for Armaments, 9 June 1915.
42. Public Record Office, Records of the Ministry of Munitions, Mun. 2, letter from William Weir to C. Addison, 8 October 1915.
43. J. Melling, 'Scottish Industrialists and the Changing Character of Class Relations in the Clyde Region', *Capital and Class* (Edinburgh, 1982), pp. 61–142.
44. Clyde Workers' Committee Leaflet, to be found in many collections including the engineering records at West Yorkshire Archives, Calderdale.
45. J.W. Muir's statement to Lloyd George, printed in *The Worker*, 15 January 1916.
46. J. Foster, *op.cit.*, pp.38–41.
47. Letter from Paterson to Ministry of Munitions in London, dated 17 January 1916, Public Record Office, Mun.2.
48. J. Hinton, 'The Clyde Workers' Committee and the Dilution Struggle' in A. Briggs and J. Saville (eds), *Essays in Labour History, 1886–1923* (1971), p. 184.
49. Melling, 'Clydeside', p. 19.
50. S. Tolliday, 'The Failure of Mass Production Unionism in the Motor Industry, 1914–39', *A History of British Industrial Relations, Vol. II, 1914–1939* (Brighton, Harvester Press, 1987), edited by C. J. Wrigley, pp. 298–322.
51. Wrigley, *op.cit.*, p. 46.

CHAPTER FIVE

TRADE UNIONISM DURING THE INTER-WAR YEARS 1918–39

The First World War marked a sharp break in the history of trade unionism, raising trade unions to a new level of importance and achievement. Most obviously, it saw the rapid rise of trade union membership from four million in 1914 to six million in 1918. By 1920, the figure had risen to its inter-war peak of eight million. This growth was the result of a variety of factors, particularly the high demand for labour and the high wages which were paid in wartime. Moreover, as the war continued, the government depended increasingly on the support of union officials and the status of trade unions rose to a level which had previously appeared unattainable. The Webbs, the first historians of British trade unionism, sensitive to this change, emphasized the point, noting the 'revolutionary transformation of the social and political standing of the official representatives of the Trade Union world – a transformation which has been immensely accelerated by the Great War.'[1] This, of course, was no more than a recognition of what most employers were keenly aware. For instance, a meeting of the North

TRADE UNIONISM DURING THE INTER-WAR YEARS

London Manufacturers' Association on 16 July 1918 was told that 'the industrial system of this country, as we knew it in July 1914, has been suspended' and that it was 'unlikely to be re-established without modification of a far-reaching nature'. Specifically, 'no part of the pre-war industrial system is more likely to be radically changed in design and practice after the war than the relationship between employers and employed'.[2] There was a widespread acknowledgement that some industrial power had been conceded to the trade unions in order to win the war. Nevertheless, it was obvious that the impetus which the trade unions gained would lead to conflict once attempts were made, by government and employers alike, to abandon the wartime regulations and to return to the competitive situation of the pre-war world.

Industrial conflict became increasingly likely after 1920 when unemployment rose quickly, due to the failure of British trade to recover to its pre-war level. Faced with the intense foreign competition, employers resorted to attempts to reduce monetary wages, eventually encouraged by the decision of Baldwin's Conservative government to return to the gold standard and reflate the pound in 1925. Indeed, it was this action, which increased the price of British exports, that encouraged employers to attempt to reduce the wages of workers by 10 per cent, causing the coal lock-out/strike and the General Strike of 1926. A galvanized trade union movement facing the problems of high unemployment and constant wage reductions was inevitably going to be in conflict with both employers and government during the inter-war years, if only because its enlarged membership was expecting it to defend their position. This is ironic, since successive political leaders in government had come to a view that the mass of workers had gone 'red' and that it was only the trade union leaders who were holding back the threat of revolution: Winston Churchill lamented, in February 1919, that:

> The curse of trade unionism was that there was not enough of it, and it was not highly enough developed to make its branch secretaries fall into line with head office.[3]

The government fear was not that there would be a general strike, nor that there would be revolution, but, as H.A. Clegg has suggested, that a coalition of local leaders would take control of national decision-making and prevent the national union leaders from reaching compromises acceptable to both the employers and government, because they had greater expectation of what could be achieved by industrial action. In the end, government actions prevented trade unions acting in the moderating role, which they hoped they would play, but also undermined the rank-and-file hopes of achievement and success through industrial action.[4]

The General Strike is often seen as the symbol of the industrial relations of these years – and is considered to be the event which brought to an end the militant trade unionism of almost two decades. Thereafter, it is argued, trade unionism was defeated and the Trades Union Congress, which had limited support before 1926, had even less support afterwards. Indeed, the militancy of the 1920s is often compared with the relative quiescence of trade union action during the 1930s. But are these generalizations justified? Did unemployment, economic depression and the General Strike reduce trade unionism to pitiful weakness? Had the trajectory of Labour's industrial growth been altered by the events of 1926? Did the General Strike marginalize the romantic image of industrial militancy, as Dame Margaret Cole has suggested?[5] Were the defeats of the coal strike/lock-out and the General Strike vital in permitting the government to return to the political economy of normalcy which was being sought by Britain's post-war governments? Can the General Strike be seen, in any sense at all, as the revolutionary strike which the Communists were anticipating? And, can the defeat of the trade unions in the General Strike be regarded as a watershed in British industrial relations? The evidence which will be offered suggests that the General Strike did not substantially reduce the power of the unions and possibly, in a fairly overt manner, projected forward a more unified trade union movement under a more cohesive and powerful leadership in the 1930s.

The Immediate Post-War Years, 1919–25

The trade union movement reached its post-war apogee in the immediate post-war years. Its membership was increasing and, in 1919, a Restoration of Pre-War Practices Act obliged employers to return to the trade practices of the pre-war years. In addition, an Industrial Courts Act set up a permanent arbitration tribunal – the Industrial Court – to which disputes could be voluntarily referred by the two parties concerned. However, the decision was no longer enforceable as it had been in wartime. The Whitley Councils, composed of both employers and union leaders, set up after 1917, were still in place in many industries and at least offered the prospect of industrial peace.[6] Yet, at the height of its success, the trade union movement was threatened. It faced a conservative-dominated Coalition government, led by David Lloyd George, which had dealt ruthlessly with the police strikes of 1918 and 1919, by dismissing the men concerned from the service. The government's decision to ignore the Sankey Commission of 1919, which advised the government to keep control of the coal industry, and to return the industry back to the coal owners in April 1921, was further proof that post-war industrial relations were likely to become bitter and protracted.[7] Added to this, the economy began to decline in 1920, unemployment rose and the government decided to return Britain to free trade and the gold standard by 1925. The deflationary policies which such an action implied, for the return was to be on the basis of a strengthened pound, added to the problem of unemployment at a time when Britain's foreign trade was depressed. Employers, therefore, resorted to the reduction of costs, most particularly in wages, in order to compete in world markets at a time when it appeared that rising unemployment made their action possible without major conflict.

Employers constantly gnawed away at the high level of wages which had been built up during the First World War. They frequently attempted to reduce the basic wage of workers and to eliminate the cost of living addition which had been paid throughout the war and in the immediate post-war years. Indeed, it was estimated that the wages of Britain's twelve million workers were reduced by about £12 million per week between 1921 and 1925, although higher estimates have also been made.[8] But this had not improved Britain's competitive position, and all such reductions had done was reduce the home demand for products, thus further increasing unemployment. Ben Turner, of the General Union of Textile Workers and soon to be president of the TUC, wrote in 1925 that:

> It's as much home trade we are suffering from as the lack of foreign trade. In fact the reduction in home trade is far bigger than the reduction in exports, and this is accounted for the ten million reduction paid out now would give a right big fillip to trade.[9]

Trade unionists had increasingly come to accept that underconsumption was the cause of stagnant trade, for, as the *Manifesto* of the woollen textile workers stated on the eve of the 1925 textile lock-out: 'There is no greater fallacy today than to think we could get back to prosperity by reducing wages.'[10] Even before the General Strike there was evidence that trade union leaders were beginning to challenge the notion that wage reductions could solve Britain's economic difficulties and an increasing willingness to threaten industrial action. Until 1925, however, industrial action did not appear to work and threatening postures had not normally been successful against employers. Trade union membership fell by more than 20 per cent, about 1.7 million in 1920 and 1921, in a period when there was more industrial conflict than at any other time in the inter-war years, apart from 1926. The implacable determination of employers had forced wages down despite the most determined efforts of the trade unions.

This swift decline of trade union power appears to have occurred because of a combination of both internal weakness and external pressure. Apart from the difficulties presented by unemployment and the trade depression, already referred to, some of the leading trade unions found it impossible to submerge their differences in a joint defence against the onslaught of both employers and government. The most famous evidence of this is offered by the events in the coal mining industry which led to 'Black Friday' in April 1921.

At the end of the First World War, the leading question in the mining industry was whether or not the state would return the coal mines to their pre-war owners. The Miners' Federation of Great Britain, which had passed resolutions in favour of both workers' control and nationalization, supported state control and, in order to avoid industrial conflict, the Lloyd George Coalition government set up a royal commission, chaired by Lord Sankey, to investigate the coal industry. Although the Sankey commission produced four different reports, the majority one – on the casting vote of the chairman – recommended that the coal industry should continue under national control. However, David Lloyd George decided that a majority of one was not sufficient, even though he had given an undertaking to implement the Majority Report. The consequence was immediate; the Yorkshire miners struck, unsuccessfully, in July 1919 and some two hundred thousand miners in South Wales and Monmouth threatened to strike in sympathy. In the final analysis, this sympathetic support did not emerge. Yet, the frustration which this 'betrayal' caused among coal miners was to dominate the industry for many years to come. As one historian has noted:

> The bitterness and the troubles of the coal mines for the next seven, or for that matter twenty-seven years, derived in great part from the feeling of both miners and owners that they had been betrayed.[11]

Vernon Hartshorn, then a Derbyshire MP and a South Wales miners' leader, asked the House of Commons:

> Why was the commission set up? Was it a huge game of bluff? Was it ever intended that if the reports favoured nationalization we were to get it? . . . That is the kind of question the miners of the country will ask, and they will say they have been deceived, betrayed, duped.[12]

Although there were several disputes in the coal industry during the next twenty months, it was not until the coal mines were formally handed back to the coal owners, on 31 March 1921, that serious conflict ensued. On the following day, the coal owners locked out those miners who would not work at lower rates of pay – of up to 49 per cent off in the badly affected export areas of South Wales – and attempted to suspend national agreements. The government also issued regulations under the 1920 Emergency Powers Act and recalled troops from Ireland and abroad in order to quell the miners and their political allies. The government feared that the Triple Alliance, forged between the Miners' Federation of Great Britain (MFGB), the National Union of Railwaymen (NUR) and the National Transport Workers (NTW) at the beginning of the war, whereby each union offered sympathetic strike support under certain circumstances, might be used to widen the dispute. It need not have feared.

The expected support of the NUR and the NTW on Friday 15 April 1921 never occurred, and that day is known, by historians of Labour history as 'Black Friday'. Although Ernest Bevin's transport workers had not come out on strike the real opprobrium of the Labour movement was held for Jimmy Thomas, the leader of the railwaymen, whose opposition to sympathetic strike action was the cause of the collapse of the Triple Alliance. He had not helped his cause when he 'trotted blithely down the steps to greet eager reporters with the news "It's all off boys"' and added, to cries of 'Jimmy's selling you' the riposte that 'I've tried boys, I've done my very best. But I couldn't find a bloody buyer.'[13]

The immediate outcome of the collapse of the Triple Alliance was that the miners were left to fight alone. Eventually, they were forced to accept some significant wage reductions, although the French invasion of the Ruhr, and the consequent interruption of coal output, plus the American coal strike of 1924 helped to check the downward trend of coal prices and the rate of decrease in the wages of coal miners. It was not until 1925 that the downward pressure in wages was to again produce the threat of a major industrial conflict in the coalfields.

As Rodney Lowe has suggested, the return of the coal industry to the employers was only a small part of the general strategy of the government to withdraw from active participation in industrial relations.[14] After the defeat of the miners, following 'Black Friday', the government's commitment to reform ended, and with it the desire to improve working conditions and wages. As a result, governments, for the rest of the inter-war years, adopted a non-interventionist policy, although not always successfully as evidenced by the General Strike.

Without government moderation, the wage levels in all industries were forced down by the more aggressive tactics of the employers operating in the harsh economic climate of the early 1920s. In consequence, the TUC was forced to form the General Council, an alternative to its parliamentary committee, as its executive body. The real purpose of the General Council was to develop its powers to intervene in major industrial disputes and to establish effective cooperation between unions. In 1922 it set up a Joint Defence Committee, later known as the Committee for the Coordination of Trade Union Effort, to accomplish this aim. By 1925, it was strongly advocating the idea of forming an Industrial Alliance by which threatened unions could call upon the sympathetic strike support of other TUC unions.[15] Indeed, the left-wing and Communist demands for 'All Power to the General Council', in 1924 and 1925, helped the General Council to strengthen greatly its demand for an 'Industrial Alliance'.[16] Gordon Phillips has stressed the way in which this objective, and the General Strike of 1926, can be seen as an 'expiation of 1921'.[17]

Yet the trade union movement faced many difficulties in the early 1920s. High levels of unemployment made it difficult for them to defend the wages of their members and forced many into amalgamations, such as the Amalgamated Engineering Union (AEU) in

1921, the Transport and General Workers' Union in 1922 and the National Union of General and Municipal Workers in 1924. There was still, however, some antipathy towards surrendering the individual powers of trade unions to a wider industrial alliance organized by the General Council. The Miners' Federation of Great Britain was particularly reluctant to invest the General Council with the power to call out all unions on sympathetic strike action. Nevertheless, in 1925 a determined effort was made by the TUC and other unions to reverse the trend. In many ways the stimulus for this came from the wool and worsted textile workers, among the least well organized of all industrial workers, whose position had been partly protected by the 'cosy relationship' which it enjoyed with the employers through their Whitley council organization, which had been formed during the First World War.[18]

The summer of 1925 was hardly the most propitious moment for the textile unions to make their stand against further wage reductions. Trade unions were already weakened, and the implementation of the decision to return to the gold standard augured badly for the staple export industries. Yet, in April, the Executive Committee of the National Union of Textile Workers declared its intention of demanding the restoration of the 5 per cent on base wage rates lost in 1925 and that the cost of living addition should be altered every three months – an action which would greatly benefit the textile workers. These demands were endorsed by the National Associatation of Unions in the Textile Trade and the matter was put to the employers who responded by suggesting that British industry was less competitive than it had been before the return of the gold standard and the reflation of the pound, and suggested that wages should be reduced by 10, later reducing to 8 and 5, per cent.[19]

The seeds of conflict were sown and, despite offers of mediation from several quarters, the employers issued notices of reduction of wages on 24 July 1925.[20] From that moment the lock-out, or standstill, in the textile trade began. It lasted just over three weeks and the immediate conflict was only resolved by the intervention of the Minister of Labour, Sir Arthur Steel-Maitland, who requested that the employers allow the existing wage rates to continue until a Court of Investigation, which had been set up, reported upon the woollen and worsted textile trades. When the body, which was composed of an independent chairman and two representatives from both sides, eventually reported, it suggested that there should be no change in conditions and wages in the industry.[21]

The significance of this dispute should not be lost. In the first place, there were probably between 135,000 and 170,000 woollen and worsted textile workers involved in the dispute, although estimates go up to 240,000, and every union and all sections of the textile workforce were unified in the action which they took. Ben Turner, the main trade union leader, was pleased to reflect that:

> I am glad to have lived to see the day when overlookers, foremen and managers, craftsmen, engine tenters, etc. joined together to defend labour's interests – when the doffer lass, the designer, the long brat man, and the woolcomber were standing together.[22]

Such unity was a remarkable achievement for an industry which was notorious for its local variation, the disunity of its workforce and the general weakness of its trade union organization.

Secondly, the outcome of the dispute was seen as a victory for the workers in their attempt to prevent wages being reduced further. Even before the Court of Investigation confirmed the workers' stand, the trade unions had smelled the scent of victory. On the eve of the agreement to call off the dispute, the *Yorkshire Factory Times* reflected that the wage retreat had at least 'been stopped'.[23] Presumptuous as this was, the feeling abroad was that government policy, as well as the employers' stand, had been defeated:

> Wages, said Mr. Baldwin, have to be brought down. This is not simply an incautious and unconsidered statement by Mr. Baldwin, a slip of the tongue: it is the settled and deliberate policy of the governing class, who have entered upon a course of action which has for its object the deliberate intensification of unemployment as a method of forcing down wages.[24]

The article even invoked the views of John Maynard Keynes as evidence of the foolishness of the government's approach.

Combined with the temporary solution of the coal crisis in 1925, which will be discussed later, the anticipated textile victory buoyed up the whole of the trade union movement. Herbert Tracey reflected that the 'defeatist' mood of the trade unions over the last few years had been transformed. Now it was felt that the General Council of the TUC had struck a blow to maintain minimum wages for all workers by its support of the woollen and worsted textile workers.

But the message went further for it was felt that the lesson to be learned was that living standards could be protected if unity prevailed:

> With the help of the Trade Union Movement, mobilised by the T.U.C. General Council, they were enabled to secure victory which they could not have won if they were left to fight alone.[25]

In other words they could not overcome the debilitating impact of high unemployment and the government's attempts at deflation which had clearly weakened the trade union movement's power of resistance during the early 1920s.

The moral seemed obvious: the reversal of the onslaught on wages and the defence of a minimum wage, if not the establishment of a living wage, could be secured by an alliance among unions. It was felt that if such unity could be achieved in the poorly organized wool textile trade then it was even more likely that it might also be achieved in better organized industries. Indeed, the threatened coal strike of 1925, which occurred at more or less the same time, appeared to confirm this impression. There was, indeed, strong support for collective action within unions in specific industries and between the unions of all industries – something which the TUC encouraged through its new journal *Trade Union Unity*.

This strategy was particularly evident in the more famous coal dispute of 1925. The events which led to this began on 30 June 1925 when the coal owners decided that they would abolish the national minimum wage, cut wages by about 10 per cent in order to compensate for the government's return to the gold standard with a reflated pound, and to maintain standard profits no matter how low wages fell. The miners refused to accept such changes and the General Council of the TUC committed itself to sympathetic strike action from Friday 31 July, and set up a Special Industrial Committee, to deal with the coal crisis, on 10 July 1925. It was this committee which conducted the TUC's activities in support of the miners between July 1925 and 27 April 1926.[26]

The intransigence of both coal owners and the union ensured that conflict was inevitable in the coal industry, and with it the threat of a wider conflict whereby the TUC would at least call for a coal embargo from its affiliated unions. Faced with the immediate prospect of a serious coal dispute and fuel crisis, the Baldwin government decided to provide a nine-month subsidy to the coal owners, during which time a royal commission, the Samuel Commission, would investigate the coal industry. The government had decided to intervene in the dispute on Friday 31 July, in order to avoid serious industrial conflict. Thereafter, that date became known as 'Red Friday'.

There was much euphoria among trade unionists. The outcome of both the wool and worsted dispute and the coal dispute convinced many that the tide of wage reductions had been changed and with it, perhaps, the course of unemployment. The *Yorkshire Factory Times*, journal of the wool and worsted textile workers, confidently predicted that the:

> General Council's action in support of the miners and wool textile
> workers signalised a turn in the tide, the beginning of a definite stand
> against the policy of wage reductions which economic conditions have
> enabled the employers to impose in the last four and a half years.[27]

Others were less convinced that the tide had turned.

Herbert Smith, President of the Miners' Federation of Great Britain, maintained that the 1925 coal dispute had been 'an affair of outposts. It was a mere skirmish. The main battle had still to be fought and won'.[28] The Communist Party of Great Britain, whose policy at this time was one of 'All Power to the General Council', also posed a question and offered an answer:

> Thirty four weeks to go – Thirty four weeks to go to what? To the
> termination of the mining agreement and the opening of the greatest
> struggle in the history of the British working class. We must prepare for
> the struggle.[29]

In 1925, then, it appeared that the position of trade unions and the pattern of industrial relations were about to change. On the one hand, trade unionists were confident that the period of post-war wage reductions was about to be halted, even if a battle remained to be fought. As a result, there would be more employment and an improvement in the condition of working-class life. On the other hand, there remained the conviction of many employers and Baldwin's Conservative government that wages would have to be reduced in order to maintain profits and to fight international competition. It was the threatened industrial conflict of 1926, the General Strike, which promised to resolve the matter.

TRADE UNIONISM DURING THE INTER-WAR YEARS

The General Strike, 1926

The General Strike, which occurred between 3 May and 12 May 1926, was the most important industrial conflict of British Labour history. It is the only occasion in British industrial history when the vast majority of the organized working class have given their industrial, financial and moral support to one group of workers for any length of time. Indeed, it is the only time when there has ever been a substantial national strike in support of any industrial group of workers in Britain. Historians have been fascinated with the General Strike, have written extensively on its causes, meticulously recorded its events and speculated about the consequences of its failure for British industrial relations. On the fiftieth anniversary of the dispute, in 1976, several books appeared on the subject, producing a surfeit of published research to which there has been no significant addition since.[30] As a consequence of this research historians know very well the variety of factors which led to the dispute. They are aware that the problems of the coal industry combined with the clash between government policy and the policies of the TUC to ensure that there would have to be some type of conflict. They are also aware of the regional and local variations in the support for the General Strike. They disagree strongly about the consequences: was it a watershed, as some Communist writers would have us believe, or did it barely change the course of TUC, and trade union policy, as Gordon Phillips has argued?[31]

The main argument presented here is that the General Strike was partly, but significantly, a consequence of the determination of successive governments to reduce wages, thus increasing unemployment in the short term, in the hope of strengthening the pound and returning to the gold standard. Secondly, it must also be appreciated that there was substantial unity within trade union ranks and that, despite the suspension of the strike on 12 May, the unions had signalled their intention not to accept further wage reductions without some resistance. In this respect, it seems unlikely that subsequent governments were given the opportunity to return to the economic normalcy which prevailed in the pre-war years. Thirdly, it is doubtful whether the General Strike could be regarded as the watershed in British trade union history, which it is often depicted as being, or that it changed in any significant way the pattern of industrial relations.

133

The immediate context of the General Strike was the return to the gold standard and the reflation of the pound which forced employers in exporting industries to contemplate ways of further reducing costs, and thus wages, by about 10 per cent. This situation had provoked the coal dispute, and matters had altered little between 31 July 1925, 'Red Friday', and 1 May 1926, when the coal lock-out began. The only change in the intervening period had been that the government had prepared for the threatened dispute while the Samuel Commission, set up to report on the coal industry during the period when the nine-month subsidy was paid, deliberated on how to make the coal industry more efficient and profitable. Anticipating further conflict, the government had divided the country into twelve divisions, distributed *Circular 636* indicating the responsibilities of local authorities, passed a Preservation of Public Order Act and received from the Home Secretary, in February 1926, the statement that 'little remained to be done before the actual occurrence of an emergency'.[32] It was also concerned to win a propaganda war and to prepare the people for what it regarded as a constitutional crisis. The Home Secretary, Sir William Joynson-Hicks, put the matter starkly when, at a meeting on 2 August 1925, he commented that:

> I say to you, coming straight from the Cabinet councils, the thing is not finished. The danger is not over. Sooner or later, this question has to be fought out by the people of the land. Is England to be governed by Parliament and the Cabinet or by a handful of trade union leaders?[33]

In contrast, the trade union movement did little until the coal subsidy ended on 30 April 1926, even though it was hoped that the Samuel Commission would be unable to offer a compromise which might be agreeable to both coal owners and the unions. The TUC Special Industrial Committee, formed in July 1925 to deal with the crisis, paid scant regard to the problem of what would happen in May 1926, once the nine-month subsidy expired, and never gave serious consideration to the problem of organizing support for the miners.[34] It was left to the TUC's Ways and Means Committee, established by the General Council on 27 April 1926, to provide plans for strike action. As John Lovell has made clear, the Special Industrial Committee was dominated by J.H. Thomas who 'believed in the fairness or neutrality of the government, and therefore rested his hopes for a peaceful settlement upon government intervention in the dispute.'[35]

This assumption was unrealistic, for the government had made clear its intention not to extend the coal subsidy and the publication of the Samuel Commission, in March 1926, made conflict inevitable. The Samuel Commission recommended the 'amalgamation of small units of production' and that the miners should accept further wage reductions as a temporary measure until such re-organization occurred.[36] This was never likely to offer a basis for a wages agreement and the employers issued notices giving the reduced wage rates on 30 April and 1 May 1926, on the expiry of the subsidy.

In response, a special meeting of the TUC on 1 May 1926 undertook to support the coal miners through sympathetic strike action, giving the General Council primary responsibility for negotiations:

> provided that there was the fullest consultation between the two bodies in respect of any developments which might occur, and no settlement would be reached without the miners' consent.[37]

And for two days officials from the General Council discussed with the government the possibility of extending the subsidy. But negotiations were broken off by the government on 3 May once the compositors at the *Daily Mail* refused to set the type for an editorial on 'For King and Country'. The General Strike began, at one minute to midnight, on 3 May 1926.

From the start, there was much confusion about who should come out on strike to support the miners. The General Council had decided that only essential, front line or group one, workers such as railwaymen and printers should be called out. In fact, many non-essential, second line, workers, such as those in textiles, came out although the General Council never called upon their services throughout the dispute. The reticence of the General Council was deliberate for it feared the violence which might ensue if all workers came out and was alarmed at the prospect of mass defections leading to the rapid collapse of the dispute if it did not immediately meet its objectives. It believed that:

> once the strike has reached its highest point . . . then we shall have dribblings back to work here and there, and possibly large desecration.[38]

Given the lack of clear and early advice, the General Council's policy was ignored by many second-line workers who came out in support of the miners. This lack of organization was compounded by the fact that many trades councils set themselves up as councils of action to run the dispute at local level. They often came into conflict with the local transport committees, formed from the local branches of the main transport unions, who correctly maintained that they alone had the right to issue permits for the movement of essential items which would otherwise have been held up in the dispute. This confusion of responsibilities had forced the National Transport Committee, at Unity House, London, to circulate a telegram on 7 May, with the approval of the General Council, stating that:

> We instruct all local transport committees to review permits which have been issued. No trades council or Labour Party council of action, strike committee or trade union branch has authority to deal with permits. Please convey to all concerned.[39]

In addition, there was great variation in the areas of support, and the surviving local strike records offer a confusing and changing picture of strike activity. Apart from the coal areas, where sympathetic strike action was strongly evident, and the rural areas, where it was not, the rest of the country displayed immense diversity. In London, there were both areas of strong support for the strike, like Battersea, and areas where support was extremely limited – although far fewer in number.[40] In Yorkshire, the coal areas and Halifax, Huddersfield, Skipton and many other textile towns supported the strike almost 100 per cent while there was much less support in Bradford, Leeds and Wakefield. In the south east the salubrious towns of King's Lynn and Eastbourne were evidently strongholds of the strike while Aldershot, Maidstone, Dorking, Lowestoft and Yarmouth displayed only lukewarm interest.

The role of the government in publishing the *British Gazette*, its resort to middle-class volunteers and the use of troops reduced the impact of the strike in many regions. The Economic League, formed in the winter of 1919 to 1920 in order to lead a counter-attack by British capitalism against the rise of a mass labour movement, also added greatly to the difficulties of the General Council. It was obsessionally hostile to trade unionism and Arthur McIvor has written that:

> During the General Strike, the League collaborated with other employers' organizations, such as the FBI, to provide information to the government on coal stocks and shortages, the availability of transport and the

organization of strikebreaking operations. Indeed, regional Leagues played an active role in strikebreaking, encouraging the enrolment of volunteer workers, providing lorry drivers and transporting foodstuffs, and publishing news-sheets and leaflets attacking 'the pernicious influence of the reds'. In the coalfields, the district League organized a more sustained propaganda campaign, touring the colliery villages with 'flying squads', vilifying 'Cookism', supporting the Spencer brand of non-political company unionism and propagating the League's new slogan: 'every man is a capitalist.'[41]

There is also little doubt that the effectiveness of the strike was greatly impaired by its internal difficulties and external opposition. The four or five hundred councils of action which were formed were often divided and inefficient. It is alleged that internal conflict made Leeds one of the worst organized towns in Britain.[42] Indeed, Emile Burns's survey of the councils of action revealed the great extent to which they were badly organized and the degree to which in Middlesborough, for instance, 'each trade acted on its own'.[43] The decision of the General Council, on 12 May, to call off the strike without any guarantee that those involved would not be victimized, might also be seen as evidence of failure. But there was also much evidence of trade union unity and achievement.

About two million workers had come out in support of the miners, a number which represented almost half the total which the TUC could have called out in support of the miners – and more than it did. There was also a great spirit of unity among the workers and, although the statements were coloured with rhetoric, it was emphasized that at Wolverhampton 'The whole of the workers stood firm and were prepared to fight to the bitter end' and that at Hull there was 'Alarm – fear – despair – a victorious army disarmed and handed over to its enemies'.[44] In Bradford, it was even suggested that the General Strike might be seen as a victory:

> We do not say that the Government has been defeated by the General Strike, for it was not directed against the Government. But we do say that its object [has] been gained, and that after all the stir and excitement, the inconvenience . . . we are back to where we wished to be, and with the miners' case under negotiation.[45]

The last comment was obviously wrong, although there remained a rather threadbare conviction that something had been achieved. Evidence mounted that, despite the TUC's negotiations with Sir Herbert Samuel and the meeting with the Prime Minister on

12 May, the strike had been called off without a guarantee of protection against victimization. In addition, there was no immediate resumption of negotiations between the coal miners and the coal owners.

Nevertheless, in the wake of the strike, Robin Page Arnot, the Communist activist, wrote that:

> In the strike there appeared something which had not been known before – UNITY – but which, once known, can easily be found again. This action was attained by the action of the workers themselves, despite their organizations, despite chains of traditions, habits, separateness, sectionalism, etc. etc. This consolidation of the workers, however temporary, was the most significant feature of the whole General Strike.[46]

Yet, little of that spirit of unity could be attributed to the activities of the Communist Party of which Arnot was a member. Though Communists claimed some influence upon the councils of action in the north east and in London, their impact was minimal. The presence of its members was normally accepted since they supported the industrial action of the TUC, because 1,200 of them were arrested during the dispute, and due to the fact that some of its leading figures did sterling work in organizing the activities of councils of action. Their influence, however, was usually patchy and short-lived.

In Yorkshire, Shipley was one of the main centres of Communist activity but most of its members were arrested early on in the dispute.[47] There was also some violence when the Castleford Communists marched to Leeds. Several Communist agitators from Castleford were arrested on this occasion for making speeches likely to cause disaffection. Typical of these arrests was the case of Isabel Brown. The *Yorkshire Observer*, shortly after the end of the General Strike, reported that:

> At Pontefract yesterday Isabel Brown, who said her last permanent address was Moscow, was committed for three months in the second division for having delivered a speech at Castleford on Wednesday likely to cause disaffection. She admitted she had come from London to gain recruits for the Communist Party, but denied any attempt to stir up strife.[48]

None of the efforts of the Communist Party amounted to anything of a significant revolutionary threat and it was Winston Churchill, editing the *British Gazette* for the government, who drummed up more revolutionary potential than really existed. The General

Strike, a title never used by the General Council, was simply an attempt to support the miners against a wage reduction. A few activists might have seen it as more than that, but that was never the view of the General Council.

It may well be argued that the government was able to defeat the General Strike by its propaganda campaigns, the arrest of Communist activists, the use of volunteers and by sheer patience, in ignoring the General Council Negotiating Committee's attempt to forge a settlement with Sir Herbert Samuel, the ill-fated 'Samuel Memorandum'. But in the final analysis, though the TUC lost some credibility and membership, the government was never able to capitalize upon the victory it achieved. This was evident in the fact that the provision banning sympathetic strike action in the 1927 Trade Dispute and Trade Union Act was never tested in the courts. In many respects the whole General Strike could be seen as an inevitable development which served notice to the government, employers and trade unions that each party was not to be taken lightly.

In what respect, then, can the General Strike be seen as a watershed in British industrial relations? It has been suggested that the government and employers were left free to reduce wages and to rationalize industry, and trade union membership did decline from 5.5 million in 1925 to about 4.8 million in 1928.[49] Railway workers and bus drivers were victimized by employers and forced to sign documents indicating their intention to leave their unions, and the miners in many, though by no means all, districts found their wages reduced in the wake of their defeat in November 1926. By the late 1920s and the early 1930s, governments were encouraging employers to rationalize coal, along the lines laid down by the Samuel Commission, whereby small units would be incorporated into larger ones, some to be closed, as in shipbuilding, cotton and other industries. It is clear that the views of unions were being ignored. Equally, employers in the wool and worsted industry, having failed to achieve wage reductions in 1929, forced the textile workers to accept a 9 per cent reduction in wage rates in June 1930, after a ten-week lock-out.[50] There were clear losses for the trade union movement, and a reversal of fortune for several years, which was amplified by the deepening depression of the late 1920s and early 1930s. Nevertheless, as Gordon Phillips and Frank Wilkinson have argued, the pattern of trade union activity and industrial relations was not altered by the General Strike.[51]

It should be remembered that there was no prosecution under the 1927 Act up to its repeal by a Labour government in 1946,[52] and that the decline in trade union activity was already occurring before 1926, as indicated in Table 1 (see page 141), and not a product of the strike. Individual trade unions had also reflected this continuous decline of membership throughout the 1920s and early 1930s; the coal miners' union declined from 936,653 members in 1921 to 885,789 in 1925 and to 554,015 in 1932 while, for the same dates, respectively, trade union membership in the railway unions fell from 560,875 to 528,764 and 399,184.[53] There also appears to have been no let up in the determination to forge a more effective industrial alliance – even though the General Council stopped short of another general strike. In addition, the pace of wage reductions fell and only one-eighth the amount was taken off the weekly wage bill between 1930–3 as was taken from the net weekly wage bill for 1921.[54] There is also little to suggest that the pattern and style of industrial relations was greatly altered by the General Strike.

As Frank Wilkinson has suggested, in his detailed study of collective bargaining in the steel industry, 'Despite this lapse during the General Strike the industry maintained its reputation for peacefully resolving its own wage disputes during the 1920s'.[55] The industry was, in fact, marked by an unusual degree of industrial peace and the General Strike does not appear to have fundamentally altered its pattern of industrial negotiations. Indeed, it appears that decision-making power within the steel union, the Iron and Steel Trades Confederation, moved from the local branch to the national executive as the focus of debate turned from the high paid open-hearth melters, earning between about £6.46 and £11.37 per week in 1925, to the low paid ancillary workers and labourers. And between 1924 and 1929, the base rates of shift pay for the lower-paid workers rose from 3 to 37 per cent.[56] Whatever the difficulties faced by the steel workers, the steel union was most effective in improving the financial position of its members in a period when trade unions felt satisfaction if they were able to preserve the *status quo*. Trade unions in other industries continued to operate much as they had done before.

Perhaps the only major casualty of the General Strike, and the pattern of industrial events of the 1920s, was the decline of the shop stewards' movement. This had risen to prominence during the First

World War, highlighted by the events on Clydeside, but had become less effective in the 1920s as the national leaders, such as J. Murphy, were absorbed into the Communist Party of Great Britain and as the downward wage spiral made it difficult to secure any gains in its former engineering strongholds. There were occasional successes for this informal system of control at the workplace, most notably at Hoe's Engineering works in London in the mid-1920s when a go-slow campaign, an overtime ban and a stay-in-strike, led by the shop stewards, ensured that the rationalization of the works was successfully resisted.[57] But even this success was short-lived and eventually the shop stewards lost their jobs, payment by results was introduced and there was a general speed-up of production in the company. Elsewhere, the picture was equally bleak. By 1923 the famous centres of wartime militancy, such as Beardmores, Dalmuir and John Brown's in Glasgow, were

Table 1 *Trade Union Membership and Rate of Unemployment, 1920–39*[58]

Year	Membership (000s)	Rate of Change (year)	(%)	Unemployment (%)
1920	8,438			7.9
1921	6,633	1920–1	−20.55	16.9
1922	5,625			14.3
1923	5,429			11.7
1924	5,544	1922–5	+2.12	10.3
1925	5,506			11.3
1926	5,219			12.5
1927	4,919	1925–8	−12.71	9.7
1928	4,806			10.8
1929	4,858			10.4
1930	4,842			16.1
1931	4,614	1929–33	−9.59	21.3
1932	4,444			22.1
1933	4,392			19.9
1934	4,590	1933–9	+43.39	16.7
1939	6,298			10.5

Table 2 *Workers Directly and Indirectly Involved in Disputes and the Number of Days Lost, 1920–39*[59]

Year	Workers (000s)	Days Lost (000s)	Year	Workers (000s)	Days Lost (000s)
1920	1,932	26,568	1930	307	4,339
1921	1,801	85,872	1931	490	6,908
1922	552	19,850	1932	379	6,448
1923	405	10,672	1933	136	1,072
1924	613	8,424	1934	134	959
1925	441	7,952	1935	271	1,955
1926	2,750	162,230	1936	316	1,829
1927	108	1,174	1937	597	3,413
1928	124	1,388	1938	274	1,334
1929	533	8,287	1939	337	1,356

without shop stewards because no one could be found to take up posts for which they would undoubtedly be victimized. The General Strike was simply further evidence of the limits of trade union militancy and, ironically, provided the basis for the unions – reduced in both finance and members – to focus support of their activities upon their leaders.

This is not to deny that there were no major setbacks. The mining dispute, which had provoked the strike, continued from the end of April 1926 until November, when the miners and their families were effectively starved back to work despite the financial support of those unions affiliated to the TUC. There is no denying the suffering of the mining families and the deep hatred which was further nurtured between the miners and the coal owners. The striking miners received no relief though 'The wives did get a few shillings from the Parish Relief (which all had to be paid back when the strike ended).'[60] The younger men 'Started what was called jazz bands through which to win prizes and raise money for the strike effort'.[61] The local branches of the miners' union set up soup kitchens, with much local help from butchers and shopkeepers. But all was to no avail. As Kenneth Maher, a miner from Caerphilly, reflected:

> Towards the end of the strike things were awful. No coal, no clothes. We were in rags and a lot of us had no shoes. I remember going with my mother and my brother to a colliery tip about four miles away. The weather was getting very cold. It took us a day to pick two buckets of tiny bits of coal. The tip had been picked clean. Then after eight months the strike collapsed in Nottinghamshire. There was a drift back to work. But in South Wales it wasn't going to be as easy as that. The miners went back completely crushed – worse off than before.[62]

The miners suffered a humiliating defeat, but this does not appear to have been true of the whole trade union movement.

1927–39

Until the 1960s historians generally accepted that the trade unions were on the retreat, toothless and passive, throughout the rest of the inter-war years which followed their defeat in the General Strike. The victimization which occurred, the loss of trade union membership, and the wage reductions all seemed to confirm this impression. The comparatively calm industrial relations which occurred in 1927 and 1928 also suggested that the militancy of earlier years had evaporated in the wake of defeat. Dame Margaret Cole, for instance, suggested that the failure of the General Strike killed off the 'romantic vision of workers' control'.[63] Clearly, there were some changes and in some industries, most notably coal mining, national wage negotiations disappeared in November 1926, after the collapse of the miners' resistance to the coal lock-out, to be replaced by district agreements. This meant that wages fell sharply in the coal-exporting districts of South Wales and the north east but remained the same in the new and expanding south Yorkshire coalfield, where new and deeper mines were producing high quality coal for the home market. Nevertheless, there were many signs that trade unions, while still losing members, were maintaining their resistance against wage reductions.

Neither side of industry was seeking confrontation after the General Strike. Indeed, the TUC began to consider the prospect of trade unions being involved with the state and the employers in running and regulating the economy. The short-lived Mond–Turner talks advocated this new spirit in industrial relations, which can be

viewed as an extension of the General Council acting as representative of the whole trade union movement in national industrial
matters.

In addition, as Jonathan Zeitlin and S. Tolliday have suggested,
while there was antagonism between the state and the labour
movement the state has played a key role in limiting managerial
prerogatives and, in particular, overcoming the opposition to trade
unionism.[64] This was partly reflected in the Baldwin government's
reluctance to pursue the draconian legislation advocated by some
Conservative extremists in the autumn of 1926 and the production
of the relatively timid Trade Dispute and Trade Union Act in 1927.
The moderation in the relationship between the state and the trade
unions arose out of the feeling in government that trade unions had
to become involved in other spheres of influence if they were to offset
any serious injury which might befall them as a result of the General
Strike. There also emerged the possibility of some common
agreement between trade unions and industry over the fact that the
economy was being run to the advantage of the City as opposed to
industry. The decision to return to the gold standard, and to operate
it, often necessitated the rise of interest rates which acted as a
burden upon the exporting industries just as the reflation of the
pound had made exporting more difficult. By the end of 1926, the
General Council was advancing the argument, with some justi-
fication, that the General Strike had only been an attempt to warn
the employers that the problems of industry could not be constantly
tackled at the expense of the standard of living of the workers.

Such a view helped trade union leaders to think in terms of
coming to an accommodation with industrialists who were feeling
the pinch of economic policy. George Hicks was well attuned to this
possible linkage when, in his presidential address to the 1927
Trades Union Congress, he asserted that:

> much fuller use can be made . . . of the machinery for joint consultation
> and negotiation between employers and employed. . . . It is more than
> doubtful whether we have seen the fullest possible development of
> machinery for joint consultation in particular industries. And practically
> nothing has been done to establish effective machinery of joint conference
> between the representative organizations entitled to speak for industry as
> a whole.[65]

Within a few months, similar statements were being made by the
King, Stanley Baldwin, Ramsay MacDonald, and many prominent

trade unionists. Indeed, Ernest Bevin, speaking at a union dinner, maintained that:

> if there is a new conception of the objects of industry, then there can be created in this country . . . conditions which will minimise strikes and probably make them non-existent for 25 years.[66]

By January 1928 the preparatory negotiations were going on between the TUC and the Confederation of Employers' Organizations and the Federation of British Industries, the two main employers' organizations. The implacable opponents of the past were now, due to common necessity, moving towards establishing a harmony of interests.

Sir Alfred Mond, of the Federation of British Industries, and Ben Turner, president of the General Council of the TUC, entered discussions while their respective bodies debated their attitude to the new alliance and the proposals which were being made. The Mond–Turner talks attempted to form a common alliance between the employers and the unions on such matters as unemployment, outlining remedies for it such as a development fund, colonial development, more liberal trade facilities, export credits, augmented pensions for those retiring at sixty-five, the raising of school-leaving age, and, above all, 'the substitution of modern plant and techniques for existing machinery and methods' – in consultation with the unions and with 'measures . . . for safeguarding workers displaced by rationalisation'.[67]

Yet, although the leaders of both sides of industry worked hard to achieve a common agreement on policies to present to the government, the talks, and the influence they exerted, began to wither away after a couple of years, and did not survive into the 1930s. The worsening economic situation, and a dramatic increase in industrial conflict between 1929 and 1932, served to sour the possibility of a long-term consensus between employers and trade unionists. Also, the introduction of scientific management, Taylorism and the Bedaux system, which introduced new wages systems and work measurement, caused many strikes in the 1930s, including ones at the car components firm at Lucas in Birmingham in 1932 and in the hosiery industry at the Wolsey works in Leicester also in 1932.

Nevertheless, as already suggested, wages did not decrease at the height of the slump of 1929 to 1933 at anything like the level of reduction which occurred in the early 1920s, and some type of stability and balance was being established. Trade unions, despite a loss of membership and their apparently weakened position, appear to have performed more effectively after the General Strike than they did before – which suggests that employers were more reluctant to become embroiled in major industrial conflict and that unions were, themselves, asserting their rights in more effective and varied ways. The defeat of the TUC in the General Strike did not have the disastrous impact which trade unionists feared. On the contrary, unions appear to have been more effective and even the loss of trade union membership may have been a consequence of the inability of the unemployed trade unionists to pay their union fees rather than due to the loss of support for the unions.

Trade unions, in fact, did rather well during the 1930s. Professor H.A. Clegg has examined the reasons for this and suggested that employers were not well organized at that time and that there were fewer jobs being lost in the early 1930s than in the early 1920s. In a particularly perceptive passage, he captures the essence of the problem faced by many employers:

> Most firms in most industries were not facing disastrous losses, nor even the prospect of disastrous losses. The worst hit firms might decide that they must have a reduction in pay in order to stay in business. Their colleagues, or enough of them, might agree that a reduction in labour costs would improve their prospects too, so that negotiations with the unions could begin. However, when the unions proved reluctant to make concessions, the employers would have to consider the possibility of a lockout. Those who were not hard pressed and in no immediate danger of running at a considerable loss might have no strong incentive to vote in favour of a course which threatened them with heavy losses in the immediate future. The conditions of 1930–3 were unfavourable to unity among employers.[68]

Trade unions were, in fact, in a much stronger position in 1933 than they had been in 1921 or 1922. There had been many amalgamations, the Transport and General Workers and many other large unions had absorbed small unions to form a formidable barrier to employers, there was less inter-union rivalry and the authority of the General Council of the TUC was accepted and practically unchallenged. In addition, in some trades there had been strong rank-and-file reaction to changing conditions and wages, most particularly in the cotton industry where employers attempted to reduce wages and speed up work rather than invest in new machinery between 1928 and 1935.

In this new atmosphere, employers responded more readily to a centralized and more powerful trade union leadership. Indeed, Ernest Bevin drew the contrast, emphasizing that the 'industrial policy of [our] opponents has changed. The old bitter hostility . . . has gone. It is a new technique which is being introduced.'[69] And again, he added that 'Those [the 1920s] were the days of advocacy. Ours [the 1930s] is the day of administration.'[70]

The majority of unions found their membership increasing as the 1930s progressed, a fact already reflected in the increase of total trade union membership from 4.4 million in 1932 to 6.3 million in 1939. This growth is partly reflected in Table 3, where it can be seen that trade unionism in practically all industries, except for textiles and water transport, increases significantly in the mid- and late 1930s.

Table 3 *Union Membership by Industry, 1932–9*[71]

Industry	1932	1939	% Change 1932–9
Coal-Mining	554,015	707,012	+28.05
Paper & Printing	184,218	224,188	+21.69
Railways	399,184	470,033	+17.75
Transport and General Labour	660,180	1,288,911	+84.64
Furniture, woodwork and building	332,469	420,105	+27.89
Water Transport	77,441	74,277	− 4.09
Textiles	492,473	419,559	−14.81
Engineering, Shipbuilding and iron and steel	526,234	936,125	+77.89

The figures for individual industries do hide the fact that some individual unions did experience decline in membership in industries where trade unionism was increasing. The Miners' Federation of Great Britain, for instance, had about 200,000 members fewer in 1939 than in 1929, and was faced with opposition from a Scottish Communist miners' union and the Spencer Union, formed in 1926 and named after George Spencer MP, a non-strike union which was powerful in organizing the miners in the Nottinghamshire coalfield.[72]

Nevertheless, there were many factors which favoured the trade unions after the detrimental impact of the 1929 to 1933 world slump began to fade. The economy began to revive and, from the mid-1930s, the re-armament policies began to favour some sectors, particularly engineering. Also, despite the fact that there were many difficulties in organizing the new industries, it was the car and electrical industries, in particular, which encouraged the expansion of some unions. The winning of trade union organizations in these industries was not easy, as is testified by Arthur Exell, who was employed at Morris Motors in the 1930s at a time when 'there was no trade union and the factory was ruled by a mixture of tyranny, favouritism and paternalism'.[73] Not surprisingly, it was ardent agitators from within the Communist ranks who took the lead in organizing the car workers and it was due partly to their efforts that the car industry, and other new industries, were unionized. As a result, the Electrical Trade Union and the Amalgamated Engineering Union experienced rapid increases in their membership figures, the latter seeing its membership doubling between 1933 and 1939 to a total of 390,873. It was, indeed, in this climate of expansion that the TUC introduced the 'Bridlington Agreement', passed at the TUC conference in 1939, which laid down that no union should attempt to organize workers at any industrial establishment where another union already represented and negotiated on behalf of the majority of the workers.

Part of the reason for this revival of the movement was the dominating influence of the powerful and bullying Ernest Bevin, leader of the dockers and transport workers. He had already established his reputation as an astute and powerful trade union leader in the 1920s. He had helped mount the 'Hands of Russia' campaign in 1920 and 1921, and became the secretary of the Transport and General Workers' Union when it was formed in 1922. Projected forward by the General Strike he was, thereafter, the dominant force within the trade union movement and the Labour Party. His power was the result of a variety of complementary factors. He had a powerful union base, was closely connected with the negotiations which led to the *Daily Herald*, the Labour Party's newspaper, being taken over by Odhams press in 1929 and becoming a national newspaper, and was, from May 1928, the landlord of both the TUC and the Labour Party who took up offices in Transport House, his new union headquarters. In addition, he exercised considerable influence over the policies of the whole Labour movement through the fact that he was a member of the National Joint Council, formed in 1921 and which became the National Council of Labour from 1934, a body which was set up to coordinate the activities of the Labour Party and the TUC. After the General Strike, and with Bevin as a member, it gradually became the most powerful policy-making body within the Labour movement – reaching its zenith when dealing with foreign affairs during the 1930s, when it supported the League of Nations, attacked Italy over the Abyssinian crisis and effectively forced the Labour Party to accept that the foreign powers' policy of 'non-intervention' in Spain was working against the interests of the Spanish Republican government.[74]

Using the large block vote of the Transport and General and other unions, Bevin was also able to dominate the Labour Party annual conferences throughout the 1930s. In this forum he was able to temper or overturn the recommendations of the Labour Party leaders. This was demonstrated on many occasions but most emphatically at the Brighton conference in 1935. This took place in the climate of Italian aggression against Abyssinia, and Bevin, with the overwhelming support of the trade union movement, swept away the protests of George Lansbury and Stafford Cripps to win conference support for collective security through the League of Nations sanctions, including, if necessary, military action against Italian aggression in Abyssinia. Bevin, with the support of the major trade unions, put paid to any pacifist policies which George Lansbury still harboured for the party. Bevin dealt brutally with Lansbury and his pacifist reservations, thus forcing him to quit as leader of the Labour Party. Rather dramatically, Hugh Dalton recorded that Bevin 'hammered [Lansbury] to death'.[75]

Bevin, with Walter Citrine, the Secretary of the TUC, formed a formidable force within the Labour movement so much so that, under their leadership, trade unionism shaped the direction of the Labour movement in the 1930s. They ensured that there would be strong trade union opposition to any suggestion that Ramsay MacDonald's second Labour government should increase the unemployment contributions of the employed and reduce the benefits of the unemployed. Such suggestions had been made by the Royal Commission on Unemployment Insurance of 1930/1 and were supported by the Committee in National Expenditure, under Sir George May, at a time when the world economic crisis had increased British unemployment figures and provoked a foreign exchange crisis. This opposition to expenditure cuts and other deflationary measures was made quite plain in the famous meeting between the Cabinet Economy Committee and the General Council on 20 August 1931, which was followed by a deputation to the Cabinet, led by Citrine and Bevin, which reaffirmed this stand.[76] This opposition, which MacDonald regarded as 'practically a declaration of war', was clearly an important factor influencing Arthur Henderson to oppose MacDonald and Snowden in their demands for cuts in unemployment benefits, for it was now clear that a Labour government could not expect to carry the Labour Party with it if it agreed to cuts in unemployment benefit.[77] The split in Cabinet, when the cuts were discussed, led to the collapse of the second Labour government and the formation of MacDonald's National government in August 1931.

Bevin's domination of the trade union movement also helped to ensure that Communist influence diminished in the 1930s. His opposition operated at many levels. In the first place, he continued to limit the power of Communists within the local trades councils; both he and Citrine were determined to integrate the trades councils into a more centralized structure which would ensure that Communist influence was diminished. Centralization had begun in the mid-1920s, at a time when the Communist Party, through its minority movement, had established a powerful presence within many trades councils, such as in London, where the Communists controlled the Executive Committee in 1927, and in Barrow.[78] The General Council issued a circular in March 1927 informing trades councils that they would not be recognized if they affiliated to the minority movement, and some individual trade unions also withdrew their branches from those trades councils who maintained such a connection. Finally, in 1934, the General Council issued circulars 16 and 17, usually known as the 'black circulars', which, consecutively, informed trades councils that they would be withdrawn from the official list of recognized trades councils if they admitted delegates from Communist or Fascist organizations, and asked unions to enforce such bans within their own ranks.[79] Many trades councils, such as those at Bury and Bradford, initially refused to comply but were forced to capitulate by the end of 1935.[80]

Secondly, Bevin eventually defeated the Communists within his own union, and particularly those who were troublesome among the London busmen, where Bert Papworth had established his influence, and on the Central London Bus Committee. After the Communists had forced through an unsuccessful strike for a reduction of hours in 1937, Bevin managed to get the rank-and-file Communist leaders expelled from the union.

Thirdly, through his influence over the National Council of Labour, he was able to ensure that the Labour Party rejected the international Communist movement's campaign, begun in 1933, to form a 'united front' against fascism. After the collapse of the second Labour government in 1931, all Labour leaders were sensitive to alliances and compromises which they felt would not be in Labour's interest.

Bevin's opposition to Communism did not mean that he, and the trade union movement, were not conscious of the threat of fascism to world peace. Indeed, on the contrary and as already suggested, Bevin was in the forefront of attempts to face up to the fascist threat as posed by the Italian invasion of Abyssinia in 1935 and the beginning of the Spanish Civil War in 1936. On facing up to the threat of European fascism, Bevin reminded Labour Party conferences that it was trade unionism which would be liquidated if the fascists ever came to power in Britain and gradually moved the Labour movement to the need for rearmament.

By 1936, the fact is that the tide had turned to the right in British Labour politics. In that year Bevin became chairman of the General Council of the TUC and Hugh Dalton became the chairman of the NEC of the Labour Party. More centralized than ever before, and dominated by Bevin and the small coterie of leaders who supported his views, trade unionism began to become more effective, unified and acceptable to government.

All three National governments, which operated under the premiership of J. Ramsay MacDonald (1931–5), Stanley Baldwin (1935–7) and Neville Chamberlain (1937–40), displayed increasing respect for trade unions in the 1930s. This was reflected in many ways. For instance, MacDonald offered knighthoods to both Arthur Pugh and Walter Citrine, for their trade union work. Both accepted what might have been regarded as a rather dubious honour. By the late 1930s, the TUC was being drawn into discussions with the government and textile unions were pressed into the task of re-organizing the cotton industry, through the acts of 1936 and 1939. The highpoint of this relationship was reached on 22 March 1938 when Neville Chamberlain, the Prime Minister, invited Walter Citrine for a private conversation because 'he wanted to explain the need for an accelerated rearmament programme to the TUC General Council'.[81] Chamberlain signified that the full General Council should meet him the next day. This was the first such meeting between the General Council and the Prime Minister, with the exception of the Labour Prime Minister, since 1926.

Conclusion

During the early 1920s unemployment posed serious problems for the British trade union movement. Wages fell rapidly and the unions, despite their involvement in many long and protracted disputes, were unable to staunch the outward flow of members and funds or to stave off the savage monetary wage cuts which occurred. Ironically, the situation changed remarkably after the General Strike. Far from being the moment when British trade unionism all but collapsed, the General Strike – even though there were other factors at play – sounded a warning to employers that trade unions would resist further wage incursions and that the cost of too muscular an industrial policy could be high. Thereafter, despite high unemployment between 1922 and 1932, trade union membership remained remarkably resilient and recovered sharply during the improving trade situation of the late 1930s. Trade unions were drawn more centrally into negotiation with national employers and with the National government, with the exception of the wool unions, from 1930.

While the General Strike might be viewed as a watershed by some historians who feel that the trade union position worsened considerably after 1926, this was clearly not the case; trade unions were less frequently attacked by employers after 1926 than they were before and the pace of wage reductions slowed considerably. However, there was no change in the strategy and policies adopted by the General Council of the TUC. The purpose of the General

Council continued to be the need to unite trade unions into an industrial alliance to defend the wages and conditions of their members. The General Strike in no way deflected it from that course and it is difficult to see that event as an historical watershed in the evolution of trade union policies and attitudes. What is remarkable about the inter-war years is the consistency of trade union policies and the forthright manner in which the General Council pursued its intention of forging an effective industrial alliance between its member unions. There was no sudden change in direction even though employers and government began to modify their attitudes in such a way as to encourage negotiations at the highest level. Far from bringing about the denouement of inter-war trade unionism, the General Strike reaffirmed, in the fullest form possible, the potential power of trade unionism within the capitalist system. It was never the revolutionary strike which some ardent Communists hoped it would be but it had a cathartic effect upon government and employers, and permitted the trade unions to protect and improve the standard of living of their members. By the late 1930s the British trade union movement was probably as powerful, both economically and politically, as it had ever been and was firmly in control of its membership.

NOTES

1. B. and S. Webb, *The History of Trade Unionism* (1920 edn.), p. 635.
2. H.B. Graham, *Relations between Employers and Employed* (1918), 1, 3, *passim*, quoted in J.E. Cronin, 'Coping with Labour, 1918–1926', in *Social Conflict and the Political Order in Modern Britain*, edited by J.E. Cronin and J. Schneer, p. 113.
3. K. Middlemass, *Politics in Industrial Society: The Experience of the British System since 1914* (Andre Deutsch, 1979), pp. 143–4.
4. H.A. Clegg, *A History of British Trade Unions since 1889, Vol. II, 1911–1933* (Oxford University Press, 1985); Cronin, *op.cit.*, who argues that the trade unions were controlled due to the strength of the Conservative Party, the weakness of Labour and the structural changes which occurred in British society.
5. *Society for the Study of Labour History, Bulletin*, 34, spring 1977, pp. 14–15.
6. Named after J.H. Whitley, MP for Halifax and the Speaker of the House of Commons.
7. The Sankey Commission was set up to decide whether or not coal industry would remain under state control or be given back to the mine owners.

The Majority Report, with the casting vote of Lord Sankey, decided upon
the need for continued state control.

8. *Yorkshire Factory Times*, 23 July 1925.
9. *Ibid.*, 28 May 1925, quoting Ben Turner writing in the *Textile Record*, the
    journal of the National Union of Textile Workers, which is deposited in
    the NUTW collection, Archives Department, Huddersfield Central
    Library.
10. *Manifesto*, Amalgamated Union of Dyers' collection at Bradford Archives
    Department and the National Union of Textile Workers' collection,
    Archives Department, Huddersfield Central Library. Also *Yorkshire Factory
    Times*, 23 July 1925.
11. Quoted in C.L. Mowat, *Britain between the Wars* (Methuen, 1968 edn.),
    p. 34.
12. *Hansard*, 18 August 1919.
13. Quoted in P. Renshaw, *The General Strike* (Eyre Methuen, 1975), p. 87.
14. R. Lowe, 'The erosion of state intervention in Britain, 1917–24', *Economic
    History Review*, 31 (1978), pp. 270–86; R. Lowe, 'The Government and
    Industrial Relations, 1919–39', in C.J. Wrigley (ed.), *A History of British
    Industrial Relations, Vol. II, 1914–1939* (Brighton, Harvester, 1987). Also
    look at J.A. Jowitt and K. Laybourn, 'The Wool Textile Dispute of
    1925', *The Journal of (Regional and) Local Studies*, vol. 2, no. 1, spring
    1982, p. 13.
15. G.A. Phillips, *The General Strike: The Politics of Industrial Conflict*
    (Weidenfeld and Nicolson, 1976), chapter III.
16. *Ibid.*, p. 16.
17. *Ibid.*, p. 13.
18. C. Wrigley, *Cosy Co-operation under Strain: Industrial Relations in the
    Yorkshire Woollen Industry 1919–1930* (York, University of York Borthwick
    Papers, 1987).
19. Amalgamated Union of Dyers, Huddersfield collection, box 2, National
    Union of Textile Workers' Executive Committee Meeting, Memorandum,
    E.C. 14/249, 4 April 1925; Amalgamated Union of Dyers, Bradford
    collection, 126 D77/192, National Wool (and Allied) Textile Industrial
    Council, Minutes, Memorandum IC 196, 18 May 1925 and Memorandum
    IC, 197, 198 and 201; Wrigley, *Cosy Co-operation*, pp.20–1.
20. Jowitt and Laybourn, 'The Wool Textile Dispute', p. 15.
21. *Yorkshire Factory Times*, 19 November 1925 and the National Association
    of Unions in the Textile Trades, *Report of the Court of Investigations
    concerning the wages position in the Wool Textile Trade (Northern Counties)*
    (Bradford, 1925).
22. National Union of Textile Workers, *Quarterly Record*, 11 (October 1925)
    and also quoted in Wrigley, *Cosy Co-operation*, p. 23.
23. *Yorkshire Factory Times*, 13 August 1925.
24. *Ibid.*
25. *Ibid.*, 27 August 1925.
26. J. Lovell, 'The TUC Special Industrial Committee, January–April 1926',
    in *Essays in Labour History 1918–1939* (Croom Helm, 1977), edited by
    A. Briggs and J. Saville, pp. 36–56.

27. *Yorkshire Factory Times*, 27 August 1925.
28. C. Farman, *The General Strike, May 1926* (Rupert Hart-Davies, 1972), pp. 28–9.
29. *Workers Weekly*, 28 August 1925.
30. Most notably, G.A. Phillips, *General Strike*; M. Morris, *The General Strike* (Journeyman Press, 1976 and 1980) and J. Skelley (ed.), *1926: The General Strike* (Lawrence and Wishart, 1976), added to earlier books by Renshaw, *General Strike*, and Farman, *General Strike*, and M. Morris, *The British General Strike 1926* (Historical Association, G 82, 1973).
31. Phillips, *General Strike*, chapter xiii.
32. Cabinet Conclusions, 44 (25), 23/50, pp. 316–17, 7 August 1925.
33. Farman, *General Strike*, p. 29.
34. Lovell, 'The Special Industrial Committee', pp. 37 and 53.
35. *Ibid.*, p. 53.
36. *Report of the Royal Commission on the Coal Industry (1925), Vol. 1, Report*, chapter xxii, Summary of Findings and Recommendations, p. 233–4.
37. *Report of Special Conference of Trade Union Executives*, 29 April–1 May 1926.
38. Lord Citrine, *Men and Work: an Autobiography* (1964), p. 196.
39. Copies of the telegram are to be found in many collections, including the strike records of the Liverpool Council of Action.
40. Morris, *General Strike*, pp. 39–43.
41. A. McIvor, 'Essay in Anti-Labour History', *Society for the Study of Labour History, Bulletin*, vol. 53, part 1, 1988, p. 21.
42. T. Woodhouse, 'The General Strike in Leeds', *Northern History*, vol. xviii, 1982, pp. 252–62.
43. Emile Burns, *Councils in Action* (1927).
44. Farman, *The General Strike*, p. 237.
45. *Bradford Pioneer*, 14 May 1926.
46. R.P. Arnot, *The General Strike May 1926* (Labour Research Department, 1927, republished Wakefield, EP Publishing, 1975), p. 245.
47. D.A. Wilson, 'Personal Reminiscences from Bradford', in J. Skelley (ed.), *1926 The General Strike*, pp. 352–9; *Yorkshire Observer*, 15 May 1926, reporting the raid on the Shipley Communist Club.
48. *Yorkshire Observer*, 8 May 1926.
49. Look at Table 1.
50. *Bradford Pioneer*, 23 May 1930.
51. Phillips, *General Strike*; F. Wilkinson, 'Collective Bargaining in the Steel Industry in the 1920s', *Essays in Labour History 1918–1939* (Croom Helm, 1977), pp. 102–32.
52. H. Phelps Brown, *The Origins of Trade Union Power* (Oxford, OUP, 1986), p. 91.
53. Phillips, *General Strike*, p. 283.
54. H.A. Clegg, *A History of British Trade Unions since 1889, Vol. II, 1911–1933*, pp. 526–30.
55. Wilkinson, 'Steel Industry', p. 103.
56. *Ibid.*, p. 125.

155

57. R. Price, 'Rethinking Labour History: The Importance of Work', *Social Conflict and Political Order in Modern Britain*, edited by J.E. Cronin and J. Schneer, p. 190.
58. Phillips, *General Strike*, p. 281.
59. *Ibid.*, pp. 287.
60. N. Gray, *The Worst of Times: An Oral History of the Great Depression in Britain* (Totowa, New Jersey, 1985), p. 28.
61. *Ibid.*, p. 29.
62. *Ibid.*, pp. 29–30.
63. Look at note 3.
64. S. Tolliday and J. Zeitlin (ed.), *Shopfloor Bargaining and the State: Historical and Co-operative Perspective* (Cambridge, CUP, 1985).
65. Trade Union Congress, *Report, 1927*, pp. 66–7.
66. Transport and General Workers, *Record*, January 1927, quoted in Clegg, *British Trade Unions, 1911–1933*, p. 464.
67. Clegg, *British Trade Unions, 1911–1933* p. 464. Also refers to C. Wrigley, 'The Trade Unions between the Wars', in C. Wrigley (ed.), *A History of British Industrial Relations, Vol. II, 1914–1939* (Brighton, Harvester, 1987).
68. *Ibid.*, p. 528.
69. A. Bullock, *The Life and Times of Ernest Bevin, 1881–1940*, vol. 1, (Heinemann, 1960, 1969), p. 599.
70. Bullock, *Bevin*, p. 600.
71. Phillips, *General Strike*, p. 283.
72. A.R. Griffin and C.P. Griffin, 'The Non-Political Trade Union Movement', *Essays in Labour History 1918–1939* (Croom Helm, 1977), edited by A. Briggs and J. Saville, pp. 133–162.
73. A. Exell, 'Morris Motors in the 1930s. Part I', *History Workshop Journal*, 6, autumn 1978, p. 52; also read S. Tolliday, 'The Development of Bargaining Structure: The Case of Electrical Contracting, 1914–1939', in C. Wrigley (ed.), *A History of British Industrial Relations, Vol. II, 1914–1939* (Brighton, Harvester, 1987).
74. B. Pimlott, *Labour and the Left in the 1930s* (Cambridge, CUP, 1977); K. Laybourn, *The Rise of Labour* (Edward Arnold, 1988), pp. 95–9.
75. Pimlott, *Labour and the Left in the 1930s*, p. 73.
76. K. Laybourn, *Philip Snowden: a biography* (Aldershot, Temple Smith/Gower/Wildwood, 1988), p. 135; P. Snowden, *An Autobiography* (Ivor Nicholson & Watson, 1934), p. 941; Bullock, *Bevin*, p. 482; the Archives of the Labour Party, National Executive Committee, Minutes, 20 August 1931.
77. Public Record Office, MacDonald Diaries, 21 August 1931.
78. A. Clinton, *The trade union rank and file: Trades councils in Britain 1900–1940* (Manchester, MUP, 1977), pp. 146–56.
79. *Ibid.*, p. 152.
80. *Ibid.*, p. 155; Bradford Trades Council, Minutes, 18 October 1934; Bradford Trades Council, *Yearbook, 1934* (Bradford, 1935).
81. General Council, Minutes, 23 March 1938.

CHAPTER SIX

THE TRIUMPH OF BRITISH TRADE UNIONISM
c. 1940–69

The Second World War saw the powerful re-emergence of trade unions; their membership increased rapidly and the working conditions and wages of their members improved. Working in close harmony with government there was clearly a wartime consensus between employers, the state and unions which appears to have survived at least until the late 1960s. In this situation trade unions became increasingly conscious of their power and authority – seeking involvement in the economic decisions of governments, agreeing to wage freezes for the good of the economy and even contemplating the need for new productivity arrangements in order to ensure the continued health of British industry. They also made a conscious stand for the nationalization of the whole of industry, 'the socialisation of production', throughout the Attlee years and the 1950s, much to the annoyance of Hugh Gaitskell and the Labour Party leadership which was becoming doubtful of the relevance of that demand in the late 1950s. This enhanced position and responsibility of the trade unions often put them into conflict with their own members, who, most particularly in the coal mining and car industries, became involved in unofficial strike action as the 'responsible unionism' of their organizations apparently failed to meet the demands of their members. Combined with the economic failures of the British economy in the 1960s and the rising level of foreign competition, the emergence of such undisciplined industrial relations paved the way for both Labour and Conservative politicians to examine ways of making trade union leaders both more powerful within their unions and more accountable to the public. The Donovan Commission and the White Paper *In Place of Strife* (1969), although they were both ultimately ignored and rejected, created the mood which demanded the reduction of trade union power, under the guise of accountability for the next twenty-odd years. If the late 1960s saw a threat to the future role of trade unions, however, it is clear that for more than a quarter of a century the British trade unions enjoyed an importance in the economy which they had never previously experienced and are unlikely to experience again.

Historians have almost universally acknowledged the rising importance of trade unions between the 1940s and the 1960s. On the whole they have not sought to explain their growth but have accepted that the wartime and post-war consensus created the opportunity for trade union development. Instead, they have been concerned with three major debates and issues. Firstly, they have quarrelled over the extent to which it can be said that a wartime and post-war consensus existed at all. While most historians accept that there was a consensus, there has been some recent criticism and rejection of the whole idea of consensus.[1] Secondly, they have been deeply divided on how to approach the study of trade union and working-class history. Since the 1960s Richard Price, J.E. Cronin and Richard Hyman have all argued for a broader and less institutionally-based approach to the study of labour history, thus being dubbed the 'rank and filists'. Jonathan Zeitlin has accused them of adopting a mistaken view of class conflict, portraying trade union leaders of 'selling out' to capitalist society through compromise and cooperation. He argues that it is a flawed assumption to suggest that there is 'a fundamental division within trade unions between the interests and activities of the "bureaucracy", "leadership" or "officialdom" on the one hand, and those of the "rank and file", "membership" or "opposition" on the other'.[2] He maintains that

THE TRIUMPH OF BRITISH TRADE UNIONISM

James Hinton accepts that the majority of engineering workers followed their trade union officials in the First World War and that distinctions between the union bureaucracy and the membership were blurred in engineering in the 1970s.[3] For their part, Price, Cronin and Hyman have accused Zeitlin of adopting a rather limited, and negative, approach to the study of labour history.[4] Thirdly, many historians – Price as much as Zeitlin – have generally come to accept that labour history should be firmly set within the field of industrial relations. Indeed, in some of Price's work the economic situation and industrial relations are clearly shown to influence views about political economy.[5]

In examining the development of trade unionism for the years between 1940 and 1969 one has to be mindful of these three debates and issues in order to examine them alongside other questions which have also been considered important in the development of trade unionism and British industrial relations in this period. For instance, how strike-prone was Britain? How important were workshop problems, particularly in the development of unofficial strike action? Why, and how, did strike patterns change? To what extent did the attitudes of governments towards trade unions and industrial relations vary between Conservative and Labour administrations? Indeed, given the arguments in favour of consensus, can significant differences between the Labour and Conservative governments' policy towards trade unions and industrial relations be detected?

The Second World War

From the start of the Second World War the British trade union movement became deeply involved in operating the wartime economy. At first, under the Chamberlain government, relations were of an informal nature. A Schedule of Reserved Occupations was in operation and agreements had been forged in some industries, such as engineering where the Amalgamated Engineering Union and the Engineering Employers' Federation arranged for the 'relaxation of customs'. But once Churchill formed a government in May 1940, matters became more formal and direct. Ernest Bevin, leader of the Transport and General Workers' Union, was asked to take office as Minister of Labour and National Service. He did so and immediately created a Joint Consultative Committee of seven

159

employers and seven trade union leaders, asked trade union leaders for their support for the duration of the war, and was given extra powers to control labour through the Emergency Powers (Defence) Act and Defence Regulation 58A. With his Consultative Committee he quickly established that existing negotiating machinery should be supplemented, in the final resort, by a National Arbitration Tribunal, the decisions of which would be binding upon both parties. Strikes were thus, effectively, illegal and were formally made so under Order 1305. Also, in order to prevent the poaching of workers, Bevin obliged employers to obtain their workers through the employment exchanges or through an approved trade union, under the Restriction on Engagement Order. Also, in March 1941 the Essential Work (General Provisions) Order was passed which required skilled workers to register themselves. If they fell into the essential category they could be directed to enter employment, although all 'essential undertakings' had to meet minimum requirements of wages and conditions. Trade unions were further encouraged to drop their trade restrictions through the passing of the Restoration of Pre-War Practices Act of 1942.

Trade unions accepted these changes with remarkable equanimity, and the level of strike activity in 1940 was at its lowest level since records had begun. Apart from the obvious experience of war, the reason for this appears to have been the way in which trade union leaders had been drawn into government committees. Consultative committees began to spring up at factory level, especially in engineering production, and trade union organization positively benefited from the new legislation. This was evident in the catering industry, which had always been difficult to unionize, where the Catering Wages Act of 1943 created wage determination in the industry. The Wages Councils Act of 1945 also converted trade boards into wages councils with extended powers and range.

Trade unions did well out of these arrangements. Their powers to negotiate were improved and their rights were to be restored immediately peace was declared. The wages of their members rose faster than the cost of living and there was, of course, full employment. Also, trade union membership increased from 6,053,000 in 1938 to 7,803,000 in 1945, the great beneficiaries being the Transport and General Workers' Union (TGWU) and the Amalgamated Engineering Union (AEU). In this climate, the TUC and many trade unions saw the need for amalgamations and structural changes to improve trade union efficiency, although little was actually achieved. The General Council of the TUC also produced an interim report on Post-War Reconstruction, which contemplated trade union involvement in the process of running industries in public ownership: 'It will be essential for the Trade Union Movement to participate in the determination of all questions affecting the conduct of an industry and the well-being of its workpeople, as well as in the operation of all economic controls.'[6]

Inevitably, there were problems with such trade union activity. The most obvious was that the commitment of trade union leaders to the war effort meant that some of the legitimate grievances of their members were ignored. Not surprisingly, towards the end of the war this led to a rise in the number of unofficial strikes. The problem was most acute in the coal industry, which was to maintain its level of unofficial strike action well into the post-war years. In 1943, half the unofficial strikes were in coal and in 1944 the proportion had risen to two-thirds. It appears that the Greene Award, which guaranteed miners a minimum wage of £5 per week, had not been immediately implemented. When piece rates in mining were made up to the new level, strike activity declined quickly. Yet here was an omen for the future, for after the immediate post-war years during which the strike levels remained low, the major problem that emerged, at least until the 1960s, was the dichotomy between the 'responsible' actions of trade unionism and the expectations of the rank and file.

The Labour Governments of 1945–51

The new-found strength of the trade union movement was further enhanced by the return of a Labour government at the 1945 general election. The trade union movement was, of course, well represented in the new government, with 120 trade union sponsored MPs, six of whom were in Attlee's twenty-member Cabinet. These included Aneurin Bevan (of the Miners) who became Minister of Health, Ellen Wilkinson (of the Distribution Workers) who became Minister of Education, and George Isaacs (of the Operative Printers and chairman of the TUC) who became Minister of Labour, and Ernest Bevin (Transport Workers) who became Foreign Secretary. The new Labour government also decided upon the creation of a modern welfare state and moves towards the public ownership of industry. Trade unionists began to secure places on the boards of the newly-nationalized industries, although Manny Shinwell, Minister of Fuel and Power, suggested that the miners had given up the opportunity to play an even bigger role in the organization of the industry. None the less, the National Coal Board, formed on 1 January 1947, offered a seat to Sir Walter Citrine, representing the General Council, and Ebby Edwards, who had been secretary of the Miners since 1932. And, other prominent trade unionists were subsequently appointed to regional boards. Soon afterwards, Citrine became chairman of the Electricity Authority, the general secretaries of the Railwaymen and Locomotive Engineers left the General Council for posts on the Transport Commission, and other trade union appointments were made. Furthermore, almost the first action of the new Labour government was to repeal the Trade Dispute and Trade Union Act of 1927 despite the fact that the Lord Chancellor sent a memorandum to the Cabinet advising it that it 'would, of course, arouse considerable political controversy'.[7]

There was a price to pay for this involvement of the trade union movement. The Labour government was faced with the vital need to increase productivity and develop its export trade. In order to do this, it asked the General Council to accept the continuance of Order 1305, which made strikes illegal, and it also agreed that the Restoration of Pre-War Practices Act would not be implemented for the time being. The General Council was further drawn into the post-war production effort and nominated a number of its own members to the National Production Advisory Council on Industry, which met under Sir Stafford Cripps, the president of the Board of Trade.

The foreign-exchange crisis of 1947 and the fuel crisis of the winter of 1947 made such cooperation all the more necessary. Joint production committees, which had faded away after the war, were reconstituted in factories and the General Council urged wage restraint, in line with Attlee's speech in February 1948 demanding a voluntary stabilization of prices, profits and wages. The 1949 financial crisis, which led Britain towards devaluation, necessitated the new Chancellor of the Exchequer, Sir Stafford Cripps, to ask the General Council to make wage restraint even more vigorous. In November 1949 the General Council, therefore, agreed to recommend that existing wage rates be held stable while the Interim Index of Retail Prices remained between the upper and lower limits of 118 and 106. The Cabinet was well pleased.[8] But the strains which this placed upon relations between union officials and their members led the TUC to abandon wage restraint in 1950, at a time when the economy was doing well, even though the General Council had suggested that it be kept with greater flexibility. There was a point beyond which consensus could not go.

The perceived problem of these years, at least from the government and the TUC's point of view, was the rising level of Communist activity in Britain which, it was claimed, was designed to undermine the British economy. There has, indeed, been a substantial debate about the extent to which this problem existed. The traditional viewpoint is that Communist activity was a serious problem, and was most clearly evidenced in the London Dock strike of 1949.[9] More recently, however, this view has been challenged by Peter Weiler,[10] and on balance, it would appear that there are good grounds for believing that the Communist threat was exaggerated and that 'rank and file' workers were frustrated at the actions of their unions.

There is no doubting a Communist presence in British trade unionism. A few unions, such as the Electrical Trade Union (ETU), the Foundry Workers and the Fire Brigade Union, were under their control as well as a small number of unions with prominent Communist activists, such as the dockers' section of the Transport and General. Bert Papworth, who had led the Communist-inspired London busmen section of the Transport and General Workers in the 1930s, was a member of the General Council of the TUC, though he was the only Communist in such a position.

Limited as Communist activity was, it still worried both the government and trade union leaders, who felt that Communists were responsible for much of the industrial unrest that was occurring. In October 1948, the General Council of the TUC denounced the Communist aim of 'sabotage of the European Recovery Programme' and followed this up with a fuller statement of this position in *Defend Democracy*, urging unions to keep Communists out of key posts. This led to problems in dealing with the Communist leader of the Mineworkers, Arthur Horner, and to the eventual conflict between Arthur Deakin of the Transport and General and Bert Papworth, which led to the Biennial Delegate conference in July 1949 which decided to remove Communists, including Papworth, from holding office in and for the union. As a result, nine full-time officials lost their jobs and Papworth lost his seat on the General Council. However, even with such cleansing of the trade union movement, concerns about the Communist threat persisted, encouraged by a variety of strikes, including the famous Smithfield Drivers' Strike of June 1950 (which led to the use of the military as strike breakers). But it was in the docks where most concern existed, since strikes here directly damaged Britain's vital export drive.

The Labour government felt that all the major dock disputes, in 1947, 1949 and 1950, were inspired by Communist activists. The London dock strike of 1949 came in for particular attention in this regard. The dispute had originally begun in the Canadian ports with the Communist-inspired Canadian Seamen's Union in early 1949 and had spread to London in the summer of 1949, when fifteen thousand dockers struck for a month, refusing to unload ships affected by this dispute. Eventually, the Labour government sent in twelve thousand servicemen to unload the affected ships on 7 July 1949. The Labour government's opinion was clearly presented by George Isaacs, who stated that the Communist Party aimed 'to destruct the flow of merchandise' in British ports.'[11] Chuter Ede, the Home Secretary elaborated:

> The only reason we are having to deal with the trouble in this country is that the Communists see in it a chance of fomenting unrest, injuring our trade, and so hampering our recovery and with it the whole process of Marshall Aid on which the recovery of Western Europe depends. The issue with which we are faced is not one of a legitimate industrial dispute.[12]

Arthur Deakin, General Secretary of the Transport and General Workers' Union, concurred.[13]

Such assessments are hardly surprising. The 'cold war' had developed from 1947 onwards, Bevin was involved in attempting to develop the emergent North Atlantic Treaty Organization, and the whole attitude of Attlee's government was anti-Communist. And, above all, there were Communists active in the London docks. But, as Weiler quite rightly stresses, the activities of the Communists involved in the London docks ignore the fact that the London dockers had genuine grievances. The dockers were concerned at the National Dock Labour Scheme. This had developed from Bevin's decision, in 1940, to get rid of casual labour. In July 1947 this commitment was extended under the Dock Workers (Compulsory Regulation) Order. The gist of the scheme is that it offered security of employment and a minimum standard of living for dockers but they had to work for minimum periods, comply with the lawful orders of employers and, on failure to accept work, could be dismissed. As a result, there were 118 stoppages in English ports between January 1948 and June 1949 over pay, overtime, methods of loading and unloading and the employers' power to discipline men.[14] The London dock strike could be seen as a culmination of these events. In addition, the Leggett Committee, examining the impact of this scheme on industrial relations, commented that:

> the participation of union officials who are members of the Board in the exercise of the Board's disciplinary powers and particularly the powers of dismissal, has had the effect of changing the standing of these officials with their Union membership.[15]

In other words, it was the conflict between 'responsible union' and the interests of the rank and file which was contributing to the conflict.

Weiler suggests that there was no evidence of a Communist plot in the 1949 London dock strike and that there were other factors at play, and this seems fair comment. Nevertheless, he seems rather wide of the mark in his assessment that the government was well aware that this was not a Communist-inspired dispute. An examination of government records does not confirm this view. If anything, government ministers and their civil servants appear to be blinded by their belief that a Communist plot was afoot, driven on in this view by the outbreak of the 'Cold War' in 1947. This was particularly evident in the industrial disputes of 1950. The London docks were convulsed by a variety of industrial disputes in March and April 1950 and these rumbled throughout the year. The most important dispute began as a result of the unofficial Port Workers' Defence Committee organizing a stoppage in favour of three men who were being expelled by the TGWU for their part in the 1949 London dock strike. There was also a dispute between the Stevedores' Union and the shipping company, which wished to engage some gangs by the week instead of by the day.[16] On 15 September 1950, Sir Frank Soskice, Solicitor General, wrote to

Herbert Morrison, Lord President of the Council, and effectively deputy Prime Minister, that:

> . . . you are presiding over a Committee which is considering action to counter Communist manoeuvres directed at causing industrial unrest. . . .
> At present, as you know, they do find themselves at liberty to get their agents inside such trade union meetings or, for instance, by disguising themselves or issuing false Union cards, and the result is that it is hardly ever possible to obtain legal evidence of the incitement or illegal action which no doubt occurs when such meetings take place.[17]

In other words, hard evidence was difficult to find, but the Labour government was certain that the Communists were inciting workers to strike. Indeed, on 19 October 1950, it was further recorded that:

> At their morning Cabinet meeting – Cabinet agreed that a Committee of Ministers should further preside for (i) countering Communist endeavours to, promote industrial unrest, politically by means of unofficial strikes; and (ii) adapting to the current needs the everyday machinery for the negotiation of wage settlements in industry.[18]

The Labour government clearly felt that there was a Communist plot even if it could not find evidence of it and was also keenly aware that there were other industrial problems. Indeed, it was reminded of this by P. Jordan, on 6 October 1950, who wrote that:

> It is argued that, under a Socialist government, the power of the Trade Unions to hold the loyalty of their members must inevitably wither, because the Unions are so completely connected with the government that they must attempt the impossible task of running with the hare and hunting with the hounds. The argument concluded that so long as wage restraint is necessary unofficial strikes will become more numerous because men and women who are mainly preoccupied with their immediate living conditions will lose faith in a leadership that must now take account of interests far wider than those they were elected to serve.[19]

The Labour government was obviously concerned about industrial unrest, whether Communist-inspired or not. On 16 October 1950, the Cabinet was considering the need to extend the contract of workers in essential industries, with either criminal or civil proceedings against those who broke such contracts.[20] On the 21 November the government was also discussing the possibility of strengthening legal safeguards against strikes, improving the machinery for settling industrial disputes, and extending the propaganda of the Labour Party and the trade union movement against the Communists.[21] On the issue of 'Wages, Prices and Full Employment', E.M. Nicholson, a prominent civil servant and adviser to Morrison, was advocating the need for 'vigorous action' by the Minister of Labour. The real concern was that the wage freeze was breaking down and a Wages Advisory Service was recommended.[22] George Isaacs, Herbert Morrison and the Attorney-General also met trade union leaders, including Sir Vincent Tewson and George Woodcock of the TUC, to discuss ways of controlling unofficial strikes, including the use of strike ballots.[23] They did not get very far, accepting the demands of the trade union leaders who wished to offer something to their members, and removing Order 1305 in August 1951. Evidently, government was concerned at the growth of industrial conflict between 1949 and 1950, but no one should exaggerate the extent of the industrial problem. In their recent study, J.W. Durcan, W.E.J. McCarthy and G.P. Redman have argued that post-war strike activity was quite low until 1953.[24] Indeed, they refer to the period 1946 to 1951 as being the 'Post-War Peace', when for over seven years there was an historical low in strikes – an average of 625 strikes each year, involving 228,000 workers and 1,300,000 working days lost for all industries except coal mining. In coal mining, unofficial strikes totalled 1,069 per year, involved about 216,000 workers and were responsible for about 588,000 days lost.[25] Excluding the mining industry these national figures were at their lowest level of strike action since well before the First World War, and much lower than in the first seven years after the First World War. The strike situation was much worse in mining than in other industries, and remained so until the early 1960s when the incidence of mining disputes declined rapidly. Nevertheless, even given that strikes were effectively illegal in the period of the post-war Labour governments, the industrial relations' record of the Labour government, in alliance with the trade unions, was impressive.

Yet, the Labour government did not see it in that way. Its records show an overwhelming concern with the challenge of the Communists, worries about the Smithfield troubles of 1949, the power stations, London strikes as well as the difficulties of the National Dock Labour Board.[26] Indeed, the draft speech of George Isaac, Minister of Labour and National Services, for his broadcast on BBC

Radio in 1950, reflects the government's concern to stress how strikes were irresponsible. The whole message of the broadcast was carefully contrived in order to explain to the nation that many of the major unofficial strikes were part of a 'deliberate plan' by the Communist Party to disrupt British industry. The draft includes reference to the 1949 dock strike, the formation of the Communist Party Road Haulage and Allied Workers' Committee. The message was loud and clear, the Communist Party was behind the outbreak of industrial unrest. This message clouded the perception that Labour's industrial record was impressive and that the Attlee years were ones of relative quiescence when compared with what came after.

They were also years when trade unions did well. Their membership had risen from less than eight million in 1945 to about nine and a half million by the end of 1951, and trade unions were often able to enforce 'closed shops', compulsory unionism, on all employees. So powerfully enhanced was trade unionism that the defeat of the Labour government and the return of a Conservative government in October 1951 did little to threaten its newly-acquired power and influence.

Conservative Trade Unionism, 1951–64

When the Conservatives came to power they were determined to relax state controls on market forces, to 'set the people free', and to ensure that the employers and trade unions had more freedom. All this was in the hope that there would be faster economic growth. These more relaxed industrial relations policies did not mean an immediate end to wage control machinery, although many of the old constraints were gone. Indeed, the new Conservative Chancellor of the Exchequer, R.A Butler, and the Minister of Labour, Sir Walter Monckton, continued to involve trade unions in working through the existing wage-negotiating mechanisms and, despite some attempts to tinker with the recommendations of Wages Councils, the Conservative government invariably confirmed the recommended awards. They did not desire conflict with the trade unions and preferred inflationary settlements to strikes. Indeed, Monckton was ordered to 'do my best to preserve industrial peace'.[27]

In response, the trade union leaders, most notably Arthur Deakin of the TGWU, Tom Williamson of the General and Municipal and

Will Lawther of the Mineworkers, ensured that the trade union movement adopted moderate policies, even if ritualistic sniping was directed at the Conservative government from time to time. They were as emphatic as the Conservative government that they would not be subject to restraint on wages, and passed resolutions at TUC conferences to that effect.

Table 4 *Strike Activity in Britain, 1946–69*[29]

(Net strikes exclude mining, gross strikes include mining)

Year	No. of strikes		No. of workers involved (000s)		No. of working days lost (000s)	
	Net	Gross	Net	Gross	Net	Gross
1946	876	2,205	312.9	529.5	1,736	2,158
1947	668	1,721	314.7	622.6	1,521	2,433
1948	643	1,759	236.9	426.0	1,480	1,944
1949	552	1,426	186.2	434.0	1,053	1,807
1950	479	1,339	161.1	303.0	958	1,389
1951	661	1,719	244.2	379.0	1,344	1,694
1952	493	1,714	142.5	416.0	1,132	1,792
1953	439	1,746	1,205.6	1,374.0	1,791	2,184
1954	525	1,989	245.6	450.0	1,989	2,457
1955	636	2,419	317.4	671.0	2,669	3,781
1956	572	2,648	266.6	508.0	1,581	2,083
1957	635	2,859	1,093.6	1,359.0	7,898	8,412
1958	666	2,629	275.5	524.1	3,012	3,462
1959	786	2,093	454.4	645.8	4,907	5,270
1960	1,166	2,832	581.4	818.8	2,530	3,024
1961	1,228	2,686	529.9	778.5	2,390	3,046
1962	1,244	2,449	4,268.2	4,422.7	5,490	5,798
1963	1,081	2,068	440.3	592.5	1,429	1,755
1964	1,466	2,524	711.1	883.0	1,975	2,277
1965	1,614	2,354	758.8	876.4	2,513	2,925
1966	1,384	1,937	493.6	543.9	2,280	2,398
1967	1,722	2,116	693.0	733.7	2,682	2,787
1968	2,157	2,378	2,227.8	2,258.0	4,636	4,690
1969	2,930	3,116	1,519.6	1,665.0	5,807	6,846

At first, this industrial policy progressed amicably and strike levels were low. But from about 1953 onwards the rising level of strikes, the constant balance of payments difficulties, and the low productivity of British industry made the Conservative government rethink its strategy. The fact is that the strategy was beginning to fail and was fuelling inflation, as was evident in the engineering, shipbuilding and railway strikes of 1953, settled by the intervention of Monckton. Indeed, between 1953 and 1959 there were, on average, 608 strikes, involving 551,200 miners and 3,407,000 working days in industries other than mining. In coal mining the annual figures averaged 1,732 strikes, 239,900 strikers and 543,000 working days lost. In other words, the number of strikes and their length increased. Mining was responsible for more strikes than before, almost three-quarters of the total number, but was now much less important in terms of the number of days lost. Also, there were years of marked industrial disturbance, such as 1953 and 1957. Durcan, McCarthy and Redman referred to this period as 'The Return to Strike'.[28]

The level of unofficial strike action remained high in the coal mining industry but the most obvious development in the 1950s and the early 1960s were the difficulties in the docks, which between 1949 and 1973 was the most strike-prone sector of the British economy with an average of one in two workers involved in strike action each year.[30] The origins of these problems arose from the 'casualism' in the docks that went back before the Second World War. The 1947 Dock Labour Scheme, which covered seventy-eight thousand dockers, had attempted to deal with this but had increased the tensions. The cost of the scheme was paid for by an additional levy on the employers of about 25 per cent of their wages bill which permitted some continuity of work and the end of 'casualism' in return for an arrangement which guaranteed some flexibility of employment schedules for employers. The board itself registered the dockers but the arrangements were organized between twenty-two local boards. The Devlin Report (1966) suggested that 'decasualisation' had failed and needed to be improved, but as Durcan, McCarthy and Redman had noted, it was the changing patterns of traffic and some of the varying work practices which complicated matters.[31] And, indeed, certain issues had arisen which helped to increase industrial tensions in the docks. Most obviously, there was a concern to restrict overtime, which led to the 'overtime ban' strike in the London docks in 1954. There was also the concern about the continued presence of the Communist-inspired Portworkers' Defence Committee, which appeared regularly in disputes and produced, from 1949, the *Portworkers' News*.[32] But the most serious problem was the conflict between the unions responsible for organizing the men in the dock. For the most part, dockers' unions kept to particular ports. The General and Municipal Workers' Union organized the ports of the north east, the Scottish Transport and General Workers' Union organized Glasgow, while the Watermen, Lightermen, Tugmen and Bargemen's Union organized many dockers in London. Within these unions there was comparatively little rivalry. But this was not the case between the Transport and General Workers' Union (TGWU) and the National Amalgamated Stevedores' and Dockers' Union (NASDU). Conflict flared up between these two unions in 1954 when NASDU attempted to extend its influence to Hull, Liverpool and Manchester.

The Hull dockers dispute of August 1954 is representative of this conflict. The dockers objected to the hand technique of unloading. Against the will of the TGWU, which ordered that they should go back to work since they were in breach of an agreement, they persisted with an unofficial strike against the continuance of the work practice. About four thousand Hull dockers took strike action and sixty ships were affected. In their frustration at the TGWU, some of these men joined NASDU. Others did likewise at Birkenhead, Liverpool and other ports and in October 1954 many dockers followed NASDU's decision to oppose overtime in the London docks and to take strike action. Although the London dock strike failed, it is estimated that upwards of ten thousand dockers changed their allegiance from the TGWU to NASDU in 1954. As a result, the TGWU informed the TUC that the Bridlington Agreement had been broken by NASDU, which was suspended from the TUC in October 1954. However, the dispute rumbled on for the next four years with NASDU attempting to restore dockers to the TGWU and those dockers refusing to do so, until it was finally expelled from the TUC in 1959.

Other inter-union disputes also emerged in the newspaper printing trade in March and April 1955 and in the railways in May and June 1955. Both effectively emerged from inter-union rivalry, as had the dockers' unions. All three disputes, relatively minor as they were, encouraged discussion of the need for trade union reform. Indeed, such views were more than encouraged by an overall rise in industrial conflict in the late 1950s. The changing pattern of strikes in the car industry more than added to these concerns.

The British car industry had no significant strike record before the Second World War. However, between 1955 and 1960 the level of industrial conflict, measured in days lost, increased about seven-fold and continued to intensify until the early 1970s. Most of these strikes were over in less than six days. These developments have attracted the interest of a large number of writers. Turner, Clack and Roberts, in a study of the major assembly shops, suggest that irregularity of employment, both cyclical and seasonal, resulting from fluctuations in production, was an important factor in causing this industrial disturbance.[33] The variation in the level of earnings within and between firms added to the problem. In addition, it was felt that changes in the expectations of workers contributed to the disputes especially when the process of collective bargaining failed to meet those needs. With the failure of that formal collective bargaining machinery, it is hardly surprising that the workers accepted the leadership of their shop stewards rather than their trade union officials. Durcan, McCarthy and Redman also endorse some of these views, noting the fluctuations in employment in the industry within a general climate of expanding employment opportunities; the workforce increased from 294,600 in 1953 to 499,800 in 1966 and 508,100 in 1973.[34] Yet, rather more than Turner et al., they suggest that external, rather than internal, factors were behind the industrial problems of the car industry. In other words, the changes in company organization with, for instance, eight major companies slimming down to four through mergers between 1965 and 1968, may well have created the tensions where car workers were concerned for their job rights and fair wages.[35] In the end, it might not be the defective internal machinery which generated strike activity but external pressures and developments.

Whatever the cause of industrial unrest, there is no denying the development of the 'unofficial' and 'informal' system of industrial relations. This has been examined by many historians, most obviously Richard Price, who has noted that there were links between workshop organizations in the various plants.[36] For instance, in Standard Motors in the early 1950s, the shop stewards' committees were joined together through a system of committees that tried to coordinate the actions of various plants. The British Motor Company Combine Committee, which was formed in 1951, held regular bi-monthly meetings attended by forty delegates and apparently possessed a formalized structure and a constitution. The extent to which such workshop organization could affect industrial relations varied but, as Price suggests, the eventual collapse of Standard Motors was due to its inability to gain sufficient flexibility in production to meet competition, in which the shop stewards system played its part.[37]

Table 5 *Strike Activity in Motor Vehicles, 1949–73*[38]

Year	No. of strikes	No. of workers involved (000s)	No. of working days lost (000s)	% of workers involved	Days lost as % of potential time
1949	24	3.6	14	1.2	0.02
1955	36	34.7	70	10.5	0.04
1960	124	183.0	513	42.0	0.48
1965	159	215.0	857	43.3	0.70
1970	336	271.4	1,105	52.9	0.90
1971	241	340.3	3,100	67.5	2.56
1973	297	442.6	2,082	86.8	1.70
Average	125	131	614	33.9	0.60

With the rising level of industrial conflict emerging in most parts of the economy, the position of trade unions becoming more openly questioned, and widespread concern about the economy, the Conservative government decided to reverse its industrial policy. In the spring of 1956, the government appears to have decided to impose an incomes policy upon public-sector wages, although it initially found it difficult to do so in any consistent manner. The severe sterling crisis of September 1957 provided the final push necessary for concerted action. Soon afterwards the government created a new institution, the Council for Prices, Productivity and Incomes, which, in its first report in February 1958, suggested that sharp wage rises were causing excessive demand and rising prices and needed to be controlled.

The government was now contemplating the possibility of fighting strikes rather than accepting inflationary settlements. It had already encouraged the Engineering Employers' Federation to stand firm against a 10 per cent wage demand by the Confederation of Shipbuilding and Engineering Unions in March 1957, although it intervened and conceded to the workers' demands when the electricity supply, the docks and other sectors of the economy were threatened. When its policies failed with the well-organized workers, it moved towards imposing an incomes policy of type on the less powerfully organized sectors. Already, in October 1957, the Minister of Labour had made it clear that in sectors where the state was the employer it would apply the most stringent tests to wage increases. Choosing to avoid the miners, electricity workers, and other powerful groups, it focused its attention on the National Health Service. In November 1957, it overruled a rather modest pay agreement negotiated for employees in the National Health Service by their own Whitley Council.[39] The civil service unions were also informed that all pay increases in government departments would have to be 'offset by corresponding economies'. Other groups of workers, including workers at the BBC were similarly affected.

Yet when the government was faced with excessive wage demands from the miners, the railwaymen and the London busmen in 1958, it compromised with the first two groups and only chose battle with the busmen, who eventually stuck out and won their demands. By this stage Frank Cousins, the TUC, and the trade union leaders were convinced that 'fair play' was at an end and that success in wage negotiations would now depend upon the industrial muscle of the union involved. It was fully in line with the new policy being adopted by the government that, in October 1958, the Minister of Labour should announce that he was allowing the National Arbitration Tribunal, which had survived the abandonment of Order 1305 in 1951, to go out of existence. Consequently, this was seen as the ending of a compulsory arrangement which had often earned the unions small wage increases. The Industrial Court still remained, but was not now compulsory. Industrial relations thus became rather less certain than they had been before.

The expansion of the economy in 1959 and 1960 allowed a less stringent government policy towards wages but, in July 1961, another sterling crisis forced the government to deflate the economy and to introduce a 'pay pause' for nine months. When it ended, the powerful unions gained wage increases but the less powerful organizations, such as the health unions, came in for similar treatment as that they had received in 1958. In the end, it became clear to organized workers that the power to organize an effective strike was the only way to bargain with Macmillan's Conservative government.

In order to reduce the risk of such potential conflict, the Conservative government did offer George Woodcock, who had become general secretary of the TUC in 1959, the prospect of trade union membership of the National Economic Development Council, which would plan the long-term growth of Britain. It was an offer he and the TUC could not refuse, for it created a tripartite agreement between the unions, the government and the employers in the future running of the economy. In effect, consensus politics, although not all measures introduced by the government were welcomed by the unions. The unions rejected the views of the White Paper, published in February 1962, which suggested that wages should not rise faster than output and that certain criteria should be adopted for wage increases. The establishment of the National Incomes Commission ('Nicky'), an independent body aimed at examining wage claims put to it by government, was equally ignored by the unions, the organization disappearing with the return of a Labour government in 1964. In the final analysis, the government was intent upon maintaining some type of consensus with the unions but, forced by the economic difficulties between 1957 and 1962, it found that it was compelled to deal unfairly with the weaker public sector unions in order to secure some type of wage restraint. The larger, more powerful unions were not prepared to play ball and it is not surprising that the level of industrial conflict rose, even though the government normally backed down where strike resistance was determined.

At a time when its relations with government and employers were changing, the trade unions were also under attack because of their close relationship with the Labour Party. The real problem, as it remained for many years to come, was that the trade unions operated the 'block vote' of their members at Labour Party conferences. By casting the millions of votes of their members, unions could easily determine Labour Party policy if they so wished. There had been much concern on this issue in the 1930s when the Constituency Labour Party movement challenged the 'block vote' and, in post-war years, this issue was further challenged by Nye Bevan and the Bevanite group of left-wing MPs which emerged in the 1950s. Of course, the unions were reluctant to give up their power and both Arthur Deakin and Frank Cousins, of the TGWU, made no concessions to the opponents of the 'block vote' system. In the early 1950s it was the left-wing group who were challenging the dictatorship which the 'block vote' system imposed, but by the late 1950s, with the emergence of Frank Cousins as leader of the TGWU in 1956 and with the changing direction of the General and Municipal Workers to the middle and the left of the party, it was the right-wing who began to challenge the tyranny of the 'block vote'.

Indeed, the new, more left-wing, slant to trade unionism became evident at the Labour Party conference in 1959 when the unions blocked the attempts of the Labour leader, Hugh Gaitskell, to reduce Labour's commitment to the 'socialisation of industry'. In 1960, the unions also ensured that the Labour Party conference committed itself to supporting unilateral disarmament in the face of the opposition of Gaitskell and the majority of Labour MPs.[40] The decision was reversed the following year when the TGWU was isolated and the only one of the six major unions to continue to support unilateralism.

Despite these switches in political persuasions it is clear that the 'block vote' system of the unions remained firmly in place and a weapon with which to criticize the limited nature of democratic controls within the Labour Party. The Labour Party was also subject to criticism from those who argued that it was under the control of the trade unions, a charge which Gaitskell was at pains to refute in a speech to the TUC on 10 September 1959, in which he emphasized that:

> We are part of the same great Labour Movement in Britain. We are comrades together, but we have different jobs to do. You have your industrial job and we have our political job. We do not dictate to one another. I should get the brush off pretty quickly if I started trying to dictate to Bob Willis. And believe me, any leader of the Labour Party would not be worth his salt if he allowed himself to be dictated to by the trade unions.[41]

Further damage was done to the trade unions by the weaknesses of the democratic processes which operated within the trade unions.

THE TRIUMPH OF BRITISH TRADE UNIONISM

Only a small percentage of union members ever attended trade union meetings. This meant that a small number of organized members, such as Communists, could effectively take control. The most famous case of this occurring was the Communist takeover of the Electrical Trades Union (ETU), the seventh largest union with a membership of about a quarter of a million in 1960. This union had first fallen under Communist control during the Second World War and attempts to change this situation in the early 1950s had failed. But the Hungarian revolt of 1956 led to the resignation of about one-third of card-carrying Communists in Great Britain, among them Les Cannon and Frank Chapple, two leading members of the ETU. Combining with John Byrne, an ardent opponent of communism, they challenged the Communist leadership who, in order to retain power, forged ballot papers, arbitrarily disqualified union branches and falsified returns. With wide attention being focused upon this affair in 1958, the General Council of the TUC intervened and asked the ETU to clear its name of the accusations of ballot-rigging by taking its accusers to court. All the ETU did was to produce its own inquiry exonerating its members of the accusations laid against it. At this point Byrne and Chapple issued writs against the union and its officers for alleged fraud in the 1959 election for general secretary, at which Byrne had stood against the retiring secretary, Frank Haxell, and was supposedly defeated. On 28 June 1961 Mr Justice Winn gave the judgement that a group of Communists, including Frank Foulkes and Frank Haxell, had conspired in a fraudulent and unlawful manner to prevent the return of Byrne, who he thus declared to be general secretary. But even then the battle was not ended. The majority of the union executive were Communists, as was its president, Foulkes, and they sought to prevent the new general secretary acting freely. As a result, the TUC expelled the ETU in September 1961 and the Labour Party did the same in October 1961. But shortly afterwards, the autumn vote of the union replaced most of the old executive with Byrne's supporters and in 1962 both the TUC and the Labour Party re-admitted the union.

The whole issue of undemocratic and illegal trade union practices had been effectively opened up by the case of the ETU. In addition, the sensitive issue of the 'closed shop' was subjected to legal examination, by the Spring case of 1955, the Bonsor v. Musicians Union case of 1956, the Huntley v. Thornton and Others case of

1959 and, most effectively, by the Rookes v. Barnard case, which came to fruition in 1964. In the last of these cases, Douglas Rookes, a draughtsman employed by British Overseas Airways Corporation at Heathrow Airport, decided to leave his union, the Association of Engineering and Shipbuilding Draughtsmen. The local union threatened to strike if Rookes was not dismissed. Once dismissed, Rookes brought and won an action for damages against the officials of his local union, but found the decision reversed in the Court of Appeal. However, in 1964 the original appeal was upheld in the Lords. Trade union leaders were apparently no longer protected from damages despite the Trade Disputes Act of 1906.

By 1964, major changes were afoot. The poor economic performance of Britain and the recurrent sterling crises were placing the tripartite consensus under strain, although as one link was lost another was being forged. In the new harsh economic climate, strong trade unions were learning the value of strikes in winning wage increases, and the 'post-war peace' in industrial relations evaporated. In addition, trade unions, in associating themselves with government in a number of ways, began to frustrate their members, some of whom desired to move to other unions and others of whom preferred to follow the lead of shop stewards rather than their own union officials. In one sense, trade unions had never been so strong with their membership increasing from nine and a half million in 1951 to just under ten and a quarter million in 1964. But, in another sense, they had never been so vulnerable to unofficial strike action and it was becoming increasingly clear that a significant amount of power in many unions was falling out of the hands of trade union officials and into those of the unofficial shop stewards' movement. Governments, both of the Conservative and the Labour Party, were concerned to re-establish trade union control and responsibility and the issue of how to curb the increased level of strike activity became the prime concern of the Labour government which was returned in October 1964.

The Labour Governments, from 1964 to 1969

Harold Wilson, who became Labour's leader in 1963 on the death of Hugh Gaitskell, formed two Labour governments, in 1964 and 1966, the latter leaving office in June 1970. From an industrial point of view, however, his efforts to reform the industrial relations pattern of Britain lasted from 1964 to 1969, coming to an end with the publication and failure of the White Paper, *In Place of Strife* (1969). Wilson promised to use the latest scientific and technological know-how to solve Britain's economic problems but quickly found his efforts thwarted. It may well have been that the British economy was incapable of matching the task and that there was something fundamentally wrong with the structure of British industry. But many members of the Labour government, as well as the Conservative Party, began to question whether or not the real problem of the British economy was the widespread existence of unofficial strikes and restrictive practices together with the inflationary costs of collective bargaining. There were many subsidiary questions arising from this assumption that trade unions were to blame for Britain's poor economic performance. Should the government intervene in industrial relations or leave it to managers and trade unionists? If the government needed to intervene, what form of intervention should occur? The widespread public debate which emerged led to the most comprehensive examination of the pattern of British industrial relations for almost a century.

Immediately the Labour government assumed power it was faced with a serious balance of payments deficit, resulting from the Conservative government's push for economic expansion, and was forced to impose a 15 per cent surcharge on all imports except for food and raw materials. At the same time it was becoming abundantly clear that the real economic problem of Britain was the inefficient use of manpower meaning that British productivity was low and that wage increases, by comparison, were excessive. Therefore, the first action of the new Labour government was to work out with employers and trade unions a 'Joint Statement of Intent on Productivity, Prices and Incomes', signed in December 1964, to promote higher productivity and to facilitate close relations with a watch committee on prices and incomes, which became the National Board for Prices and Incomes (NBPI), chaired by the moderate Conservative ex-minister Aubrey Jones. In this document the government declared its intent to 'maintain a rapid rise in output and real incomes combined with full employment' and to prepare a 'general plan for economic development'.[42] George Brown, the First Secretary of State linked with the Ministry of Economic Affairs, eventually drew up a National Plan on the assumption that the economy would grow at 4 per cent per annum.

The basic machinery of the Labour government's more interventionist approach was in place and the norm for wage increases for 1965 was set in place at 3 to 3.5 per cent. But the real problem of dealing with the collective bargaining system had yet to be tackled.

From the start, the Labour government went out of its way to restore something of the old relationships that had existed between government and unions in the late 1940s. One of its early acts was in fact to introduce the Trade Disputes Act of 1965, to close the loophole in the 1906 Trade Disputes Act opened up by the Rookes v. Barnard case. This set the tone of the new cooperation which would permit the government to persuade trade unions to accept the need for a Royal Commission on Trade Unions and Employers' Associations. Trade union acceptance of this body relied upon the guarantee of a place on the commission for George Woodcock and the assumption that the body would not be unfriendly to the trade unions. The appointment of Lord Donovan, a former Labour MP, as chairman was crucial to building up the confidence of the unions. The commission was set up in April 1965 and eventually reported in June 1968. It was formed at a period of good relations between the Labour government and the trade unions but reported at a time when relations had deteriorated. Government policies between 1965 and 1968 had created serious tensions within the wider Labour movement.

There were difficulties over the government's intention to submit all wage claims and price increases to the NBPI. The new Labour government of March 1966, with its increased Labour majority, soon found its plans for wage restraint challenged by the seamen's strike of May to July 1966. The National Union of Seamen had let the wages and conditions of their members deteriorate compared with other workers and were demanding improved conditions at a time when the government was attempting to operate an incomes policy. In the end a compromise was arranged, under the strong pressure of the government, which faced a sterling crisis in July 1966, forcing it to deflate the economy and to introduce a six-month 'wage freeze'. But matters worsened considerably when George Brown got the Cabinet to approve his Prices and Incomes Bill, which required prospective price, wage and dividend increases to be announced in advance to the NBPI. This provoked Frank Cousins to leave the government and return to his post as secretary of the TGWU, leading his union into staunch opposition against compulsory wage bargaining. Driven on by the sterling crisis, the government pressed Brown's bill through Parliament and, faced with further wage demands, introduced a six-month 'wage freeze' in the autumn of 1966, to be followed by an equal period of 'severe restraint'.[43]

The TUC continued to advocate a voluntary wage system and was clearly on course to clash with a government whose concerns for the economy were heightened by the Six-Day War, which closed the Suez Canal, and other developments which adversely affected the British balance of payments. The government, therefore, replaced the standstill clauses of the Prices and Incomes Act, which lapsed in August 1967, with a new Act which allowed the delaying of a proposed wage increase for six months if the IBPI reported against the proposed increase. In 1968, after devaluation, the period was extended to one year. In addition, a ceiling of 3.5 per cent was imposed while the Act was in force. The chief way in which such levels of wage increases could be justified was through productivity agreements of which there were four thousand covering seven million workers by 1969. However, despite the intention of linking wages and productivity to control inflation, it is clear that this device permitted unions and management to negotiate pay deals above the level of inflation, a factor which Professor Hugh Clegg suggests was responsible for the wage explosion which began in 1969.[44]

The tone and scope of this legislation did not find approval among the trade union sponsored MPs and the Amalgamated Union of Engineering and Foundry Workers (the new amalgamation of the engineers and foundry workers) held a one-day stoppage in protest against the new powers. The conflict between government and the trade unions intensified when, in April 1968, Harold Wilson decided to replace Ray Gunter with Barbara Castle at the Ministry of Labour. Barbara Castle also took over the Department of Economic Affairs, which had responsibility for the incomes policy, and the Ministry of Labour now became known as the Department of Employment and Productivity, with Mrs Castle as Secretary of State and First Secretary.

The Donovan Commission thus reported in June 1968, into an atmosphere of mistrust and conflict between the unions and government. Its main recommendation was that the key to a better system of industrial relations lay in the reform and extension of collective bargaining by management initiative and trade union agreement.[45] Apparently, the overriding need was to reconstruct the framework of employee relations at the workplace level through individual management and trade union representatives. Therefore, it argued that industrial relations were unlikely to improve as a result of working between the formal institutions of trade unions and employers' organizations. In other words, shop-floor agreements in plants and factories had to replace industry-wide agreements, which often limited suitable procedures at plant and company level.[46] And, since trade unions were essentially democratic bodies whose power derived from the wishes of their local members, it was unrealistic to expect that they could act as a police force to impose the collective bargains which they had entered into on their behalf. In effect, the informal system developed around the shop stewards had to be fully incorporated into the new pattern of industrial relations. In consequence, it was argued that trade unions should be more concerned with minimum conditions of employment for the industry. The Donovan Report also maintained that these changes in collective bargaining arrangements could not be forced into being by legal enactment but only encouraged. It therefore advised the need to create an advisory body to be known as the Industrial Relations Commission and, in order to ensure that all employers recognized trade unions, the commission might be given powers to enforce arbitration where collective bargaining arrangements were absent.[47] In essence, it followed that there was no point in making unofficial strikes illegal, imposing 'cooling-off periods' and 'conciliation pauses'. Such actions simply ignored the problems that had led to disputes.

The Donovan Report was not well received. For some, its conclusions did not appear to be mindful of the evidence and reports which it had been presented with.[48] In the mid-1960s, the number of unofficial strikes was falling while the number of official disputes was rising which suggested that the analysis might be out of date. There was also an extremely uneven development of strike-proneness between industries. For instance, from 1957 the strike-proneness of the coal mining industry declined rapidly as that industry continued its long-term decline and as the creation of a standard wage replaced the pit-based incentive schemes. In other industries similar changes were also taking place. In other words, the whole pattern of unofficial strike activity was diminishing and changing in its distribution. Even in the engineering and car industries, where there had been an upsurge in strike activity, there was immense variation between Fords, where there were few but large strikes, and BMC, where strikes were frequent but small, at its Longbridge and Cowley plants, and Vauxhall which enjoyed more or less strike-free labour relations up to 1966. McCarthy, in his survey of workshop relations across a variety of industries, produced for the Donovan Commission, also played down the importance of strikes, which were often seen as part of the procedure of negotiation, and noted the exaggerations about the militancy of the shop stewards.[49] The gist of this criticism was that the strike problem was changing and that the importance of strikes in causing Britain's industrial problems had, in any case, been exaggerated.[50] Donovan, for many in the academic world, foundered on the shifting sands of industrial relations and the popular mythology about the extent to which strikes presented a problem to the British economy.

Others rejected the findings of the Donovan Commission for more partisan reasons. The trade union leaders were hesitant of losing power and influence. The public was increasingly encouraged, by the press, to gloat upon the chaos in British industrial relations. The Conservative Party wanted more state intervention. It had already published its policy statement, *Fair Deal at Work*, which suggested that collective bargaining agreements should be enforced by law, that a sixty-day 'conciliation pause' should be enforced before a strike could take place, and that strike calls should be subject to compulsory ballots. Even the Conservative Party, once committed to voluntary industrial relations, had come to accept the Labour Party's view of the need for firm state intervention in order to ensure industrial peace. But, above all, the Labour government was adamant that industrial relations had to be regulated immediately, and that there was no way in which collective bargaining arrangements could be settled in a piecemeal fashion over many years.

The Labour government, with no prominent trade unionist in the Cabinet and with Barbara Castle at the helm, plumped for a more interventionist approach and produced the White Paper, *In Place of Strife*, in January 1969. It ignored the main recommendations of the Donovan Commission and provoked the trade unions. Although it offered a number of advantages to trade unions, most notably the protection from 'unfair dismissal', they were sensitive to the suggestion that they would be registered and that their rights to strike action would be impaired. The White Paper suggested the need for a 'conciliation pause' for twenty-eight days, advocated that powers be given to the Secretary of State to impose a settlement on inter-union disputes, if such disputes could not be settled by the TUC or the Commission for Industrial Relations, and that the Secretary of State should have the power to order a strike ballot if that was deemed necessary. Thus the whole package suggested that trade unions would no longer be able to conduct industrial relations on the voluntary basis which they had enjoyed for almost a century in peacetime Britain. In consequence, the TUC held a special conference, mobilized its opposition to the White Paper, got the Trade Union Group in the House of Commons to vote against the measure in the Commons in March 1969, and even forced the NEC of the Labour Party to vote against its acceptance.

Frank Cousins and Hugh Scanlon, a left-winger who was by now president of the Engineers and Foundry Workers, ensured that George Woodcock and the TUC vented its opposition to the White Paper. In any case, Woodcock left the TUC to become chairman of the Commission on Industrial Relations, and was replaced by Vic Feather whose position could not be confirmed until the September annual Congress, thus leaving real power in the hands of Cousins and Scanlon.[51] Clearly, the trade union movement was not going to accept the White Paper. The Labour Party and the Labour government were faced with splits, as Harold Wilson and Barbara Castle refused to compromise on their proposals. Indeed, compromise did not seem possible until Vic Feather, an old Bradford friend of Barbara Castle (Betts), came up with a draft statement of the General Council entitled *Programme for Action*, which suggested that the TUC would be prepared to give its constituent unions 'opinion and advice'. The TUC's willingness to intervene was hardened at a special conference at Croydon in June 1969. This provided the basis upon which Robert Mellish managed to get Wilson, Castle and ministers to drop the White Paper at a Cabinet meeting on 17 June 1969, thus avoiding a potential split within the Labour Party.

The Labour Party had been humbled by the trade unions. In its desire to make British industry more efficient it had tackled an issue on which it could only lose. If it took action against strikes then it threatened the link between class, union and party. If, on the other hand, it did not face up to the problems of strikes then, to the electorate at large, it demonstrated its incapacity to govern and its unwillingness to move beyond sectional interests. Was the Labour Party to be a party of the unions or a party of the nation? The events surrounding the White Paper suggested that it might be neither. Its trade union support fell as did its credibility in the nation at large. The fragility of Labour's hopes and aspirations in the 1960s had been exposed both by its inability to achieve significant growth and to deal effectively with the trade unions. Consequently, Edward Heath's Conservative government replaced the Labour government in June 1970, inaugurating a period when trade union rights and practices came under even closer scrutiny.

The attack upon trade unions and strike activity in the 1960s obscured many of the improvements and developments that were occurring in trade unions. Trade unions, many of whose members had adopted racialist attitudes throughout their history,[52] declared their opposition to racialism and, ultimately, Jack Jones became chairman of the Community Relations Commission which was set up under the Race Relations Act of 1968. The movement broadened its similar attitude towards women, although the position of women within the trade union hierarchy continued to be weak. The structure of trade unionism began to change as traditionally powerful groups, such as the railwaymen and miners, whose membership fell between 40 and 46 per cent between 1959 and 1968, gave way to the rapidly developing white-collar unions, such as the National and Local Government Officers' Association and the National Union of Teachers, who joined the TUC in the 1960s and whose membership rose by about a third.[53]

There was also an attempt to improve the poor industrial relations in the docks. The Devlin Report (1966) argued that this situation had arisen from the lack of security, defects in management and the failure of the National Dock Labour Board scheme. Therefore, it maintained that the 'decasualisation' of dockers had been a disaster and that reforms should be brought to eliminate the insecurity of employment by the return to full-time contracts, and other reforms. However, these reforms did not work and it has been suggested that the move towards containerization and the changing pattern of trade might also help to explain the continued high level of strike activity in the docks.[54]

The trade unions also began to change and modernize in two other respects. In the first place, there was an increasing tendency to amalgamation, especially after the passing of the Trade Union

(Amalgamation) Act of 1964, whereby a simple majority in a ballot of each union concerned was required. In the 1960s the Engineers and Foundry Workers amalgamated, as did the Typographical Association and the London Typographical Association, to form the National Graphical Society. Indeed, during the years from 1962 to 1970 trade union membership increased from 9.9 million to 11 million and the number of trade unions fell from 626 to 538. The second development was the increasing move towards productivity agreements. As already indicated, there were about four thousand such agreements by 1969 affecting seven million workers, most of which had emerged in the wake of the Fawley refinery agreement at the Esso plant which negotiated two comprehensive productivity agreements between 1959 and 1963, abolishing overtime, reducing hours of work, raising output and wages, and increasing the flexibility of the workforce to new technologies.[55]

Conclusion

Recent writers have been correct to re-examine the whole issue of how one tackles trade union history. The 'rank and filist' debate is particularly appropriate in the context of trade union history for the years from 1940 to 1969, given that it has been perceived that the real industrial problem of Britain in this period has been the rise of unofficial strike action, which the Donovan Commission placed such store by in attempting to suggest how collective bargaining agreements could be made to work. At the same time, however, one must be aware that this concern may have been more relevant in the 1950s and early 1960s than in the late 1960s. Yet, the confrontational nature of the current debate does appear to be rather unnecessary since it must be apparent that a full study of post-war Labour history must take account of all sides of industrial relations now that the topic has been set firmly at the centre of the study of trade union history. It is no longer sufficient to look at TUC and trade union policy alone, and management strategies have been just as important as trade union objectives in the development of recent industrial relations, and may well explain the differing strike response in the car industry. In addition, the history of trade unions since 1970 has been littered with evidence of the way in which the national unions have come to the aid of local branches, a fact that is indicative of the way in which the power of trade unionism has, in any case, moved from the centre to the region and locality.

The issue of the post-war consensus is always a relative matter, for there is always evidence of conflict between government, trade unions and employers as well as strong indications of cooperation. Yet, on balance, Coalition, Labour and Conservative governments all sought to work with employers and trade unions from 1940 onwards and it was not until the economic problems of the late 1960s that that relationship was seriously challenged. Cooperation was the hallmark of trade unionism in this period, but since this was often of a general nature it seems unfair to suggest that trade union leaders were selling their members short. Trade union members had, in many instances, developed their own plant and factory arrangements. Consensus was only challenged when both the 1960s Labour governments and the Tory Party began to see the need to legally enforce collective agreements and to interfere in the pattern of voluntary collective bargaining when faced with the intensification of foreign competition and a worsening balance of payments situation.

On strikes and the trade union relationship with the Labour Party several points could be made. In the first case, the apparent breakdown of industrial relations in the mid- and late 1960s promoted the impression that Britain was strike-prone, but strikes generally formed a small proportion of the days lost at work and may deflect attention from other factors which might be more appropriate as explanations of Britain's relative industrial decline. Secondly, the trade unions worked closely with the Labour Party, although it is obvious, from the events of that time, that a Labour government could in no sense be regarded as the tool of the trade unions.

There is no doubt that the trade union movement was on the defensive by 1970. The defeat of *In Place of Strife* obviously contributed to Labour's defeat in the 1970 general election and paved the way for a new era of industrial relations in which the Conservative demand for a *Fair deal at Work* became paramount.

NOTES

1. K. Middlemass, *Politics in Industrial Society: The Experience of the British System since 1911* (Deutsch, 1979).

2. J. Zeitlin, ' "Rank and filism" in British Labour history: a critique', *International Review of Social History*, 34, 1989, p. 45.

3. *Ibid.*, also J. Zeitlin ' "Rank and filism" and labour history: a rejoinder to Price and Cronin', *International Review of Social History*, 34, 1989.

4. J.E. Cronin, ' "The rank and file" and the social history of the working class', *International Review of Social History*, 34, 1989. In the same volume are R. Hyman, 'The sound of one hand clapping: a comment on the "rank and file" debate' and R. Price, 'What's in a name? Workplace history and the "rank and file"'.

5. R. Price, *Labour in British Society* (Croom Helm, 1986), chapter 8.

6. General Council of the Trades Union Congress, *Interim Report on Post-War Reconstruction, 1944* (TUC, 1944).

7. PRO, Cab. 31 (45), 13 September 1945.

8. PRO, Cab. 66 (49), 14 November 1949.

9. H. Pelling, *A History of British Trade Unionism* (Penguin, 4th edn., 1988), pp. 217–20.

10. P. Weiler, 'British Labour and the Cold War: The London Dock Strike of 1949', *Social Conflict and the Political Order in Modern Britain* (Croom Helm, 1982).

11. *Parliamentary Debates*, Commons, 5th Series, 28 June 1949, 466: 982.

12. *Ibid.*, 8 July 1949, 466: 2593.

13. TUC, *Annual Report*, 1949, p. 325.

14. Weiler, *op.cit.*, p. 156.

15. *Ibid.*, p. 163, quoting *Parliamentary Papers*, 1950–1, vol. xvi, cmd 8236, 'Unofficial Stoppages in the London Docks: Report of a Committee of Inquiry', p. 13.

16. PRO, Cab. 22 (50), 20 April 1950.

17. *Ibid.*, Cab. 124, 1196.

18. *Ibid.*, Cab. 124, 1196.

19. *Ibid.*, Cab. 124, 1194.

20. *Ibid.*, Cab. 124, 1196, letter to Lord President, 4 November 1950.

21. *Ibid.*, Cab. 124, 1196, Restrictive Note to Prime Minister, 21 November 1950.

22. *Ibid.*, Cab. 124, 1196, letter from E.M. Nicholson to the Lord President, 25 November 1950.

23. *Ibid.*, Cab. 124, 1196, letter from George Isaacs, 13 December 1950.

24. J.W. Durcan, W.E.J. McCarthy and G.P. Redman, *Strikes in Post-War Britain: A Study of Stoppages of work due to industrial stoppages, 1946–73* (George Allen & Unwin, 1983). Also look at K.C.G. Knowles, *Strikes: A Study of Industrial Conflict* (Oxford, 1952) and P.S. Bagwell, *The Railwaymen* (1962).

25. *Ibid.*, p. 26.

26. PRO, Cab. 124, 1194, dealing with Labour's industrial relations record 1946–50.

27. Quoted in R. Price, *Labour in British Society: An Interpretative History* (Croom Helm, 1986), p. 218.

28. Durcan, McCarthy and Redman, *op.cit.*, pp. 26, 59.

29. *Ibid.*, pp. 28, 59, 93, 133.

30. *Ibid.*, pp. 305–8.
31. *Ibid.*, pp. 281–6.
32. Weiler, *op.cit.*, p. 167.
33. H.A. Turner, G. Clack and R. Roberts, *Labour Relations in the Motor Industry* (George Allen and Unwin, 1967).
34. Durcan, McCarthy and Redman, *op.cit.*, p. 325.
35. *Ibid.*, p. 349.
36. Price, *Labour*, pp. 216–17.
37. *Ibid.*, p. 217.
38. Durcan, McCarthy and Redman, *op.cit.*, p. 315.
39. K. Hawkins, *British Industrial Relations, 1945–1975* (Barrie and Jenkins, 1976), p. 40.
40. TUC, *Annual Report*, 1959, p. 398, motion 38 and p. 415, motion 43.
41. *A Message from Hugh Gaitskell to trade unionists, 1959* (Labour Party, 1959).
42. *Parliamentary Debates*, Commons, 5th Series, 704: 385–8.
43. Hawkins, *op.cit.*, pp. 65–6.
44. H. Clegg, *How to Run an Incomes Policy* (Heinemann, 1971) pp. 61–7.
45. Royal Commission on Trade Unions and Employers' Associations, 1965–8, *Report* (HMSO, Cmnd 3623, 1968).
46. *Ibid.*, para. 191.
47. *Ibid.*, para. 201.
48. Hawkins, *op.cit.*, pp. 71–8.
49. Royal Commission, Research paper No. 10, *Shop Stewards and Workshop Relations*, W.E.J. McCarthy and S.R. Parker (HMSO, 1967).
50. H.A. Turner, *Is Britain really Strike-Prone?* (Cambridge, Occasional Papers, CUP, 1969).
51. *Ibid.*, pp. 81–4.
52. K. Lunn, 'Immigration and British Labour's Response', *History Today*, xxxv, 1985.
53. G.S. Bain, *The Growth of White-Collar Unionism* (Oxford, 1970).
54. Durcan, McCarthy and Redman, *op.cit.*, pp. 281–8.
55. Hawkins, *op.cit.*, p. 62.

CHAPTER SEVEN

THE CHALLENGE TO TRADE UNIONISM AND ITS DECLINE IN THE 'THATCHER YEARS' c. 1970–90

Since 1970 the trade union movement has been on the defensive. Throughout the 1970s it was taken aback by the determination of both Conservative and Labour governments alike to instil some type of discipline into the pattern of industrial relations, but it retained a degree of influence despite the fact that the 'Winter of Discontent' of 1979 turned much of the British public against trade unions. But it was less effective in fending off such a challenge in the 1980s, when the declining position of Britain in world trade and the consequent mass unemployment eroded both union membership and economic power. The problems were compounded by the determination of the Thatcher administrations to reduce the power of trade unions and to set them within a balanced framework of rights and obligations framed in eight acts, six of them specifically designed to deal with trade unions on issues such as the closed shop and strike ballots. The challenges of the 1980s have undoubtedly altered the strength, position and attitudes of British trade unionism. They have forced unions to work with the new arrangements, in what has been referred to as the 'new realism', in an age when the old consensus has disappeared. They have forced some modifications in the balance of power between trade unions and the Labour Party, and helped to change the relationship between the trade union centre and its regional and local branches. Indeed, it could be argued that just as the national trade unions are being asked to discipline their members more effectively, and to develop their bureaucracy further, the extension of democratic rights into collective bargaining have given their members more scope for ignoring the demands of union bureaucracy. In effect, much of the power which trade unions sedulously accumulated after the Second World War has been stripped away and trade unions are currently less confrontational than they have been in the past.

Thus, for the last twenty years trade unions have been buffeted by the government, employers and the public to follow a new course and to adopt new strategies. From the multitude of arguments which have gone on, it is clear that most writers feel that the trade union movement has adapted to the exigent needs of the moment in order to survive and, as yet, has not found itself a new role. To the left, compromise with the Conservative government's demands has been seen as some form of betrayal of the membership and that the movement needs to find a new crusade in order to protect jobs, peace and democracy.[1] To the right, compromise has been evidence of the essential need of the trade union movement to adapt to change. Consequently, debates about its history over the last twenty years have been rife, and numerous questions have been asked. For instance, how has the trade union relationship with government altered in recent years? How and why has trade union power diminished so markedly? Have the 'rank and file' assumed more importance? Has trade union bureaucracy led to tensions with the membership? To what extent have trade unions accommodated themselves to government policies? How has the decline of the trade union movement, and the internal conflicts within the wider Labour movement in the late 1970s, affected the position of trade unions *vis à vis* the Labour Party? To what extent was the miners' strike of 1984–5 a turning point in the attitudes of the trade union movement in dealing with the government? Such questions as these have led to many bitter debates.

The 'rank and file' debate was referred to in the previous chapter. In essence, it revolves around the extent to which trade unions and their members are in tune with one another – one school of thought emphasizing the integration of the union bureaucracy with the members, the other schools noting the rank and file's exercise of union democracy. Related to this has been the debate about union bureaucracy; was it a product of the conflict between trade union leaders and the rank and file or should it be regarded as an evolving social relationship which develops at all levels within a union, and, indeed, out of conflict?[2] There has also been a third debate on the resilience of trade unions throughout this period. Contrary to popular opinion, it has recently been argued that the trade unions have survived the 1980s remarkably intact, their financial position remaining viable and their workplace strength largely unimpaired. Indeed, some historians have argued that local management continues to seek the support and cooperation of the local union leadership.[3] And certainly there is evidence that trade unions and the TUC have modified their attitudes towards the new legislation since about 1987.

The evolution of trade unionism over the last twenty years has been subjected to extensive academic debate. This might pre-occupy the minds of historians, political scientists and sociologists, but the fine detail of debate is less relevant to those who are primarily concerned with the fundamental question of why trade unionism has declined and can anything be done to arrest this trend? On balance, as R.J. Price has implied, there is nothing inevitable in the trajectory of labour history and the changing industrial and political environment greatly determines the effectiveness of trade unionism.[4] Consequently, the worsening economic situation of Britain, the spectre of mass unemployment, and the resolve of governments to encourage 'responsible' and 'democratic' trade unionism, which may be contradictory terms, have undermined the position of trade unions. If unions impose settlements they may lose the support of their members but, if their members take action in their own right, legislation may exist to prevent union leaders imposing discipline. In short, trade unions are unable to win in the present climate, for the odds are stacked against them. But even the return of a new Labour government may not change the situation greatly since Labour governments have always claimed to be, and often acted, independently of trade unions and even the Labour Party has moved to reduce the direct influence of the trade union movement. Faced with less power, trade unions will either become more democratic or more bureaucratic in the 1990s. The one thing that is sure is that trade unionism has undergone a more rapid change in its organ-ization, philosophy and attitude towards other bodies than it has faced for more than a century. Out of this re-appraisal of its position, and the evolving nature of trade union organization, there may emerge a movement which, even if it cannot recapture the influence it exerted in the 1950s and 1960s can still exert considerable influence upon the British pattern of industrial re-lations and force governments to take account of the demands and needs of its members.

The Conservatives and the Industrial Relations Act, 1970–4

In 1970 and 1971 the trade union movement reaped the whirlwind of its furious opposition to *In Place of Strife*. Faced with continued industrial unrest, and the doubts that a Labour government could deliver the goods on the need for industrial peace, the British electorate returned Edward Heath's Conservative government in June 1970, which immediately resolved to put some legal teeth into industrial relations. The outline of its new approach appeared in a consultative document in October 1970 and the Industrial Relations Bill became law in 1971. It established the National Industrial Relations Court (NIRC), which was to have jurisdiction over most industrial disputes, could advise the Secretary for Employment to impose a 'cooling-off period' in industrial disputes and require a ballot in cases where strike action would be a serious threat to the economy. The Court could also impose fines of from £5,000 to £100,000, according to membership, on unions that undertook 'unfair industrial practices', and the closed shop became an issue of some importance. The rights of individuals to belong or not to belong to a union were emphasized, and they could not be forced to join a union before entering employment, the pre-entry closed shop. The post-entry closed shop was replaced by the idea of an 'agency shop', as a result of which a union could obtain sole bargaining rights if it secured the agreement of the employer or won the support of a majority of workers in a secret ballot. Written collective agreements, unless they contained clauses to the contrary, were to be legally binding and the union could face prosecution through the NIRC if they did not prevent the breach of the agreement. The trade unions were also expected to register with a new Registrar of Trade Unions and Employers' Associations, whereby workers sacked unfairly could claim compensation, and unions could force employers to recognize them through NIRC.

The underlying assumption of the Act was that unofficial strikes represented the major weakness of British industrial relations, a dubious suggestion as previously noted. It was also assumed that union officials were failing to control their shop stewards. Consequently, it was decided that trade unionists were abusing their freedom to strike in breach of voluntary agreements. The right to strike had, therefore, to be limited by the Industrial Relations Act.

Inevitably, the trade unions objected to this challenge to the voluntary system of industrial relations which they so much preferred. As the bill was going through Parliament, the General Council of the TUC held regional conferences and two special rallies in London. On 21 February 1971, there was a march through London from Hyde Park to Trafalgar Square. There was a national petition against the intended act and the General Council called a Special Congress at Croydon on 18 March. The main decisions of the conferences were that unions were strongly advised not to become registered and to boycott the NIRC and the already established Commission on Industrial Relations, from which George Woodcock, the former TUC General Secretary, resigned. Once the bill became law, the Labour Party pledged to repeal it.

By the end of 1971 the General Council was instructing its member unions not to register and, indeed, to de-register. Nevertheless, thirty-two unions remained registered, to obtain tax advantages and to comply with their own rules, and, as a result, they and their half a million members were suspended at the 1972 TUC Congress. Twenty of these, including the British Air Line Pilot's Association and the National Union of Bank Employees, remained registered and were eventually expelled from the TUC in 1973.

Without union registration and union recognition of the NIRC, there was little real prospect of the 1971 Industrial Relations Act establishing the more peaceful industrial conditions which the Conservative government was aiming to promote. Indeed, the very presence of the new industrial relations machinery provoked conflict. The real problem was the NIRC, presided over by Sir John Donaldson. Most unions refused to put their case to the Court. Their presence was often assumed rather than real. The Transport Workers were brought to the Court by Samuel Heaton, who maintained that they were 'blacking' his container lorries. The NIRC held the union to be responsible for its shop stewards since the latter were acting with the union's implied authority. Donaldson based his judgement upon the handbook of the Transport and General Workers' Union, which contained a section stating that:

> As a shop steward there is no doubt that the eyes of the members in your shop are upon you. You are the union as far as they are concerned. You should therefore conform to the union policy as laid down in the branch and, as required, report to the branch on your activity. In dealing with many of your problems the union will expect you to be able to manage on your own. If you cannot, you know you have the power and resources of the TGWU behind you.[5]

The TGWU was instructed to end the 'blacking' of Heaton's lorries but refused to comply and was fined £5,000 and a further £50,000 for its continued refusal. The TGWU won its case in the Court of Appeal, which decided that a union was not liable for its shop stewards when they acted outside the scope of the authority delegated to them. But when the case went to the House of Lords, Donaldson's decision was confirmed.

Other cases followed along a similar line. Maurice Macmillan, the new Secretary for Employment, asked the NIRC to impose a twenty-one day 'cooling-off period', when the railway unions decided to 'work-to-rule' in pursuit of an increased pay offer. The Court responded by imposing a fourteen-day 'cooling-off period', after which Macmillan asked the Court to impose a secret ballot on the members of the union. This ballot revealed that the union members were divided six to one in favour of the policy of the union leadership – 130,000 to 24,000. As a result the unions were in a stronger position than before, and the government refrained from using the 'cooling-off period' and the union ballot again.

The Act was clearly ineffective; the vast majority of trade unions did not register, the NIRC was being ignored, the 'cooling-off period' was ineffective and the strike ballot simply played into the hand of the unions, whose members rallied to their leaders. The weakness of the whole fabric of the Act was further exposed by the problems on the docks which led to the case of the 'Pentonville Five'. This arose in July 1972 when the NIRC ordered dockers to stop 'blacking' vehicles using the Midland Cold Storage Company depot at Stratford in East London. When the dockers refused the order, five of them were arrested and gaoled, actions which resulted in a national strike of 170,000 dockers. The 'Pentonville Five' were released after only two days and, as Richard Barber has written, 'No sooner were the dockers in Pentonville than the Official Solicitor appeared like a fairy godmother to "spring" them from jail and in the process deal the Act a mortal blow.'[6]

Non-cooperation with the Act and the Court continued and, as Barber implied, the whole act was effectively dead by 1972. It was a failed experiment which had not addressed the real problems of trade unions and industrial relations. As Table 6 (see page 201) indicates, the number of disputes increased after 1971 as did the number of working days lost, which reached almost twenty-four million in 1972. In the same year, Paul Ferris suggested that moderate unions would have to compromise with the government to avoid a disaster and that 'Compromises must lie ahead for all parties.'[7] In the final analysis the unions did not compromise and made the legislation redundant.

Despite the active resistance directed against the 1971 Act, many of the important industrial conflicts of this period arose from the normal pattern of wage demands. The Post Office workers went on strike in early 1971 and, although forced back to work, managed to secure a wage increase of 9 per cent, which was below the going rate at the time thus setting a maximum figure for the public sector. But the major problem faced by the Heath government was how to deal with the miners. In January and February 1972, the miners called their first official strike since 1926. They were demanding an increase of £9 per week for underground workers, £8 for surface workers and £5 for face workers. The Coal Board replied with £1.75 (8 per cent) on all basic rates, an offer which led miners to picket the power stations. Arthur Scargill, who organized an unofficial strike committee in Barnsley, masterminded the action which led to the eventual closure of the Saltley power station in Birmingham, where considerable violence occurred between the police and the pickets.[8]

A state of emergency was declared, black-outs began from 11 February and about one million workers were laid off from 14 February. There was a three-day week in industry and eventually Lord Wilberforce was appointed to head a Court of Inquiry into the miners' claim. Wilberforce gave the miners most of what they asked for – £6 per week for underground workers, £5 for surface workers and £4.50 for face workers – and direct discussions with the Prime Minister secured further gains.

The victory of the miners had major consequences for the government's attempts to impose some type of incomes policy. Although the Conservative Party had been disdainful of Labour's attempts at imposing a compulsory incomes policy, and had abandoned the Prices and Incomes Policy in 1972, it reversed its policy by imposing a ninety-day standstill on prices, dividends and rents towards the end of 1972 to be followed by the enforcement of strict controls with a Price Commission and a Pay Board from April 1973. Later that year, a third stage was to be introduced whereby a limit of 7 per cent on wage increases was imposed, with allowances to be made for 'unsocial hours' and threshold agreements to allow for the cost of living until November 1973. This created further tensions in industrial relations when the miners claimed a wage increase far in excess of the government's limits. Anticipating a long conflict with the miners, and faced with an impending conflict with the power workers and the quadrupling of Arabian oil prices, the government began its 'Switch off Something' campaign in December 1973, also enforcing a speed limit of 50 miles per hour and a heat limit of 63°F. The government also introduced a three-day week from 31 December 1973. After a ballot, held under the rules of the National Union of Mineworkers, a strike was called for 10 February 1974 but this was overtaken by the government's decision to call a general election for 28 February 1974. The return of a minority Labour government brought to an end the sad shambles of the Conservative government's industrial strategy. That policy had failed to recognize the problems of British industrial relations, for it had challenged the voluntary system of collective bargaining without providing evidence of tangible benefits for the majority of British workers. The new Labour government aimed to proceed by a voluntary arrangement with the unions, the 'Social Contract', but unable to meet its part of the bargain found that its efforts to resolve the industrial problems of Britain were as equally ineffective as those of the Conservative government.

The Labour Governments 1974–9

The Labour Party had narrowly won the election on the basis of its manifesto *Get Britain Back to Work*, in which it announced a new round of nationalization and urged the generous treatment of the miners' claim. The manifesto also referred to a new arrangement with the trade unions, the 'Social Contract'. It was hoped that this new arrangement, which had been evolving since 1972, would remove the damaging impression that the Labour Party could not deal with the unions. Although our picture of the events which led to the introduction of this policy may not be complete until government records become available next century, the records of the TUC, diaries and other accounts have been used to demonstrate the failure of this policy.

The fact is that the Labour governments, formed in March 1974 and October 1974, after two general elections, were never able to sustain economic growth, partly because of the difficulties they faced in dealing with industrial relations. This was not from a lack of hope and good intent from the Labour party and the trade union movement. Wilson appealed for the unions to accept 'the economic realities and understand the political responsibilities we face in government'.[9] Trade unions were quick to respond and even the normally cautious Hugh Scanlon of the Amalgamated Union of Engineering Workers acknowledged the need for unity: 'There had been too much blood letting, too much acrimony, too much disillusionment – and trade unions were not blameless for this – with all the harmful effects that accrued in June 1970, for these mistakes ever to be repeated again.'[10]

The Labour Party and the TUC moved towards *rapprochement* when the 1973 party conference at Blackpool accepted the Labour Party's *Programme for Britain*, which stated that once rid of the Tory legislation 'we can begin to implement our programme of voluntary industrial relations reform, with the co-operation of trade unions'.[11] Such an arrangement depended upon economic growth, a healthy balance of payments and a willingness by the trade unions to accept a voluntary incomes policy. The Labour programme accepted that:

> there is a need for a far-reaching *social contract* between workers and the government — a contract that can be renewed each year as the circumstances change and as new opportunities present themselves.[12]

The Blackpool resolution accepting this policy had, however, been foreshadowed by the TUC–Labour Party Liaison Committee whose policy statement, *Economic Policy and the Cost of Living*, had advocated such a voluntary policy.[13] And the Labour Party announced the 'Social Contract' in the widest sense to the public in its election pamphlet *Britain Will Win with Labour*.[14] Such accord was short-lived once Labour was in office. At first, it appeared that the government was attempting to make it work when compulsory wage restraint imposed by Heath's government was jettisoned in July 1974, a new Ministry of Prices and Consumer Protection and Fair Trading was established, and food subsidies were introduced in Denis Healey's first budget. The Industrial Relations Act was repealed and, with it, the NIRA was abolished in July 1974. The miners' strike was also settled more or less on their terms, although Stage III of the Conservative government's incomes policy, with its threshold policy, was briefly retained. As Barbara Castle suggested, in her published diaries, the Cabinet and Wilson were intent upon playing it straight down the line of agreed policy, at least until the spring of 1975 when inflationary pressures became too great.[15] But Castle rightly perceived that there would be penalties to pay in adopting a voluntary policy at a time of balance of payments difficulties.

Coates, Taylor, Holmes and other writers of both the left and the right, have traced the decline of the 'Social Contract'.[16] They all agree that it occurred quickly. A. Taylor suggests that it effectively broke down in July 1975 when the £6 wage rise limit, with zero increase for those above £8,500 per annum, was imposed. David Coates suggests that it lasted a little bit longer but that it more or less ceased to be meaningful by 1977:

> When the government had reached the point, as it had in the summer of 1977, of publicly leaving the design of the next stage of the incomes policy to the TUC, only to find the TUC unwilling and unable to cooperate in this way, it is hardly surprising that people like Professor S.E. Finer could begin 'to wonder whether free collective bargaining [was] still compatible with the traditional practices of parliamentary democracy . . . and to wonder what, if this [was] the case, parliamentary democracy [could] do about it'.[17]

Whichever view is taken, it is clear that the process of breakdown had begun early in the life of the 1970s governments.

The reasons for the Labour government's failure to achieve economic growth against a background of rising unemployment and inflation had forced it to abandon its promises of increasing public control over private industry and of extending and improving social welfare measures. Unemployment rose from 678,000 to 1,129,000 during the course of 1975, at a time of rising inflation. The government panicked and, as early as April 1975, introduced an austerity budget which transferred resources from the public to the private sector, reducing public expenditure for 1977–8 by £900 million, at the expense of about 20,000 jobs. This was followed by a £6 wage increase limit in July 1975. This arose partly as a result of a suggestion for flat-rate increases suggested by Jack Jones, secretary of the TGWU, and accepted by the General Council of the TUC in June 1975. The TUC conference approved of the measure in September 1975. But the Labour government had returned to an old-style incomes policy and matters grew worse when Denis Healey, the Chancellor of the Exchequer, was forced to approach the International Monetary Fund (IMF) to secure a massive loan of £1,000 million and £700 million standby credit in December 1975. When the deal was struck, the Labour government was faced with the necessity of pruning government expenditure and in December 1976 it needed to cut £2,500 million in order to secure a further loan of £3,000 million from the IMF. The Labour government was forced to abandon any idea of extending public control, a position enforced by its political arrangement with the Liberal Party in 1977.

Almost inevitably, industrial relations grew worse, although the TUC agreed to Stage II of Healey's pay policy in 1976, whereby tax reductions would be offered in return for an agreement that wages would be raised by only 5 per cent, with a £4 ceiling and a £3.50 minimum. Yet it was not until the autumn of 1978 that the TUC formally decided to return to free collective bargaining and rejected totally any wage restraint.[18] In a climate of rising unemployment and reduced public expenditure, industrial unrest rocketed in the autumn of 1978 and early 1979 and the 'Winter of Discontent' put paid to any hopes that Labour had of winning the 1979 General Election.

It is Taylor's view that the débâcle of the 'Social Contract', and its obvious collapse in the 'Winter of Discontent' was predictable, and hence avoidable. It happened, none the less, because of the failure of both the trade unions and the Labour government to realize the extent to which their fates were inextricably linked up with the need to achieve an understanding which would stimulate economic growth. This seems a realistic assessment of the 1970s Labour governments, especially given the swift abandonment of their commitment to the 'Social Contract'. These governments expected the benefits of trade union cooperation without accepting the responsibilities which that involved. Yet, their record of defeat was hardly exceptional, for apart from the governments of 1945–51, the record of Labour governments has shown an enormous gap between promise and performance. Indeed, the Labour governments of the 1960s and '70s failed to encourage rapid economic growth, did not deliver their promises and found themselves embroiled in conflict with the unions.

The trade unions had in fact delivered their side of the bargain. Wage increases were much lower than price inflation, and they had shown a determination to try to work with the government to overcome the economic problems which the nation faced. Also, as Table 6 reveals, the years between 1974 and 1978 had seen a lull in strike activity. Yet there had been earlier signs of unrest, largely

Table 6 *Strikes, 1970–81*[19]

Year	No. of strikes		No. of workers involved (000s)		No. of working days lost (000s)	
	Net	Gross	Net	Gross	Net	Gross
1970	3,746	3,906	1,683.2	1,801	9,890	10,980
1971	2,093	2,228	1,155.4	1,178	13,488	13,551
1972	2,273	2,497	1,392.9	1,734	13,111	23,909
1973	2,572	2,873	1,148.0	1,528	7,107	7,197
1974		2,922		1,161		14,750
1975		2,282		570		6,012
1976		2,016		444		3,284
1977		2,703		785		10,142
1978		2,471		725		9,405
1979		2,080		4,121		29,474
1980		1,330		702		11,964
1981		1,338		1,326		4,266

connected with the refusal of employers to recognize the trade unions. The most famous of these was the Grunwick strike of 1976.

Grunwick was a mail order film-processing laboratory in Willesden, which did not have the benefit of new equipment. In order to compete, it employed a predominantly black and female labour force as casual labour. The pay was low, the workforce was compelled to work overtime and the employers denied any right to unionization. On 20 August 1976 the workers walked out after the management refused to accept unionization. Eventually, on 2 September 1976, the management locked out 137 of the workforce who had attempted to join the Association of Professional, Executive, Clerical and Computer Staff (APEX). The locked-out workers responded by picketing, an action which was mainly conducted by Asian women, although for four days the Post Office workers refused to handle the Grunwick mail, until there was a threat of a High Court injunction. The management attempted, unsuccessfully, to gain a High Court injunction to stop the strikers picketing retail outlets, such as chemist shops, and Jayaben Desai (one of the strike leaders) was arrested in an exchange with George Ward, the managing director, who took out a private summons for assault. However, the quashing of other summonses against six strikers and the award of £3,500 against the police for wrongful arrest raised the morale of the strikers. But a Court of Inquiry, chaired by Lord Scarman, which recommended the reinstatement of the strikers, was ignored by the management and a conciliation report recommending union recognition was declared null and void by the House of Lords. Even under a Labour government it appeared that trade unions would find the law fighting against their interests.

The change of trade union leaders also brought about a less amenable attitude to the continuance of the 'Social Contract'. Jack Jones, of the TGWU, was replaced by Moss Evans, and Hugh Scanlon, of the Engineers, was replaced by Terry Duffy. Neither of the new leaders appear to have expressed much support for the 'Social Contract' and Len Murray, general secretary of the TUC, lacked the authority to do so. With its collapse, trade unions began to re-assert their right to demand wage increases, without constraint, from the end of 1978 and through the winter months of 1979.

The 'Winter of Discontent' began on 24 August 1979 with the Ford car workers putting forward a claim for a £20 per week increase and a 35-hour week, amounting to an overall claim of 25 per cent.

They were only offered a 5 per cent increase and on 22 September they struck work. Four days later, the AUEW made the strike official, as did the TGWU on 5 October. After a nine-week strike the Ford workers accepted a 16.5 per cent wage increase. Other unions followed suit. In January (1–14) 1979, twenty thousand railwaymen held four one-day strikes. There were strikes by haulage drivers and petrol tanker drivers. The former settled for 25 to 20 per cent and the latter for 15 per cent. Secondary pickets at the docks were accused of attempting to starve the country. On 22 January 1979, 1,250,000 local authority workers organized a one-day national strike. The most notorious incident which the press picked up on was the grave-diggers' strike on Merseyside. A casual remark by a councillor hit the headlines as 'Burial at Sea', and conjured up the image of the dead not being buried. The strike action, by poorly paid, essential workers such as grave diggers, school caretakers and the refuse collectors, was widely supported. As the crisis deepened, however, and with a hostile media projecting a scenario of death and illness, public opinion moved against the strikers. Indeed, Shirley Williams, the Education Secretary, fuelled this image when she stated that:

> Tomorrow, many children will not be able to attend [school] because of the caretakers' strike, coupled with the appalling threat from some NUPE officials that children will be physically stopped from crossing the picket line.[20]

Despite the fact that none of the anticipated disasters occurred, the strikers were identified and pilloried as 'folk devils'. And the Labour government had demonstrated that it was no more successful in dealing with the unions than the Conservatives had been. Not surprisingly, Margaret Thatcher was returned as leader of a Conservative government in the General Election of May 1979, and formed three administrations which were to fundamentally weaken the position of British trade unions.

The 'Thatcher Years', 1979–90

Between 1979 and 1990 the Conservative government introduced eight acts, including the Wages Act of 1986 and the Public Order Act of 1986, which have brought about a radical change to the employment laws of Britain and thrown trade unions on to the defensive. The introduction of new legislation designed to make trade unions more accountable was central to the new government's economic philosophy which aimed to deregulate and 'free' the economy from constraints in order to achieve the economic renaissance of Britain. In other words, the attack upon trade union power was part of the process of rolling back the modern welfare state and the state control which was perceived to be the cause of Britain's post-war economic decline. Such a sea-change in government policies meant that the old tripartite relationship between government, trade unions and employers, the 'old consensus', was dead. Yet such a change was not surprising given the events which led to the defeat of Heath's Conservative government in 1974 and the reaction to the 'Winter of Discontent' of 1979. Such events allowed the fringe of Conservative thinking of the 1970s to occupy the centre-stage of industrial policy throughout the 1980s.

With their defeat in the 1974 general election, many Conservatives had begun to feel that they could not operate an economic policy without the consent of the trade unions. This was not a view endorsed by the Bow Group, a small fringe body, which advocated a far more aggressive attitude towards trade unions based upon outlawing the closed shop, making postal ballots mandatory for union officials and forcing trade unions to face up to the economic consequences of their actions. With the emergence of Thatcher as the Conservative leader and the events surrounding the 'Winter of Discontent', it is not surprising that these fringe ideas became more important. In a general sense, these policies formed the framework of the attack upon trade unions which has been the central tenet of the Thatcher years: demanding a greater accountability from trade unions by requesting that they should seek approval for strike action through secret ballots; making secondary action illegal; and by imposing fines and the sequestration of the funds of those unions which ignored the courts. The Employment Acts of 1980, 1982, 1988, 1989 and 1990 and the Trade Union Act of 1984 have imposed these Conservative policies in a step-by-step approach. To the Thatcher administrations these acts have ensured that all workers have basic rights in dealing with trade unions, but to trade unionists they have seemed quite otherwise — appearing to remove basic rights from employees under the banner of deregulation and the 'freeing' of the markets. Consequently, trade unions and government were in constant conflict throughout the 1980s, in dispute over the requirements of new legislation but also over the Conservatives' new economic experiment which has changed the character of state intervention by imposing monetarist policies, with their cash limits acting as an alternative to a formal incomes policy.

Initially, James Prior, the Secretary of Employment, was given the task of paving the way for the Conservative government's legislative programme on employment and trade unionism. In July 1979, he issued a consultative document which called for the limitation of picketing to the employees involved in the dispute and to their place of work. In addition, it advocated the extension of exemptions from the closed shop and declared an interest in providing public funds for secret ballots before strikes and for the election of full-time trade union officers. These recommendations formed the basis of the 1980 Employment Act which introduced a limited definition of lawful picketing, made secondary action illegal, required an 80 per cent ballot for a closed shop, offered unions funds to hold ballots and allowed people to become members of trade unions and not to be unreasonably expelled from them. The trade unions were powerless to resist this Act when faced with rapidly rising unemployment and the patchy response to its 'Day of Action' on 14 May 1980.

Yet, the legislation did not go far enough for the Conservatives on the thorny question of the 'closed shop'. When Norman Tebbit replaced James Prior, as Secretary for Employment in 1981, he extended the restriction on trade unions through the 1982 Employment Act, which banned the pre-entry closed shops, only permitted closed shops if 85 per cent of those voting favoured them, provided compensation for dismissals due to a closed-shop arrangement operating, and gave employers the right to take action for damages against trade unions. Tebbit was also concerned to control the provision of trade union funds for political purposes. Through a Green Paper, entitled *Democracy in Trade Unions* and the 1984 Trade Union Act, Tebbit initiated a policy which was eventually implemented by Tom King, Tebbit's successor. The 'Beloff' amendment, passed in the House of Lords, emphasized the need for postal ballots as the normal and primary way of conducting elections, with workplace ballots as a second possible method but subject to strict safeguards. Legal immunities were offered to trade unions as long as they held secret ballots not more than four weeks before industrial action. The 1984 Trade Union Act also made executive committee elections by ballot compulsory every five years, introduced ballots on political funds and before industrial action could be called.

There were many important issues here but the largest concern arose from the government's attempt to control trade unions providing funds for the Labour Party. Trade unions saw this action to be a direct attack upon the financial link between the trade unions and the Labour Party and to smack of unfairness since no equivalent limits were to be expected of companies providing funds for the Conservative Party. On the other hand, Norman Tebbit argued that 'The present members of trade unions should not be bound for ever by a ballot that may well have been taken before any of them were born.'[21]

Derek Fatchett, Ken Coates and Tony Topham have examined this attempt to control political funds.[22] Fatchett's main theme is that while the 1984 Trade Union Act made the continuation of trade union political funds conditional upon the members' approval, exercised through secret ballots, in 1985 and 1986 these ballots demonstrated, overwhelmingly, that trade union members were still committed to providing political funds for the Labour Party. He argues that the government saw the ballot as an attractive way of depriving the Labour Party of funds. Of course, a mass rejection of the political fund being paid to the Labour Party could have been extremely damaging as, according to the Labour Party Annual Accounts, trade union contributions represented 89 per cent of the total national income in 1978, or £1.5 million, 74 per cent in 1984 and 78 per cent, or £3.5 million, in 1985.[23] In 1978, just over eight million trade unionists paid contributions to the political fund out of a total of 9,888,000 trade union members who were in unions which paid the political fund. There were other unions, with just under three and a quarter million members, who paid no political funds.[24] In other words, 60 per cent of trade unionists paid the political fund to the Labour Party.

Because of the seriousness of the challenge to Labour's financial position, the twelve months from April 1985 saw the trade unions campaign to get members to maintain the political fund link with the Labour Party. By March 1986, all thirty-seven unions holding political funds had balloted their members and gained a YES vote in favour of continuing to provide funds for the Labour Party, 83 per cent voting in favour. Only two of the thirty-seven unions recorded a level of support less than 70 per cent of the ballot and six recorded support of 90 per cent or more.[25] In total, 6,984,603 ballot papers were issued, 3,561,321 members voted, with 2,957,235 voting YES and 656,534 voting NO.[26] The Amalgamated Union of Engineering Workers had an 84 per cent YES vote, the Transport and General Workers recorded 78.9 per cent YES vote, the Confederation of Health Service Employees 91.3 per cent and the National Union of Public Employees 84.1 per cent.

The Conservatives continued with their anti-trade union legislation towards the end of the decade. The Employment Act of 1988 threatened the normal democratic activities operating within the trade union movement since trade union members now had the right to ignore a trade union ballot decision on industrial action. It also further specified that members would not have indemnity against unlawful conduct although they had the right to stop employers deducting their union dues. It also outlawed industrial action which was designed to establish or preserve closed shops and also introduced new restrictions on industrial action and election ballots.

The Employment Act of 1989 undermined the rights of individual workers rather than challenged the position of unions. It introduced a pre-hearing review of cases going to Industrial Tribunals and imposed a £150 deposit to prevent groundless applications. It also removed restrictions on the work of women and children, exempted employers with fewer than twenty staff from including disciplinary procedures in employment contracts, restricted time off for union representatives, and required employees to have two years service before being given written reasons for dismissal. However, the Employment Act of 1990 returned to the attack upon trade union rights. It renewed the challenge on the closed shop by making it unlawful for an employer to refuse to employ non-union members. It also made all secondary action other than picketing unlawful. There was also a widening of the scope of ballots, which had to include all regular casual workers. More stringent measures required unions to repudiate unofficial action and the Act allowed for the selective dismissal of staff taking unofficial action.

At this time the European Economic Community was developing its European social charter of workers' rights. Included in this charter was a legal minimum of four weeks annual holiday, a ban on children aged under fifteen working full-time, and a variety of measures including mandatory quotas for the employment of handicapped workers. Although the Employment Acts of 1989 and 1990 did not directly challenge many of these proposals, the spirit of the new laws cut against the grain of the intentions being laid out in the European social charter. And the Employment Secretary, Norman Fowler, denounced the European proposal to legislate on social standards as 'a threat to jobs'.[27] Indeed, Fowler took particular exception to the inclusion of a right to strike in the draft charter, stating that 'The right to strike conflicts with our national traditions since 1906 when there has been no right to strike in Britain but a limited immunity under certain conditions for those who organize strikes.'[28]

The 'Thatcher' legislation has clearly reduced the protection given to trade unions and individuals operating within the industrial framework and it has raised two key, and related, questions connected with this legislative attack upon trade union rights. First, how have the unions responded to this challenge? Secondly, how resilient have the unions been? The evidence suggests that the trade unions initially opposed the legislation until, due to a combination of factors, they turned direction in 1986 and 1987. There is also sufficient evidence to suggest that this change of approach, the move towards trade union mergers and the greater interest in attracting and keeping members, has left the trade union movement more resilient than its loss of membership would imply.

The first ten years of Conservative rule saw the dramatic decline of trade union membership. In 1979 there were almost thirteen and a half million trade union members in Britain, 12,172,508 of them being members of the TUC. By 1989 there were about ten million trade union members of whom about 8.6 million were members of the TUC. The decline has been rapid and worrying, although it may have more to do with the rise of mass unemployment than the failures of the trade union movement. In 1979 and 1980, despite rising unemployment, trade union membership fell little but thereafter it began to fall at about half a million a year until the mid-1980s. Indeed, between 1979 and 1985 the proportion of the workforce which was unionized fell from 57.3 per cent to 49.5 per cent, a trend which has continued since. In this climate, industrial conflict declined from about twenty-nine and a half million days lost in 1979 to three and three-quarter million days lost in 1983, before the level rose once again to more than twenty-seven million days as a result of the miners' strike of 1984–5. Despite the relative industrial peace, there were some well-publicized challenges to the government's new legislation and a policy of general resistance to the government's attempt to impose rigorous financial constraints on the nationalized industries.

The TUC organized a 'Day of Action' on 14 May 1980, although the response was rather patchy. The new stringent economic policies of the government to the nationalized steel industry led to a three-month strike from January 1980, after which the steelmen got a 16 per cent rise rather than 2 per cent that was initially offered. The TUC helped to galvanize support for the steelmen, and a new, and symbolic rather than effective, Triple Alliance was formed between the Steel Trades Confederation, the Railwaymen and the Miners in January 1981. The TUC held a special Wembley conference in early April 1982 to organize the campaign against the 1980 and 1982 Employment Acts; it was agreed that the unions would not seek or accept public funds for union ballots under the 1980 Employment Act and a Campaign and Defence Fund was raised by levying 10p per member on all affiliated unions. It was obviously just a matter of time before the more militant unions came into conflict with the new legislation.

The first major conflict of this type was that between Eddie Shah and the National Graphical Association (NGA). The NGA attempted to enforce a closed shop at Shah's Warrington printing works by mass picketing but Shah sought an injunction against the union and, subsequently, a £50,000 fine for contempt.[29] Later the Court imposed another fine of £100,000 and the union assets were sequestrated. The union attempted to ignore these actions, continued with violent picketing and was fined further amounts of £150,000 and £375,000. In response, it called a national newspaper strike for 24 December 1983, which was supported by the TUC's Employment Committee until the action was declared unlawful by the High Court. In the end, the NGA was forced to admit defeat and to purge its contempt in order to unfreeze its assets.

Further conflict ensued in January 1984 when the government announced that trade unions would be banned at the Government Communication Headquarters at Cheltenham. In a protracted affair, the General Council of the TUC called a 'Day of Action' for the 28 February 1984 and withdrew its representatives from the National Economic Development Council. The High Court, the Court of Appeal and the House of Lords were also drawn into the case, and Len Murray threatened to take the case to the European Court of Human Rights. In the end, the government's will prevailed by the use of both the 'carrot and the stick'.

Yet, by far the biggest test of the new legislation was with the miners' strike of 1984–5. The immediate context of the conflict was the fact that Ian MacGregor and the National Coal Board offered the miners a 5.2 per cent wage increase in October 1983. The National Union of Mineworkers (NUM) rejected this and imposed an overtime ban from 30 October. Matters came to a head when MacGregor proposed to cut coal output and employment in the mines. There were spontaneous strikes, such as that at Cortonwood, where pits had been informed of their imminent closure. Effectively, the coal strike began on 9 March 1984 at the pits in Scotland and Yorkshire where notifications of closures had been made. However, there was to be no national ballot. Instead, the NUM sent flying pickets from Yorkshire, Scotland and Kent to persuade the working miners, particularly those in Nottingham and the Midlands, to join the dispute, despite a High Court injunction forbidding such action.[30] This led to mass picketing and violence, notably in Ollerton in Nottinghamshire, where a Yorkshire striker on picket duty was crushed to death in the demonstrations outside the pit, and later at the Orgreave coke plant. There were many twists and turns throughout the dispute. On 14 March 1984 the High Court gave the National Coal Board an injunction against flying pickets, though the NCB chose not to use it. The government also maintained a police presence to stop the movement of flying pickets. At this stage, trade union support for the miners was mixed, although Arthur Scargill drew immense personal support at the 1984 TUC conference.[31]

Yet as the strike ground on, court action began to take its effect. The South Wales Mineworkers were fined £50,000 for contempt over picketing and when this was not paid the sequestrators seized their funds of £707,000. The national union was also fined £200,000 on 10 October for breaking an order declaring their strike unofficial, and when it failed to pay its assets were seized – at least those assets which had not been salted away to Luxembourg, Dublin and other financial centres.

There was much violence and many incidents of high emotion during the strike. Arthur Scargill was much criticized for his refusal to hold a national ballot and there was much criticism by the NUM of the decision of a substantial proportion of the Nottingham miners to form the Union of Democratic Mineworkers (UDM), which sought to do business with the government. Scargill and the NUM were also intensely hostile to the decision of the National Coal Board to offer a Christmas bonus pay-packet to any miner who worked for four full weeks before Christmas. The violence which ensued included the much publicized incident when a concrete block was dropped from a motorway bridge on to a taxi taking a miner to work in South Wales, killing the driver and leading to two strikers being sent to gaol for twenty years. Despite the NUM's opposition fifteen thousand miners did return to work under this offer.

Eventually the strike came to an end, in a ragged fashion, and without any settlement, when a special delegate meeting of the mineworkers decided to return to work without agreement on 3 March 1985. The government had remained firm, the strike had not forced any power cuts throughout the winter and at the end of February 1985 the Welsh miners had returned without accepting an offer. There was no other outcome available, unless the NUM was willing to force the dispute through to another winter. After the ending of the dispute it was clear that the power of the NUM had been irrevocably destroyed and that it would be unable to prevent the rapidly developing pattern of pit closures which reduced the number of miners by half over the next six years.

In many respects the mining dispute became the turning point in the attitude of trade unions and the TUC towards the government's industrial legislation. In 1986 the Electrical, Electronic, Tele-communications and Plumbing Union (EETPU) and the Amalgamated Engineering Union (AEU) decided to accept funds for ballots as allowed under the 1980 Employment Act. Also, the same year, a special TUC conference of 'union officers with executive authority' decided to adopt a more positive policy towards government legislation and the 1987 Congress established a Special Review Body (SRB) to consider future policies. This body encouraged the TUC to offer a wide range of pension services, personal insurance and legal services. It also encouraged a change in the relationship between unions and modifications to the Bridlington Agreement.[32]

The changes in the Bridlington Agreement arose as a result of the issues raised by the conflict between Rupert Murdoch's News International Group and the Print Unions over the enforcement of new working arrangements and no-strike agreements for work on *The Times*, the *Sun*, the *News of the World* and the *Sunday Times*. Murdoch dismissed 5,500 of his Fleet Street staff in January 1986 and distributed his newspapers from Wapping using lorries owned by a separate distribution agency. This was in response to the action of the print unions who were attempting to restrict the use of the new technology and the movement of the newspaper industry from Fleet Street to Wapping in the East End of London and at Murdoch's Kinning Park plant, as they had done successfully in an earlier dispute in 1983.[33] There was mass picketing and violence at the Wapping plant, with fines and threats of sequestration of unions' funds. The major event was the violent mass demonstration at Wapping on 24 January 1987, the anniversary of the beginning of the dispute. Murdoch, who had used the Courts to threaten the print unions throughout the dispute, then threatened to seek Court sequestration of the unions' funds. As a result, the Society of Graphical and Allied Trades (SOGAT) ended the dispute on 5 February 1987. The AEU withdrew the same day and the National Graphical Association called off its dispute on 6 February. Government legislation and the intransigence of employers had been effective in destroying the powerful print unions. Nevertheless, the trade union movement had cooperated in this destruction.

The ability of the print unions to prevent Murdoch's actions had been severely hampered by the fact that the EETPU had made arrangements to operate Murdoch's Wapping plant in the event of a dispute between Murdoch and the print unions. Indeed, Murdoch bused in a team of electricians daily from Southampton. Throughout this period the TUC had been relatively ineffective in resolving the differences between the EETPU and the print unions, despite much negotiation and censure of the EETPU. In the end, due to the unwillingness of the EETPU to accept the outcome of two inter-union disputes awarded by the TUC under the Bridlington Agreement, the EETPU was expelled from the TUC at the 1988 TUC conference, regardless of Eric Hammond's protest that his union had been the victim of a conspiracy by the major unions to isolate it and despite the fact that:

> In disputed membership situations, the individual concerned should have the right to choose their union and together with their employer the type of agreement covering their employment.[34]

Hammond's point was well made in the context of the new industrial climate and, subsequently, the TUC began to modify the Bridlington Agreement to allow for the more competitive recruitment which was occurring between unions. Indeed, the TUC modified Principle 5 to allow the opinions of the workers concerned to be taken into account by the TUC's Disputes Committee. In order to control inter-union arrangements, however, the TUC also introduced a *Code of Practice* to force unions considering single union agreements to inform the TUC and to prohibit no-strike agreements. In the end, faced with the end of the 'old consensus' the TUC has turned towards policing inter-union relations more effectively.

The re-assessment of the TUC's position has also led to its attempt to strengthen its links with the Labour Party.[35] Although the power of the trade union block vote is going to be reduced the influence of the trade union movement should remain undiminished as the Labour Party's 1989 conference effectively accepted a 'Charter of Rights for Employees', agreeing to set up a national minimum wage and the reform of existing legislation on areas concerning union activity and organization, including the permitting of secondary industrial action where workers have a 'genuine' interest. The Labour Party also accepted that the trade union movement should no longer be subject to sequestration, but there has been no commitment to repealing existing balloting requirements.

Trade unions have also clearly become more bureaucratic in the attempt to retain their membership and to protect their position. They have sought to attract more women into their ranks and have attempted to organize managers and professionals from the private sector into unions, as, for instance, in the case of the Institution of Professionals, Managers and Scientists (IPMS) (formerly the Institution of Professional Civil Servants). Mergers absorbed 126 unions, and 967,769 members, between 1980 and 1988, some of which cut across the manual and non-manual divide as in the case of the Technical, Administrative and Supervisory Sections (TASS) which absorbed four manual craft unions from engineering.[36]

Despite these attempts at revitalizing and defending the movement, there have been challenges to the position of the trade union movement in the workplace. A few unions have lost recognition by the employers, the Labour Research Department indicating in a survey that thirty-nine such cases occurred between 1984 and 1988.[37] There have also been moves towards single union recognition and an attempt to avoid unions altogether. In some cases, as among some of the unions organizing teachers in higher education, appraisal has been used to limit the scope of trade union activity and, more generally, there have been attempts to by-pass trade union activity by taking workers, on new contracts, outside the normal negotiating arrangements. Indeed, many employers have been more willing to recognize workshop organizations rather than national unions and, contrary to the above evidence, P. Edwards has recently argued that there has been no sign of a widespread attack upon shop stewards or any assault on the closed shop.[38] And, indeed, in some sectors, particularly in the public sector, the move from the centre to the locality may have strengthened the positions of some shop stewards.

Conclusion

The balance of evidence suggests that the trade unions are in a turmoil. On the one hand, they have lost national influence as the 'old consensus' has evaporated, their powers to strike have been diminished, their control of their own members has been undermined by the new industrial legislation, their membership has declined, their influence in the workshop is less evident than it once was, and their control of the Labour Party has been challenged. Yet on the other hand, they have been readjusting their position to the new challenges, have organized recruitment drives, redefined the Bridlington Agreement, established new mergers, organized more widely among women and the white-collar workers, maintained workshop control in some sectors of British industry, and, in some ways, actually strengthened their influence upon the Labour Party. In other words, there are signs that while the trade union movement as a whole has been weakened by the events of the 1980s it has responded well to the challenge. Having rejected the Conservative legislation in the early 1980s, trade unions have adjusted their organization in a positive manner since the mid-1980s and have shown remarkable resilience. Obviously, the movement is weaker than it once was but, for trade unionists, there is also evidence that the movement still retains some influence and a faith that the movement will revive. In the end Professor R.J. Price's suggestion that there is no trajectory in trade union history may be correct; if the objective conditions change and trade unions adapt to these changes then the assault on trade unions over the last twenty-one years may be halted and reversed. In any case, even in a weakened state trade unions continue to be vitally important to industrial relations and in some future scenarios may still need to be consulted on industrial matters. Even the most resolute of governments has not destroyed the power of trade unions, whose central and local organizations still remain important in the process of industrial bargaining.

NOTES

1. K. Coates and T. Topham, *Trade Unions and Politics* (Oxford, Blackwell, 1986), p. 21.
2. R. Michels, *Political Parties: A Sociological Study of the Oligarchical Tendencies of Modern Democracy* (New York, Free Press, 1962); R. Hyman, 'The Politics of Workplace Trade Unionism', *Capital and Class*, No. 8, pp. 54–67.
3. P. Fairbrother and J. Waddington, 'The politics of trade unionism: Evidence, policy and theory', *Capital and Class*, 1990, p. 33.
4. R.J. Price, *Labour in British Society* (Croom Helm, 1986).
5. K. Hawkins, *British Industrial Relations 1945–1975* (Barrie & Jenkins, 1976), p. 108.
6. R. Barber, *Trade Unions and the Tories* (Bow Group, 1976), p. 2.
7. P. Ferris, *The New Militants: Crisis in the Trade Unions* (Harmondsworth, Penguin, 1972), p. 112.
8. A. Scargill, article in *New Left Review*, 93, July–August 1975.
9. Labour Party conference, *Report*, 1971, p. 165.
10. A. Taylor, *Trade Unions and the Labour Party* (Croom Helm, 1987), pp. 9–10.
11. *Loc. cit.*, p. 4.
12. Taylor, *op.cit.*, p. 25.
13. *Loc. cit.*, (February 1973), paragraph 20, p. 7.
14. *Loc. cit.*, (1974), p. 5.
15. B. Castle, *The Castle Diaries 1974–6* (Weidenfeld and Nicolson, 1980), pp. 85, 121, 224, 252–6.
16. D. Coates, *Labour in Power; A Study of the Labour Government 1974–1979* (Longman, 1980); Taylor, *op.cit.*; M. Holmes, *The Labour Government 1974–9: Political Aims and Economic Reality* (New York, St. Martin's Press, 1985).
17. Coates, *op. cit.*, p. 20.
18. Taylor, *op.cit.*, pp. 101–3; Holmes, *op.cit.*, pp. 126–30.
19. J.E. Cronin, *Labour and Society in Britain, 1918–1979* (Batsford, 1984), p. 242.
20. *The Times*, 22 January 1979.
21. *Hansard*, 12 July 1983, col. 763.
22. D. Fatchett, *Trade Unions and Politics in the 1980s: The 1984 Act and Political Funds* (Croom Helm, 1987), chapters 3, 4 and 5; Coates and Topham, *op.cit.*, chapter 4.
23. *Ibid.*, pp. 46–7.
24. *Ibid.*, p. 47.
25. *Ibid.*, p. 121–30.

26. *Ibid.*, p. 121.
27. *Guardian*, 31 October 1989.
28. *Ibid.*
29. *The Times*, 18 November 1983.
30. *Guardian*, 15 March 1984.
31. TUC, *Annual Report, 1984*, pp. 399–400, 403, appendix 5.
32. Fairbrother and Waddington, *op.cit.*, pp. 22–6; Trades Union Congress, *Organising for the 1990s: The Special Review Body's Second Report* (TUC, 1989).
33. *Guardian*, 22 January 1991, article by P. Wintour.
34. TUC, *Annual Report, 1988*, p. 411, quoting a letter sent to the TUC.
35. Labour Party, *Meet the Challenge Make the Change; A New Agenda for Britain* (1989).
36. Fairbrother and Waddington, *op. cit.*, p. 27.
37. Labour Research Department, 'New Wave Union Busting', Labour Research, 13–15 April 1988.
38. P. Edwards, *Managing the Factory* (Oxford, Blackwell, 1987).

POSTSCRIPT

The study of British trade unionism has come a long way since the Webbs first delivered their analysis of trade unionism to the world in the late nineteenth century. Historians no longer accept, without question, their Whiggish findings about the inevitable growth of the trade union movement nor their description of many of the stages of trade unionism, although vestiges of their ideas and the terminology are still used widely. They now demur at the sweeping statements of national histories, and make more concessions to the increasing local evidence which has emerged on regional trade union developments and on major strikes, such as the General Strike. It is now more common for historians to point to the diversity of trade union history, its contradictory and quarrelsome nature and to the suggestion, raised by Professor R.J. Price, that its position changes according to the prevailing economic, social and political conditions. In other words, it is now unfashionable to refer to trade unionism following one particular trajectory. Indeed, even in the 1980s there is evidence of trade unionism improving its organization and influence which can be measured against the undoubted evidence of its overall decline in influence and membership.

There have been two main stimuli for changing approaches to, and interpretations of, British trade union history. In the first place, there are now more records available: trade union records are being deposited in libraries; many unions (such as the NUM) have kept large collections of their own records; government records and Cabinet papers are now available up to the beginning of the 1960s; and many trade union leaders have committed their lives and diaries to print. Some trade union records have been consciously gathered together in important depositories, one of the most important being that at Warwick University. But many archive libraries have done similar work and the Calderdale section of West Yorkshire Archives has one of the best collections of local trade union documents in existence. These rich seams and deposits of new information have encouraged historians to scrutinize the major events in British trade union history more carefully.

Secondly, it is clear that the study of trade unionism has gained increased legitimacy in recent years. In many respects, the work of Professor Chris Wrigley and others has incorporated its study within the developing study of industrial relations. And political scientists, sociologists, and others, have incorporated the study of trade unionism within their own theoretical works.

Given these developments it is not surprising that the focus of trade union history has begun to change. There is, for instance, far more interest in the grass roots, rank-and-file and workshop basis of trade union history than was formerly the case. The eulogistic grand history of a trade union is far less common than it once was, and rightly so. It is now far more common for historians to detect trends in trade unions and to discount broad and general descriptions that the Webbs and earlier historians ascribed to them and their movements.

What is clear from recent research is that the history of trade unionism is not one of continuous growth. For the best part of two centuries the movement exerted a rather limited impact upon the economy — despite the frequent concerns expressed by employers. Indeed, it is only in the last one hundred years that the movement has achieved a significant industrial presence, and only for about forty years, from 1939 until the late 1970s, that its position, related to government and employers, has been in the ascendancy.

Currently, the British trade union movement has to reassess its position. Quite clearly, there has been change and adjustment. But even now they face a new challenge as John Major's Conservative government contemplates the future of industrial relations in the 1990s. In *Industrial Relations in the 1990s*, the Green Paper which was produced on 24 July 1991, the government continues to see the law being used to provide a balanced framework of rights and obligations, arguing that Britain cannot afford to risk slipping back into the inflationary pay settlements, low productivity, and strike-prone industrial relations of the 1970s. It suggests that employers might negotiate directly with individual employees in the 1990s, while for trade unions the real challenge will be to retain members and to convince employers that they are worth recognizing. Arising from this might be 'no strike' and 'single union' arrangements. The Green Paper also considers the need to impose new financial and balloting constraints upon trade unions. On financial matters, and in the wake of the Lightman Report into alleged irregularities within the National Union of Mineworkers, the government intends to give the trade union Certification Officer increased powers to inspect union accounts. On balloting and strikes, the Green Paper threatens to impose the requirement, following a ballot, that a trade union will have to give seven days' notice in writing of its intent to call industrial action, identifying the groups involved and indicating the date on which the action would begin. In the case of one-day strikes, seven days' notice would have to be given for each. Also, in line with John Major's 'Citizen's Charter', members of the public whose daily lives are disrupted by industrial action will have the right, in the absence of action by the employer, to restrain unlawful organization of action affecting public services such as education and health. The recommendations also include the possible suspension of the Bridlington Agreement to ensure that individuals are allowed to leave one union and join another. In essence, then, the trade union freedom to call industrial action may be even more restricted in the future and in effect the individual will be even less well represented in dealing with employers within the Conservative notion of what is meant by extending the rights of the individual.

Given this scenario for the 1990s, it is not surprising that the trade union movement has obtained from the Labour Party a commitment to reverse some, but by no means all, of the legislation once it returns to power – a position accepted by the overwhelming vote of the TUC on 3 September 1991. Thus, even if a Labour Party forms a future government it seems unlikely that it will permit a return to the strike mentality of the 1970s, which cost it dear then and would almost certainly cost it dear in the future. Whatever the political complexion of the governments of the 1990s, it seems likely that trade unions will have to become even more bureaucratic to exert the sort of control over their members which is required in the new political environment even if that may cut against the trend towards increased democracy within the movement. The individual freedoms of the workers will undoubtedly reduce the power of the trade unions. Yet the trade union movement can still advocate issues which can attract and inspire support. At the September 1991 TUC conference there was strong backing for the Labour Party's minimum wage policy. One report stated that:

Labour's electoral support would get a 6 per cent boost if it campaigned on its policy of a £3.40 hourly national minimum wage, an opinion poll commissioned by the general union, GMB, has found.

More than three-quarters of voters back the £3.40 minimum wage pledge, including 69 per cent of Conservatives, the MORI opinion poll recorded. Labour's weekend popularity rating of 40 per cent to the Tories' 42 per cent is reversed to a Labour lead of 44 per cent to the Conservatives' 40 per cent once the minimum wage policy is mentioned.

John Edmonds the GMB's general secretary presented the poll findings yesterday as a propaganda torpedo aimed at sinking Employment Secretary Michael Howard's continuing campaign against a statutory minimum wage.

'The extravagant attacks by Michael Howard have done us a great service,' Mr Edmonds told delegates. 'The more he directs attention to the minimum wage, the more people know about it. And the more they know about it, the more they like it.'[1]

Campaigns of this type may be one future direction for the TUC and its affiliated unions to follow, and may still prove the saviour of both the trade unions and the Labour Party.

NOTE

1. *Guardian*, 5 September 1991.

BIBLIOGRAPHY

PRIMARY SOURCES

Amalgamated Society of Engineers, *Abstract Report of the Council's Proceedings from June 1st 1870, to December 31st 1872.*

Amalgamated Society of Engineers, minutes and records of the Halifax branches, Calderdale branch of West Yorkshire Archives.

Amalgamated Society of Engineers, rules.

Amalgamated Society of Engineers, *To All Classes of Workmen in the Engineering Industry* (1892).

Amalgamated Society of Engineers, minutes and records of the Halifax branches, Calderdale branch of West Yorkshire Archives.

Amalgamated Society of Railway Servants, Misc. collection British Library of Political and Economic Science.

Amalgamated Union of Dyers' Collection, Bradford branch of West Yorkshire Archives.

Barber, R., *Trade Unions and the Tories* (Bow Group, 1976).

Barnsley Chronicle.

Bee-Hive, The.

Beveridge Collection on Munitions, British Library of Political and Economic Science.

Board of Trade, *Strikes and Lockouts Report*, various.

Bradford Trades and Labour Council, Minutes.

Bradford Typographical records, J.B. Priestley Library, University of Bradford.

British Worker, The.

Cabinet Papers, Public Record Office.

Citrine, W., *Men at Work* (1964).

Clarion, The.

Communist Party of Great Britain, circulars, South Yorkshire.

Conservative Political Centre, *Industrial Advance* (1966).

Gast, J., *Calumny Defeated: or, A Compleat Vindication of the Conduct of the Working Shipwrights, during the late Dispute with their Employers* (Deptford, 1802).

Gallacher, W. and Paton, J., *The Collective Contract: Towards Industrial Democracy. A Memorandum on Workers' Control* (Paisley Trades Council, 1917).

Glass Bottle Makers of Yorkshire United Trade Protection Society, *National Conference Reports, 1893–5, Vol. 1 (First to Twenty-Third Inclusive)* (1908) and various circulars.

Guardian, The.

Hansard.

Home Office records, Public Record Office.

Huddersfield Examiner.

Illustrated London News, The.

In Place of Strife: A Policy for Industrial Relations (Cmnd, 3888, 1969).

Labour Magazine.

Labour Party, *Britain Will Win with Labour* (1974).

Labour Party, *Labour Party Leaflet, no. 49*.

Labour Party, *Labour Programme For Britain* (1972).

Labour Party, *Meet the Challenge Make the Change; A New Agenda for Britain* (1989).

Leeds Intelligencer.

Leeds Mercury.

Leeds Trades and Labour Council, Minutes.

Liverpool Council of Action collection.

London Trades Council, Annual Reports.

Loveless, George, *The Victims of Whiggery being a statement of The Prosecution Experienced by the Dorchester Labourers in 1834*.

Mann, Tom, *What a Compulsory Eight-Hour Day Means to the Workers* (1886).

——, *Tom Mann's Memoirs* (1923).

Mann, Tom and Tillett, Ben, *The 'New' Trade Unionism* (1890).

Miners' Federation of Great Britain, Minutes and Correspondence, copies in the Miners' Office, Barnsley.

Ministry of Munitions records, Public Record office.

Murphy, J.T., *The Workers' Committee* (Sheffield, 1918).

National Association for the Promotion of Social Sciences, 1860.

National Clerks' Association, The, 1893.

National Left Review.

National Review.

National Union of Railwaymen's Strike Committee, Minute Book, Birmingham 1926, British Library of Political Science.

National Union of Textile Workers, records, Bradford Archives.

National Union of Textile Workers, records, Kirklees branch of West Yorkshire Archives.

O'Keefe, T.J., *Rise and Progress of the National Amalgamated Labourers' Union of G.B. & Ireland.*

Pioneer, The.

Place, Francis, mss.

Potters' Examiner and Workman's Advocate, The.

Read, W.J., *The Clerk's Charter.*

Records of the Borough of Nottingham 1800–1835 (1952).

Royal Commission on Labour, reports 1892–1895.

Royal Commission on Trade Unions, 1867–9.

Royal Commission on Trade Unions and Employers' Associations, 1965–1968.

Saddleworth Union records.

Sheffield Independent.

South Wales Miners' Reform Committee, *Miners' Next Step* (1912).

Special Bulletin of the Merseyside Council of Action, 1926.

Spencer–Stanhope Collection.

Statutory Laws, including Combination Acts and others.

St Helen's Labour News.

Sunday Times.

Tester, J., 'History of Bradford Contest', mss.

Thorne, W., *My Life's Battles.*

Times, The.

Trades Newspaper.

Trades Union Commission: Sheffield, 1867.

Trades Union Congress *Annual Reports: proceedings of . . .*

Trades Union Congress, *Report to Congress: Trade Union Structure* (1965).

Trades Union Congress, *The General Council of the Trades Union Congress: its Powers, Functions and Work* (TUC, 1925).

TUC General Council, *Guidelines to Negotiators* (1978).

TUC-Labour Liaison Committee, *Economic Policy and The Cost of Living.*

TUC, *Organising for the 1990s: The Special Review Body's Second Report* (TUC, 1989).

United Trades Cooperative Journal, The.

Voice of the West Riding.

Webb Collection, British Library of Political and Economic Science.

Wiltshire General and Agricultural Workers' Union, *The Report of the Inaugural Meeting held at Swindon. December 12th 1892: Speeches by Keir Hardie MP* . . .
Workers' Bulletin.
Workers' Chronicle.
Workers' Weekly.
Worsted Committee records, J.B. Priestley Library, University of Bradford.
Yorkshire Factory Times.

SECONDARY SOURCES

Anderson, G., *Victorian Clerk* (1976).
Arnot, R.P., *The Miners*, vol. 1 (1949) and subsequent volumes.
——, *The General Strike May 1926* (Labour Research Department, republished Wakefield EP, 1975).
Aspinall, A., *The Early English Trade Unions: Documents from the Home Office Records*, Public Record Office (Batchworth Press, 1949).
Bagwell, P.S., *The Railwaymen* (1963).
Bain, G.S., *The Growth of White-Collar Unionism* (Oxford, 1970).
Benson, J., *The Working Class in Britain 1850–1914* (Longman, 1989).
Berg, M., *The Machinery Question and the Making of Political Economy 1815–1848* (Cambridge, CUP, 1980).
Bevan, G.P., 'The Strikes of the Past Ten years', *Journal of the Royal Statistical Society*, xliii, 1980.
Biagini, E.F., 'British Trade Unions and Popular Political Economy, 1860–1880', *Historical Journal*, 30, 4, 1987.
Boyer, G.R., 'What did unions do in nineteenth-century Britain?', *Journal of Economic History*, 48, 1988.
Braverman, H., *Labor and Monopoly Capital* (1974).
Bullock, A., *The Life and Times of Ernest Bevin 1881–1940*, vol. 1 (1960).
Challinor, R.C., *The Origins of British Bolshevism*.
Challinor, R.C. and Ripley, B., *The Miners' Association: A Trade Union in the Age of the Chartists* (Lawrence and Wishart, 1968).
Church, R., 'Edwardian Labour Unrest and Coalfield Militancy, 1890–1914, *Historical Journal*, 30, 4, 1987.
Citrine, W., *Men and Work: An Autobiography* (1964).

Clegg, H.A., Fox, A. and Thompson, A.F., *A History of British Trade Unions since 1889*, vol. 1 (Oxford, OUP, 1964).

Clegg, H.A., *A History of British Trade Unionism Vol. II, 1911– 1933* (Oxford, Clarendon Press, 1985).

——, *How to Run an Incomes Policy* (Heinemann, 1971).

Clements, R.V., 'British Trade Unionism and Popular Political Economy, 1850–1875', *Economic History Review*, 1961.

Clinton, A., *The trade union rank and file: Trades Councils in Britain 1900–1940* (Manchester, MUP, 1977).

Coates, K. and Topham, T., *Industrial Democracy in Great Britain* (1968).

——, *Trade Unions and Politics* (Oxford, Blackwell, 1986).

Cole, G.D.H., 'Some Notes on British Trade Unionism in the Third Quarter of the Nineteenth Century', *International Review of Social History*, 1937.

Coltham, S.W., 'George Potter, the Junta, and the Beehive', *International Review of Social History*, ix, 1964 and x, 1965.

Cronin, J.E., *Industrial Conflict in Britain* (1979).

——, *Labour and Society in Britain, 1918–1979* (Batsford, 1984).

——, 'Strikes and Power in Britain, 1870–1920', *International Review of Social History*, vol. 32, 1987.

——, '"The rank and file" and the social history of the working class', *International Review of Social History*, 34, 1989.

Cronin, J.E. and Schneer, J. (eds), *Social Conflict and the Political Order in Britain* (Croom Helm, 1982).

Dangerfield, G., *The Strange Death of Liberal England* (1935).

Davis-Smith, Justin, *An Uneasy Alliance: Volunteers and Trades Unions in Britain since 1945* (Volunteer Centre, 1991).

Dobson, C.R., *Masters and Journeymen: A prehistory of industrial relations 1717–1800* (Croom Helm, 1980).

Duffy, A.E.P., 'New Unionism: a re-appraisal', *Economic History Review*, 1961–2.

——, 'The Eight-Hour Day Movement in Britain 1886–1893', two parts in *Manchester School of Economic and Social Studies*, xxxvi, 1968.

Durcan, J.W., McCarthy, E.J. and Redman, G.P., *Strikes in Post-war Britain study of stoppages of work due to industrial disputes, 1946–1973* (Oxford, George Allen & Unwin, 1983).

Edwards, P., *Managing the Factory* (Oxford, Blackwell, 1987).

Exall, T., *A Brief History of the Weavers of the County of Gloucestershire* (Stroud, 1838).

Exell, A., 'Morris Motors in the 1930s. Part I', *History Workshop Journal*, 6, autumn, 1978.

Fairbrother, P. and Waddington, J., 'The politics of trade unionism: Evidence, policy and theory', *Capital and Crisis*, 1990.

Farman, C., *The General Strike May 1926* (Rupert Hart-Davis, 1972).

Fatchett, D., *Trade Unions and Politics in the 1980s: The 1984 Act and Political Funds* (Croom Helm, 1987).

Foster, J., *Class Struggle and the Industrial Revolution: early industrial capitalism in three towns* (Weidenfeld & Nicolson, 1974).

——, 'Strike Action and Working-Class Politics on Clydeside 1914–1919', *International Review of Social History*, xxxv (1990).

Fox, A., *A History of the National Union of Boot and Shoe Operatives* (Oxford, 1958).

Fraser, W.H., *Trade Unions and Society: The Struggle for Acceptance, 1850–1880* (Allen & Unwin, 1974).

Gallacher, W., *Revolt on the Clyde* (1936).

George, M.D., 'The Combination Laws', *Economic History Review*, 1st series, vi (1935/6).

Gregory, R., *The Miners and British Politics 1906–14* (Oxford, Clarendon press, 1968).

Hammond, J.L. and B., *The Skilled Labourer*, ed. by J.G. Rule (Longman, 1979).

Hanson, C.G., 'Craft Unions, Welfare Benefits, and the Case for Trade Union Law Reform, 1867–1875', *Economic History Review*, second series, xxviii, May 1975.

Hawkins, K., *British Industrial Relations, 1945–1975* (Barrie & Jenkins, 1976).

Hay, D., Linebaugh, P., Thompson, E.P., *Albion's Fatal Tree: Crime and Society in Eighteenth-Century England* (Penguin, 1977).

Hinton, J., 'The Clyde Workers' Committee and the Dilution Struggle' in A. Briggs and J. Saville (eds), *Essays in Labour History, 1886–1923* (1971).

——, *The First Shop Stewards' Movement* (George Allen & Unwin, 1973).

——, 'The Rise of a Mass Labour Movement: Growth and Limits', *A History of British Industrial Relations 1875–1914* ed. by C. Wrigley (Brighton, Harvester, 1982).

History of Labour (Weidenfeld and Nicolson, 1984).

History of the TUC 1868–1968 (1968).

Hobsbawm, E.J., *Labour's Turning Point 1880–1900* (Brighton, Harvester Press edition, 1974).

——, *Labouring Men* (Weidenfeld and Nicolson, 1964).

——, *Worlds of Labour: Further Studies in the History of Labour* (Weidenfeld and Nicolson, 1984).

Holton, B., *British Syndicalism 1900–1914: Myth and Realities* (Pluto Press, 1976).

Horn, Pamela, *Joseph Arch* (Kineton, The Roundwood Press, 1971).

Hunt, E.H., *British Labour History 1815–1914* (Weidenfeld and Nicolson, 1981).

Hyman, R., *The Workers' Union* (Oxford, 1971).

——, 'The sound of one hand clapping: a comment on the "rank and file" debate', *International Review of Social History*, 34, 1989.

——, 'The Politics of Workplace Trade Unionism', *Capital and Class*, 8.

Jaffe, J.A., 'The state, capital and workmen's control during the industrial revolution: the rise and fall of the North-East Pitmen's Union, 1830–1', *Journal of Social History*, 21, 1988.

James, J., *History of Worsted Manufacture in England* (1857).

Jowitt, J. and Laybourn, K., 'The Wool Textile Dispute of 1925', *The Journal of (Regional and) Local Studies*, vol. 2, 1, spring 1982.

Joyce, P., 'Labour, Capital and Compromise: A Response to Richard Price', *Social History*, ix, 1984.

Knowles, K.C.A.G., *Strikes: A Study of Industrial Conflict* (Oxford, 1952).

Knox, W., 'Apprenticeship and De-skilling in Britain 1850–1914', *International Review of Social History*, vol. 32, 1986.

Lane, T., *The Union Makes Us Strong* (Arrow Books, 1971).

Laybourn, K., *The Rise of Labour* (Edward Arnold, 1988).

——, *Philip Snowden* (Aldershot, Temple Smith/Gower, 1988).

Laybourn, K. and Reynolds, J., *Liberalism and the Rise of Labour 1890–1918* (Croom Helm, 1984).

Leeson, R.A., 'Business as usual – craft union development 1834–1851', *Bulletin of the Society for the Study of Labour History*, 49, 1984.

Liddington, J. and Norris, J., *One Hand Tied Behind Us* (Virago, 1978).

Lindert, P.H., 'English occupations, 1670–1811', *Journal of Economic History*, xl, no. 4 (1980).

Lovell, J., *British Trade Unions 1875–1933* (Macmillan, 1977).

Lovell, J. *Stevedores and Dockers* (1967).

——, 'The TUC Special Industrial Committee, January–April 1926', *Essays in Labour History* (Croom Helm, 1977), edited by A. Briggs and J. Saville.

Lunn, K., 'Immigration and British Labour's Response', *History Today*, xxxv, 1985.

McCarthy, T., *The Great Dock Strike 1889* (Weidenfeld & Nicolson, 1964).

MacDonald, G.W. and Gospel, H.F., 'The Mond-Turner Talks, 1927–1933: A Study in Industrial Co-operation', *Historical Journal*, xvi, 4 (December 1973).

McIvor, A., 'Essay in Anti-Labour History', *Society for the Study of Labour History, Bulletin*, vol. 53, 1, 1958.

McLean, I., *The Legend of Red Clydeside* (Edinburgh, 1983).

Malcolmson, R.W., 'Workers' combinations in the eighteenth century', in M. and J. Jacobs (eds), *The Origins of Anglo-American Radicalism* (Allen & Unwin, 1984).

Mason, A., 'The Government and the General Strike, 1926', *International Review of Social History*, xiv (1967).

Mather, F.C., 'The general strike of 1842: a study of leadership organisation and the threat of revolution during the plug plot disturbances' in R. Quinault and J. Stevenson (eds), *Popular Protest and Public Order* (Allen & Unwin, 1974).

Melling, J., 'Scottish Industrialists and the Changing Character of Class Relations in the Clyde Region', in *Capital and Class* (Edinburgh, 1982).

——, 'Whatever happened to Red Clydeside? Industrial Conflict and the Politics of Skill in the First World War', *International Review of Social History*, xxxv (1990).

Middlemass, K., *Politics in Industrial Society: The Experience of the British System since 1914* (Andre Deutsch, 1979).

Milne-Bailey, W., *Trade Union Documents: Compiled and Edited, with an Introduction by W. Milne Bailey* (Bell, 1929).

More, C., *Skill and the English Working Class* (1980).

Morris, M., *The General Strike* (Journeyman Press, 1976).

Musson, A.E., *British Trade Unions 1800–1875* (Macmillan, 1972).

——, 'Class Struggle and the Labour Aristocracy 1830–1860', *Social History*, 3 (1976).

——, *The Congress of 1868: Its Origins and Establishment of the Trades Union Congress* (1955).

Musson, A.E. *The Typographical Association* (Oxford, 1954).

O'Day, A. (ed.), *The Edwardian age: conflict and stability* (1979).

Oliver, W.H., 'The Consolidated Trades Union of 1834', *Economic History Review*, xvii, 1, 1964.

Orth, J.V., 'The legal status of English trade unions 1799–1871', *Law Making and the Law-Makers in British History* (1980), ed. by A. Harding (Royal Historical Society, 1980).

Pelling, H., *The Origins of the Labour Party 1880–1900* (Oxford, OUP, 1965 edn.)

——, *A History of British Trade Unionism* (Penguin, 4th edn., 1987).

Phelps Brown, E.H., *The Growth of British Industrial Relations* (Macmillan, 1959 and 1965).

——, *The Origins of Trade Union Power* (Oxford, OUP, 1986).

Phillips, G.A., *The General Strike: The Politics of Industrial Conflict* (Weidenfeld and Nicolson, 1976).

——, 'The Triple Industrial Alliance in 1914', *Economic History Review*, 2nd series, xxiv, 1 (February 1971).

Porter, J.H., 'Wage Bargaining under Conciliation Agreements, 1860–1914', *Economic History Review*, 2nd series, xxiii, 3 (December, 1970).

Postgate, R., *Builders' History*.

Pribicevic, B., *The Shop Stewards' Movement and Workers' Control, 1910–1922* (Oxford, 1959).

Price, R.J., *Masters, Unions and Men* (1980).

Price, R., *Labour in British Society: An Interpretative History* (Croom Helm, 1986).

——, 'What's in a name? Workplace history and the "Rank and file"', *International Review of Social History*, 34, 1989.

Prothero, I., *Artisans & Politics in Early Nineteenth-Century London: John Gast and His Times* (Folkestone, Dawson, 1979).

——, 'London Chartism and the trades', *Economic History Review*, xxxiv, no. 2 (1971).

Read, D., *Edwardian England* (1982).

Reid, A., 'Dilution, Trade Unionism and the State' in S. Tolliday and J. Zeitlin (eds), *Shop Floor Bargaining and the State* (Cambridge, 1985).

Renshaw, P., *The General Strike* (Eyre Methuen, 1975).

Reynolds, J. and Laybourn, K., 'The Emergence of the Independent Labour Party in Bradford', *International Review of Social History*, xx, 1975.

Royal Commission Research paper, 10, *Shop Stewards and Work-shop Relations*, W.E.J. McCarthy and S.R. Parker (HMSO, 1967).

Rubin, G., *War, Law and Labour* (Oxford, 1987).

Rule, J., *The Experience of Labour in Eighteenth Century Industry* (Croom Helm, 1981).

——, *The Labouring Classes in Early Industrial England 1750–1850* (Longman, 1986).

——, (ed.), *British Trade Unionism 1750–1850* (Longman, 1988).

Skelley, J., *1926 The General Strike* (Lawrence and Wishart, 1976).

Stedman Jones, G., *Languages of Class: Studies in English working-class history 1832–1982* (Cambridge, 1982).

Taplin, E., *The Dockers' Union: A study of the National Union of Dock Labourers, 1889–1922* (Leicester University Press, 1985).

Thompson, E.P., 'Homage to Tom Maguire', *Essays in Labour History* (Macmillan, 1960).

——, *The Making of the English Working Class* (Penguin, 1968 and several other editions).

Tolliday, S. and Zeitlin, J., *Shopfloor Bargaining and the State* (1985).

Turner, H.A., Clack, G. and Roberts, R., *Labour Relations in the Motor Industry* (George Allen & Unwin, 1967).

Turner, H.A., *Is Britain really Strike-Prone?* (Cambridge, Occasional Papers, CUP, 1969.

——, *Trade Union Growth, Structure and Policy* (Allen & Unwin, 1962).

Webb, S. and B., *Industrial Democracy* (1920 edn.).

——, *The History of Trade Unionism* (1894).

Wrigley, C. (ed.), *A History of British Industrial Relations 1875–1914* (Brighton, Harvester Press, 1982).

——, *A History of British Industrial Relations, Vol. II, 1914–1939* (Brighton, Harvester Press, 1987).

——, *Cosy Cooperation under Strain: Industrial Relations in the Yorkshire Woollen Industry 1919–1930* (York, University of York Borthwick Papers, 1987).

Zeitlin, J., '"Rank and filism" and labour history: a rejoinder to Price and Cronin', *International Review of Social History*, 34, 1989.

——, '"Rank and filism" in British Labour history: a critique', *International Review of Social History*, 34, 1989.

INDEX

231

INDEX

INDEX

233

INDEX

INDEX

111, 131–2; strike (1912), 105; strike (1921), 108; strike (1984–5), 210–11
Miners' Association of Great Britain, 34
Miners' Federation of Great Britain, 60, 75, 83, 91, 103–4, 107–8, 112, 126–7, 132, 147–8
Moher, J., 3, 7, 16, 18, 21–2, 36–7
Molestation of Workmen Act, 1867, 59
Monckton, Sir W., 168
Mond, Sir A., 145
Mond–Turner talks, 143, 145
More, C., 68, 92
Morrison, H., 166–7
Muir, J.W., 115
Munitions of War Act/Acts, 110, 113–14
Murphy, J.T., 141
Murray, L., 209
Musson, A.E., 3, 6, 10, 23, 28, 35, 37, 64–5

National Agricultural Labourers' Union, 60, 62
National Amalgamated Union of Labour, 74
National Amalgamated Union of Labour on Tyneside, 72
National Arbitration Tribunal, 160
National Association for Plasterers, 40
National Association for the Protection of Labour, 25
National Association of Union of Textile Trades, 129
National Board for Prices and Incomes, 179–80
National Clerks' Association, 77
National Clerks' Union, 87
National Council of Labour, 149
National Dock Labour Scheme, 164, 167, 185
National Economic Development Council, 5, 175, 209
National Federation of Labour, 71
National Federation of Shop Workers and Clerks, 91
National Federation of Women Workers, 78

National Free Labour Association, 73, 90
National government, 150, 152
National Graphical Association, 209
National Incomes Policy, 175
National Industrial Relations Council, 194–5
National Joint Council, 149
National Reform League, 49, 60
National Transport Committee, 136
National Transport Workers' Federation, 127
National Union of Bank Employees, 194
National Union of Dock Labourers, 72
National Union of General and Municipal Workers, 129
National Union of Mineworkers, 6, 60, 197, 210–11, 217, 219
National Union of Public Employees, 203, 207
National Union of Seamen, 180
National Union of Teachers, 87
National Union of Textile Workers, 129, 154
Nicholson, E.M., 167
North East Pitmen's Union, 29
Northern Counties Textile Trades Federation, 91
Northern Typographical Association, 31, 51
Northern Typographical Union, 29

O'Day, A., 99, 120
Odger, G., 38, 42, 60
Olcott, T., 93
Oldham, 10, 23, 29, 33
Oliver, W.H., 23, 27, 37
Operative Bricklayers' Society, 38
Operative Stonemason's Society, 40
Order 1305, 160
Orth, J.V., 7, 16, 34, 36
Osborne Judgement, 79, 86
Owen, R., 26, 28–9

Papworth, B., 151, 163
Parkhead Forge, 116
Pease, E., 71

235

INDEX

INDEX

INDEX